# TRIES AND PREJUDICE

In Memory of
Mohammad Iqbal Dilawar Butt
Mohammad Riaz Darr
Sami Mirza

Ikram Butt

# TRIES AND PREJUDICE

The Autobiography of England's
First Muslim Rugby
International

**Written with Tony Hannan**

Scratching Shed Publishing Ltd

First published by Scratching Shed Publishing Ltd in 2009
Registered in England & Wales No. 6588772.
Registered office:
47 Street Lane, Leeds, West Yorkshire. LS8 1AP

www.scratchingshedpublishing.co.uk

ISBN 978-0956007537

Unless stated otherwise, all photographs are from
the personal collection of Ikram Butt

A catalogue record for this book is available from the British Library.

Typeset in Warnock Pro Semi Bold and Palatino

Printed and bound in the United Kingdom by
L.P.P.S.Ltd, Wellingborough, Northants, NN8 3PJ

# Contents

# FOREWORD

## RAHUL BOSE
*Indian actor, film director,*
*social activist and international rugby player*

One of the most wonderful things about being an international rugby player and movie actor is that when the two come together - which as you can imagine is rare - it affords an opportunity to reach out and interact in some depth with people whom one might otherwise never have met. Ikram Butt is one of those people.

Ikram and I met on the rugby field and then found so much in common that ours has and will remain an enduring friendship. Ikram's passion for rugby, coupled with his social concerns, mirror mine and we hit it off instantaneously.

On one of my trips to London, for the opening of my film at the London Film Festival (I think it was *Everybody Says I'm Fine!*, my directorial debut), Ikram asked me to travel up to Bradford, in Yorkshire, and interact with some high school children there. I readily agreed and that was the start of a collaboration that I believe has still to realise its full potential. Yet there were many parts of Ikram's life that I was not familiar with. While the awesome significance of him being, to date, the only player of Asian origin to have played any form of international rugby for England is something that I was aware of, other aspects of his life have come to light for me only through a reading of this warm, candid and lucid autobiography.

Being an atheist myself, I had no clue of Ikram's deep commitment to Islam. Reading about his relationship with his religion fills me with such happiness that here, in these troubled times, when Islam is so very misunderstood by the non-Muslim world, is a man who has understood how enriching religion can be if one uses it to increase one's compassion towards oneself and humanity at large.

A devout Muslim, Ikram is a living, breathing example of how, if followed correctly and contemporaneously, religion can be a force of goodwill, nourishment and succour to all. U2's Bono is the other example I can think of, of a public figure who has found vibrant sustenance from his faith. The simplicity and passion with which Ikram explains his love for Islam is a lesson to religious fundamentalists the world over.

Then there is the prison episode that tells us so much about the Ikram we would never quite see otherwise. Everyone makes mistakes and Ikram is no exception. But how beautifully, how constructively he has dealt with it!

There is not the slightest trace of bitterness, rancour or ill-feeling at the, some would say, harsh sentencing he received. In its place we hear the deepest expression of contrition, an uncomplicated honesty and the learning of the most precious lesson of them all – I will never let myself or my loved ones down again. I will emerge deeper, stronger and wider for this.

Trust a rugby player to display such an attitude. Because

truly rugby is one of the only sports to lay the highest emphasis on nobility.

Let me explain. It's easy for any sportsperson in a non-contact sport to be graceful under pressure. But when your body is quite literally on the line, and you are willing to put it on that line for your team-mates day in and day out without any sign of ill will or pressure, that's class. I have had the good fortune of playing against Ikram and I can tell you this – you will never find a rugby player more committed to his team-mates, more capable under pressure and, most important, more determined to do the best he can, but within the rules.

Since we first met, my non-profit organisation, The Foundation, has had the good fortune of hosting Ikram and a bunch of students from Leeds Met at the Mumbai Marathon in 2008, where those university athletes won the half-marathons as well as the 7km Dream Run. In fact, as I write this, I am in London filming for seven weeks over the summer of 2009 and Ikram and I have spoken about my going up to Yorkshire and perhaps doing something with the children there.

No one could be more fortunate than Ikram in the job that he does, as it combines the two purest, most illuminating aspects of his life – sport and integration of peoples from different cultures. I'd go even further and say that the good fortune is England's, and the global community in general.

The world needs ambassadors like Ikram Butt, who go about their jobs imaginatively, selflessly and tirelessly, knowing that the ultimate reward is in creating a deeper well of happiness and understanding in these strife-torn times. He has my best wishes for this book, his work and, last but not least, he has my shoulder for any ruck in life that may come his way.

# INTRODUCTION

## PETER RODGERS
### *Dean of Sporting Partnerships*
### *Leeds Metropolitan University*

My first experience of racial prejudice in rugby league was as a seven year old in the early 'fifties, watching Leeds play Wigan at Headingley. I was sitting on the wall between the South Stand and what is now the Carnegie Stand. It was the first time I had ever seen a black sportsman or indeed seen a black man in the flesh at all. Not surprising really, given that, according to the 1951 census, only eighty-five Africans lived in the city.

The player was, of course, Billy Boston - the Wigan legend who went on to play in 564 games and score 571 tries. Back then, I was in awe, not only of his size and speed but of his shiny black skin and piercing white eyes. The expression of determination on his face was frightening and the noise he created when his massive frame hit defenders made me jump back over the wall in both fear and excitement, as he plundered his way to several tries in the corner only yards in front of me.

After one try I heard a fan shout: 'Boston, You big black b....d!'. Even at that age I knew that was wrong and was surprised by those around him, who condoned his comment through facial expressions, nods of the head or verbal support.

In hindsight, I am uncertain whether this was inherent prejudice, an ignorant exclamation of disappointment at the opposition scoring a try or the resentful recognition of a great black player with extraordinary physical gifts.

In any case, my dad never said a word, but he did seem worried and concerned about the incident and what my own thoughts must have been on it. I think he was relieved after the match that I was more concerned to find out where Billy Boston had come from and why he was so different. He explained that Billy came from a place in Wales called Tiger Bay and, naively, for a short time after that, I believed that all black men came from there.

It wasn't until several years later, when prejudice became an important social issue, that my father talked about how he had to change his Lithuanian surname in order to get a job and survive in the Leeds community in the 1930s and that he had faced much worse than what was said to Billy Boston at the Wigan game. He said I was too young at the time to understand the complicated issues around racism both in sport and life in general, but it was important to experience and remember the event as well as reflect upon it when I grew older. I must also say that I never experienced a repeat of my experience in the 'fifties in rugby league at any game I have attended since, but that is not to say it never happened. Our own university research published around the mid-nineties concluded that there was a 'small but significant problem with racism in the game'. This resulted in the March 2000 RFL relaunch of *Tackle Racism in Rugby League* which emphasised the need for continuing awareness of the problem

I think this is a fundamental part of the value of this book, where Ikram shares his experience as honestly as he can and reflects upon his unique experience of being a young Asian developing a career in professional sport and his life afterwards. I never saw Ikram play for Leeds but did see him play for Featherstone against Leeds on a least a couple of occasions, along with his England debut.

The Ikram I know now is very different from the professional player I watched back then and our paths first crossed when he was seeking support for a BARA tour of India in 2005. It was great to learn about his work in Bradford and his passion for developing rugby (both codes) in the South Asian Community. He shared the same vision for inclusion as our university, as well as being an energetic alumnus who was determined to make a difference in rugby league and the rest of society. At times he could be difficult to deal with - a fact which comes out in the differences he had with some of his coaches - and was never afraid to express any different opinion openly. I did not agree with all his views but respected them and I learned a great deal from Ikram, particularly when we rigorously debated issues in rugby league on a number of occasions.

At Leeds Met, our largest number of international students came from South East Asia and we saw significant joint benefits from a partnership on this tour. The tour was very successful, winning the competition's Calcutta Cup as well as successfully promoting the Leeds Met brand in the region's schools and communities. We went on to support a number of Ikram's activities and, in particular, his BARA tag-time games at the Twickenham Stoop.

As a University we were very proud when our alumnus was presented in December 2007 with the 'Future Leaders – One to Watch' award at London's Hilton hotel. That summed up the way Ikram had developed his leadership skills and ability to make a difference.

Ikram also introduced us to Saima Hussain, almost his female equivalent in the sport, who was the first Asian woman to play rugby league for Great Britain. A stunning talkative atypical female rugby league player with the broadest Keighley accent, Saima was making a difference in West Yorkshire communities by inspiring young women - Asian or otherwise - to take up the game. As a player, she probably had even more challenging confrontations with prejudice than Ikram, not just outside her community but within it.

Harry Jepson OBE, writing in this book, makes the point that: 'If we are to get any progress in attracting more South Asians into rugby league, it is going to have to start in schools building pathways into clubs'. Saima was at the heart of this each year, working with several hundred girls after school with a level of enthusiasm that, to onlookers, was exhausting but brilliantly effective. She remains an icon in those communities, demanding of others, as much as she demands of herself. I know that Ikram mentored Saima and supported her through difficult times, particularly when governing bodies did not understand or share her methods of getting things done. Despite organisational management challenges, she continues to be as determined as ever to make a difference in the communities she serves.

Whilst I agree with Harry that, if we are to increase Asian participation in rugby league, we must start in schools, I would add that without the Ikram Butts and Saima Hussains of this world we will never inspire other young Asians to take up the game. It is therefore important to support, develop and celebrate these sporting role models as the university has tried to do in some small way.

It is equally important to listen to and understand the stories being told, simply and honestly, in a book like this. Ikram's autobiography is an important contribution to our understanding of the multicultural modern society in which we live.

**Peter Rodgers, May 2009**

# PREFACE (1)

## RICHARD LEWIS
*Chair of Sport England and*
*Executive Chairman, Rugby Football League*

There can be no doubt that Ikram Butt has made a major contribution to rugby league in many different ways.

As a player, he gave tremendous service to both Leeds and Featherstone Rovers and was the first British Asian to represent England at rugby league.

During his playing career Ikram became well known as a brave and committed competitor and he has maintained this determined approach off the field when, in recent years, he has worked hard to create opportunities for young British Asians to participate in rugby league and other sports.

Ikram was the prime mover behind the creation of the British Asian Rugby Association (BARA) in 2004, an organisation which has since developed into a positive force in terms of introducing rugby league among many diverse communities, both at home and abroad.

Through BARA and his own efforts, Ikram also consistently promotes his vision of using rugby league as a means of creating identifiable role models and promoting positive lifestyle messages.

Ikram is without doubt a passionate individual when it comes to rugby league and consistently seeks to make a tangible contribution to the sport and the wider community.

His activities and his energetic approach have been welcomed and endorsed by the RFL over the years and we will continue to support him in future seasons.

The RFL is delighted to see such activity and has itself carried out a great deal of work to make our sport open to all sections of the community and accessible to everybody, regardless of race or ethnicity.

At the Rugby Football League we have a strong and clear commitment to equality, both in our working environment at Red Hall and throughout the code, backed up by the anti-racism message of our 'Tackle It' campaign. Those key objectives, that we strive to deliver, are not just vital for our sport but also for the wider society in which it takes place.

A recent project has seen the RFL working alongside rugby league clubs to develop links with faith forums and community workers in order to engage with BEM [black and ethic minority] communities. We aim to overcome barriers to participation and create a welcoming environment for all. Religious and community leaders were invited to watch the 2009 Carnegie World Club Challenge encounter and, for many, it was their first match and proved to be a huge success.

The experience sparked a real enthusiasm for the game among the guests who are now keen to work with their local clubs to introduce rugby league into their communities.

And it is that kind of enthusiasm that Ikram will surely help to sustain and develop for the long term though his personal drive and commitment.

He has been, and will certainly continue to be, a friend to the sport of rugby league.

# PREFACE (2)

## MARTYN THOMAS
### *Chairman of Rugby Football Union Management Board*

Ikram Butt is a tremendous role model and a great ambassador for rugby.

He has been extremely influential in introducing rugby union to young British Asians and having been a major mover in the British Asian Rugby Association, which he was largely responsible for creating in 2004, his positive and inclusive approach has seen him working with both codes of rugby.

Ikram has also been heavily involved in inner cities and has helped to create links with community and religious leaders, local and national government. He is dedicated to using rugby to achieve equality and is himself a fine example of what can be achieved through sport.

The RFU has been very grateful for all his enthusiasm and commitment and expects to continue to work closely with Ikram in the future, to ensure that everyone has the chance to play and enjoy rugby union.

# PROLOGUE

It is February 1, 1995. I am sitting in the changing rooms at Ninian Park, Cardiff. The smell of wintergreen - or worse - is in my nostrils. Trying not to be distracted by big-game nerves, I sneak a look at the athletes around me. Many of them are household names; in rugby league circles anyway.

Over there is our captain, Phil Clarke, who along with the latest up-and-coming wing sensation Jason Robinson and substitute Mick Cassidy has been in superb form with the all-powerful Wigan side of the day. More familiar to me are Deryck Fox and Paul Newlove, both now at Bradford Northern on the back of record transfer fees but, once upon a time, team-mates of mine at Post Office Road, Featherstone.

Also no stranger is big bad Sonny Nickle, the awesomely tough St. Helens enforcer who, while playing as an amateur, I was once either brave or daft enough to try and have an on-field scrap with. And there in the number six shirt, confidently chucking the ball from one hand to the other, is that really my hero, Garry Schofield of Leeds, the hometown club I had supported since being a boy?

Yes, that's Garry Schofield alright. And here am I, Ikram Butt, about to become the very first Muslim ever to be capped by England in either code of rugby.

\* \* \* \* \*

Not surprisingly, when the news first broke that England coach Ellery Hanley - surely the greatest rugby league icon of them all - had chosen me in his side to play Wales in the opening game of the 1995 European Championship, the media had a right field day.

What with me being the son of Pakistani parents and raised in a community that was traditionally seen as not taking any great interest in any sport that wasn't cricket, my selection was seen as ground-breaking.

It wasn't just the rugby league papers who took up the story, either. The national papers and local radio and television stations jumped on it quickly too. In fact, although there was an official signed letter waiting on the doormat from Ellery when I got home that night - followed by a letter of congratulation from the highly-respected rugby league administrator Harry Jepson - the first confirmation I heard of a call-up came in a telephone call to Yorkshire Copperworks where, thanks to my former coach Peter Fox, I was employed as a quality control inspector. On the line was someone from a local news programme - *Look North* or *Calendar*, I forget which - inviting me into their Leeds studio.

At first, being in the glare of the media spotlight felt daunting, but I have to confess that I quickly began to enjoy all the fuss. I was also invited to be a guest summariser for

Sky on their coverage of a Bradford-Wigan game for example, and did loads of radio interviews. As the moment of truth drew nearer, though, I knew that all this was just a distraction and that the biggest challenge was yet to come. But when the big day did arrive, apart from the usual pre-match jitters, I felt as ready as I would ever be.

I was never under any illusions about the reasons for my selection. Although, as a rugby league player, I was by no means a glamour boy or superstar, over the past several seasons I had been a consistent performer for my club side, Featherstone Rovers, initially under the coaching of my long-time mentor, Peter, and then as a first-team regular for Allan Agar, Steve Martin and David Ward. The fact that I was now about to pull on an England top must at least partly be a reward for that.

I also liked to think of my England call-up as payback, of sorts, for my brother Khurshid, or Tony as everyone calls him. Our Tony, a very useful prop forward in his own right, virtually sacrificed his own career so that I could go on to better things in the game. As the eldest male still living at home, he was faced with great responsibility and, eventually, opted to put our family's financial well-being ahead of his rugby career, so that I didn't have to. I could never be grateful enough to him for that sacrifice. I was determined not to disappoint him.

And one more thing giving me confidence was the fact that, some seven years before, I had already played two international games against France for the Great Britain Colts youth team. Two of my team-mates back then, Hull's Richard Gay and Sheffield Eagles back-rower Anthony Farrell, were, like me, about to make their senior international debuts in Cardiff.

More recently, I had been talked about as a potential 1992 Lions tourist under the great Malcolm Reilly. In the end, that turned out to be just paper-talk, but being spoken about like that gives a boost to any player's self-esteem.

Playing for England, then, seemed to confirm that the selectors saw in me what I saw in myself: a good, solid player who would never let anyone down.

\* \* \* \* \*

So, Ninian Park, Cardiff. Wednesday February 1, 1995. The changing room before the game. A restless, steaming crowd of over six thousand people is waiting up the players' tunnel, while an audience of several hundred thousand are at home in front of their television sets.

Me? I just can't wait to tread on that turf.

Some players have their superstitious little routines before a game, but that was never my way. I just say a little prayer, asking that I can do well and perform to the best of my ability. Apart from the clatter of studs and the odd half-hearted joke or good-natured insult, everyone is quiet and focussed on what is to come. And then, at last, the waiting is over and we get the call to walk out. In ten minutes' time I will be absolutely knackered, telling Garry Schofield to 'hang on, I'm not ready,' when - thinking three steps ahead of everyone else as usual - he tries to pass me the ball after making a break. For now, though, everything is just a blur of nerves, hope and expectation.

Having trotted out onto the field, it is not so much the cheers and chants of the crowd that gets to you - as a player you tend to block all of that stuff out. It is more about the pressure of not letting yourself and those you care about down. The night before, you have lain awake in bed and rehearsed this game and what you are going to do in it a hundred times in your head. And now here it is, actually about to get underway.

I look down the line and see my team-mates alongside me, all dressed in white and standing to attention. How can anyone not feel proud to be a part of this? For a moment, I allow myself to soak up the achievement and tell myself to give it everything I have got. From past experience I realise that, before I know it, my England international debut will be over. Nothing but a memory. So I vow that I will savour the occasion. I don't want to be thinking afterwards about what I should have done, but didn't. True, to some extent you can never avoid that. But I am determined not to fall short of anyone's expectations, least of all my own.

When the band strikes up, I belt out the national anthem as loudly as anyone and once more tell myself to relish this moment because it might never come again.

And then, I am playing for England.

# Tries and Prejudice

# 1

*

# At Home with the Butts

It all began in Headingley. Well, once they had brought me home it did. For it was in St. Mary's hospital, Leeds, that, on October 25, 1968, the world first gazed upon Ikram Butt's chubby little rosy-cheeked face.

To those readers who have ever seen me play rugby league down the years, it will come as no surprise to learn that I wasn't the first to the Butt family try-line. Four other siblings had already got there before me, with another one to follow. The eldest three, my big brother Zaman and older sisters Qudisia and Misbah, were born in Pakistan. The rest of us were 'Made in England', where our mum and dad had first settled in 1965 in a shared property near Burley and the predominantly white area of Hyde Park, Leeds. By the time I arrived, our growing clan had relocated to Manor Drive, just off Victoria Road, a stone's throw away from the famous old Headingley stadium.

Then, as now, Headingley was a well known student area. So, what with all the comings and goings, street parties and such like, there was always something happening and most of our neighbours were open-minded and friendly. Ours was a multi-cultural neighbourhood. There were plenty of South Asian families like us, from Pakistan and India, a few black Afro-Caribbeans, white Irish Catholics... you name it. In our immediate area, at least, there was little prejudice and no one seemed to feel inferior or insignificant at all.

In our street, we had one Irish family and an Italian family to whom we were particularly close. Their children used to mix with ours. We were good friends with an Indian family too. One of their boys, Ajit, who was a good few years older than me, later emigrated to Australia. In 1990, I went to visit him while I was playing there and he had a son, two or three years old. More recently, my mum told me he was back in Leeds for a wedding. I was driving past this pub and saw his brother go in. Maybe Ajit's in there, I thought. So I stopped the car and went inside and said: 'where's Ajit?' They said: 'Oh, he's not in here. He's down the road in Kirkstall.' So I shot off down Kirkstall to meet him - I hadn't seen him for years. His son was about sixteen now and we were reminiscing.

One thing we remembered was him having an argument with my older brother, Tony, and my mum coming out and giving him a rollocking. That wasn't an uncommon event in our street - and in any number of languages. Another friend, Paul, had an Italian mother and an English dad. His mum always told Paul off in Italian. As Asians, we take the mickey out of our own families for that. When we get told off they speak to us in the original lingo, then it's a few words of English and then back again. That was very common down our way. Same with the Irish family - 'begorrah' this and 'I'll tan yer backside...' that.

In our neighbourhood, the kids were all quite sporty. We played out in the street night and day. Cars seemed to be few and far between and there certainly wasn't as much trouble as there is now although, looking back, it's easy to see that the seeds of delinquency, gang culture and anti-social behaviour were there. Occasionally, we would wander over to Burley or Hyde Park and both those areas, like ours, suffered from what would now be described as high levels of deprivation and a lack of resources for young people.

Not that we kids would have noticed any of that at the time, of course. The freedom to roam suited us just fine. We could stop out as long as we liked and we felt safe because everyone knew each other. That's all we did, the entire street. Play outdoors.

Different sections of the neighbourhood would play football, cricket, rounders... and at home my dad always made sure that there were plenty of footballs, rugby balls and cricket bats and balls in the house. Unlike other Asian families, though, where the fathers had often played it themselves, cricket wasn't really drilled into us. Mum and dad watched it when it was on and supported Pakistan obviously, but my dad, in particular, preferred a bit of rough and tumble. Even when we played football or cricket together in the park, he got physical. That was just his way.

To be honest, while I was growing up I never really thought much about my family's roots in Pakistan, and I was never much of a scholar. I must have been taught the obvious things, like how, geographically, Pakistan was surrounded by Afghanistan and Iran to the west, and India and China to the east. I was also vaguely aware of how it had once come under the rule of the British Raj, but probably wouldn't have been able to tell you that British rule lasted from 1858 to 1947, until an independent state of Pakistan was created that, in 1956, became the full-blown Islamic Republic that we know today.

All that was for the school room. To me, my Leeds stomping ground was where it was at and that was more than enough to be going on with. I was just the typical snotty-nosed kid, I suppose. All that mattered was what was happening today and, maybe, if something good was coming up, tomorrow. Where was the next game of marbles coming from? The past never crossed my radar.

Yet as we get older many of us grow more fascinated by family background and that has definitely been the case with me. As an adult, I consider my heritage to be a very important part of who I am. And I am almost embarrassed to admit that, for various reasons, I didn't make my first trip to Pakistan until I was 35 years old. Happily and thanks partly to my line of work, I have been lucky enough to go back several times since then. Also, during the writing of this book, I have come to understand more about how it was that we Butts settled in Yorkshire, by talking to my beloved mum, Tahira, and other family members such as my sister, Qudisia, an Arabic and Islamic teacher by trade, who has always been virtually my second mother.

\* \* \* \* \*

As is quite common within traditional Pakistani marriages, my mum and dad were actually first cousins who came from the same village, Kunjah, in Gujrat, a district of Punjab Province that is around two-and-a-half hours away from Lahore, close to the Indian border. My dad, born Mohammad Iqbal Dilawar Butt, was a gentle giant of a man - he stood over six feet tall - who went on to be a mechanic in the Royal Pakistan Air Force. His father was a merchant, or trader, just like my mum's dad. My paternal grandfather was the oldest of three brothers; my maternal grandfather the youngest.

Sadly, I never met my grandparents, so I don't know whether my parents' characters were in any way influenced by them or not. But, either way, my dad seems to have been a romantic soul, always on the look out for adventure. Maybe that was why he joined the Air Force; he liked the idea of travel. Before I was born, he spent lots of time based all over Pakistan, leaving my mother, his young wife, back in Kunjah with her mother-in-law. It was only when one of his friends, Masood, went off to find work in England, though, that he - and she - had the opportunity to create a new life in a new country.

I dare say that, to many non-Pakistani readers, the idea of an arranged marriage between first cousins will seem unusual or maybe even problematical. For sure, even within our own communities, the practice is nowhere near as commonplace or rigidly enforced as it once was. Even so, as the chapters ahead will hopefully explain, there are many aspects of traditional Islamic faith that, although possessing an obvious religious and spiritual aspect, are also driven by down-to-earth logic and reality. In the case of arranged marriages, for instance - and arranged marriages are quite different to forced marriages by the way - the whole thing is based on the practical and respectful recognition that parental experience counts for a lot.

In Kunjah, for example, my parents were part of an extended family community of those three brothers. Each man and his wife lived in an apartment of their own, around a central courtyard. That would have been quite a typical set-up. As a result, everyone knew each other's children well enough to be aware of what their strengths and weaknesses were, so it wasn't such a gamble in wondering how their own child would fare as a particular person's husband or wife. In the case of daughters, it also guaranteed that any prospective husband would be of a similar status level in society, financially and so on because, Islamically, men must provide the standards to which the woman is accustomed.

In this instance, when my mum was sixteen, my dad's mother approached my mother's mother to arrange the marriage. There was no problem there. Apparently my grandmother liked him because he was so hard working. There was a seven-year age difference between the two.

In short, the parents took - and still do take, in a less restricted way - responsibility for any future partnership, knowing most intimately the nature and characteristics of the couple involved. Great thought was given to any proposal; no one would ever get married in a rush.

Marriage was considered a lifetime's commitment and love was expected to grow, rather than be there from the start. So, at that time, because it was generally the norm, no one considered that they were doing anything wrong. And, in any case, the ultimate decision on whether or not to proceed rests with the couple themselves. Islam states that you must see your prospective partner first. It is important that there is some physical chemistry there.

One thing is for sure, though. An arranged marriage worked a treat for my mother and father. They were a match made in heaven.

In all their time together, I can honestly say that I can never recall them having so much as a single angry word. Anyway, two years after dad travelled on ahead to join Masood in England, he called - as is traditional - for my mum and their three children to come over and join him.

\* \* \* \* \*

In Pakistan, my dad was Air Force-trained, but once he arrived in wet and windy England he quickly discovered that those hard-earned qualifications counted for very little. He obviously still had upward ambitions because he immediately applied to join the RAF. Being an immigrant must have counted against him, however, as he was turned down flat.

Although that still rankles with me after all these years, it seems that for Asian immigrants right across Britain in the 1960s and '70s, his situation wasn't all that uncommon. People coming over from Pakistan who had white collar jobs there had no choice but to step down when they got to the UK, both in terms of wages and position. Even professors would have to retrain and gain new qualifications if they wanted to continue sharing their skills with the wider community. It just wasn't possible to get a similar type of work. Not that it was all bad news, mind. One major benefit was that the currency here was worth far more than back home. It was a better life in that way.

So anyway, needing paid employment, my dad found himself work in a car wash for a few weeks until, after another more successful interview, he landed a job as a bus conductor. In later years, we kids thought that was great. If ever he saw us walking along the road, we could hop on for a lift and we didn't have to pay. He looked smart in his uniform and, being a friendly sort by nature, I am guessing he enjoyed the work, mixing with people and so on. And these being less, shall we say 'politically correct' days, the first thing one of his new colleagues did was to give him a new name. Clearly, for this bloke, Mohammad Iqbal Dilawar - or Mohammad Iqbal as he was more commonly known - was too much of a mouthful. Instead, he christened him Albert.

The funny thing is that at the time, none of us - least of all dad himself - was in any way put out by this. It might seem a bit offensive now, and maybe it was back then, but I've little doubt it was intended to be friendly and the family still chuckles at the name even today, if perhaps a little wryly. Other times, it was a bit more sinister. I remember on one occasion when I was playing football as a 14 or 15-year-old and the coach kept calling me Abdul. Again, I didn't realise until much later what was going on there. I just thought that he couldn't remember my name, that's how naïve I was. In time, of course, I came to recognise how rude, lazy and arrogant such behaviour is. My name's Ikram. It's not that hard to say, is it?

That said, unless the insults get out of hand, I've always tried to keep a sense of humour about issues like this, or else we would spend all our time at each other's throats, wouldn't we? And in any case, there's always a danger of being a bit hypocritical. When it comes to the use of dodgy nicknames, the Butt family is hardly blame free.

I mentioned before that there would go on to be eight of us in the Headingley branch - mum, dad and six of us kids, just enough for a decent seven-a-side rugby squad. Sadly, although for Asians the importance of the extended family is a huge thing, we Butts missed out on the benefits of that owing to the fact that most of our relations remained in Pakistan. In fact, the only member of our extended family that I met as a youngster was an uncle on my mum's side, and that was in unhappy circumstances that I will come to in a while.

As I hinted earlier, when my parents first set up home in Leeds, they shared a house near Hyde Park with Masood, the friend of my dad who had first invited him to England. In time, Masood would marry an English nurse and emigrate again to Canada, where he still lives with his wife and children, but not before inviting his brother, Khalid, over to this country too. With Masood gone, mum and dad continued to share the house with Khalid and his family until, having eventually saved up enough money to buy a home of their own, they upped sticks for Headingley and the Manor Drive scene of my childhood.

Although I've always regretted that I was never able to mix with and get to know my cousins, grandparents and so on, the one advantage of our situation was that, as a family, such a separation made us even more close-knit. It also helped that the community in which I spent my earliest years was so cosmopolitan and friendly. I've got no doubt that both of those things helped to shape me as the person I am today. It was very normal for us to be among different cultures and it enriched our upbringing because we got used to such integration and being accepted for who we are. As human beings, we have to rub along, don't we? It's important that we respect each other and try to understand faiths and cultures other than our own, while giving a fair chance to all.

Anyway, back to my immediate family. Top of the tree among my brothers and sisters was our big brother Zaman who, by the time us younger ones came along, was already quite grown up. In fact, Zaman spent a big chunk of my childhood living and working overseas with his own family in Denmark, so I never saw as much of him as I would have liked. Next came Qudisia, also born in Pakistan, who, as I say, pretty much took on the role of a second mother to us younger ones, especially after the tragically premature death of my dad. Qudisia was always the intelligent one and, in time, she would complete a degree in Arabic and Islamic studies. Nowadays, she knows everything there is to know about our holy book, the Qu'ran, and is particularly helpful in ensuring I get my Islamic facts right and makes sure to tell me when I don't! Like Qudisia, my second sister, Misbah, helped my mum to keep us three boys in line while we were growing up and is now married with children of her own.

Then, once we were in England, came the three amigos. First to arrive in 1966 was Khurshid who, you may recall from the prologue, is more widely known as Tony. I'll explain why in a minute. Although I have since learned to my surprise that, earlier in his life, my dad apparently dabbled in the odd game of rugby, our Tony was the real trail-blazer when it came to the oval ball game. He grew to be big and strong and, after being signed by Peter Fox, played around twenty games for the Leeds first team, who were in those days nicknamed the Loiners rather than the Rhinos.

Two years after Tony's birth, it was my turn to put in an appearance and I was followed, a year after that, by the youngest of the brood, Innam, these days better known to all as Chinky. Why Chinky? Well, believe it or not, he was given that name by my oldest brother, Zaman, because, when he was born, he had little slit eyes. It's quite interesting that, isn't it? My brother and those of us who still call him by that name (i.e. just about everyone, because it's completely embedded by now) don't mean anything derogatory by it. But it does go to show how when it comes to racial prejudice, consciously or not, one community can be just as insensitive as any another.

As for Tony, well that name came about as a result of the matriarch of our closest neighbours, a black Afro-Caribbean family called Stewart, being unable to pronounce Khurshid. So Granny Stewart, as we still call her, decided to anglicise it to David. Don't ask me how but somehow, over time, that gradually evolved into Tony. And to this day that is how everyone knows him. My mum, his brothers, sisters, family and friends - everyone calls him that. Even my late father did so. Our Tony is quite light-skinned; a lot lighter than me. I think a lot of people thought he was dual-heritage, but that's not the case. Qudisia, meanwhile, was renamed Maria, but that one doesn't seem to have stuck. Despite long since moving on, as a family we have stayed in close contact with Granny Stewart and her family. My own kids call her

Auntie. Just the other month, the Stewarts were guests at my niece's wedding.

Whatever we called ourselves, as kids playing amidst the rows of terrace houses in our narrow street, using dustbins for cricket wickets and getting into trouble for kicking balls into gardens, we three brothers were very close. We still are. Even more so, in fact, because as you mature you value the importance of that relationship so much more. When you are a kid, there can be a lack of understanding of the nature and strength of the family bond and brotherhood. Often your brother is your best mate - closer to you than anyone else can be. Blood really is thicker than water.

Another reason for the closeness of our relationship as kids is that, at home, we all shared the same bedroom. As the oldest, our Tony got the single bed whilst me and the young 'un had the bunk bed - I was on top, of course. Consequently, our house, which was a typical Victorian job - cellar below, first floor with a high-ceilinged sitting-room, second floor with three bedrooms (one for my mum and dad, one for my sisters and one for us), bathroom and, finally, a converted attic bedroom (Zaman's while he lived with us) - was always lively and noisy.

That atmosphere was also encouraged by the open-house policy adopted by my parents. My mum and dad would never lock the door and there was always someone walking in. Our home's real claim to fame, though, was that my dad had turned our cellar into a kitchen long before anyone else did. Later on, he did the attic and we became upwardly mobile! But it was the cellar kitchen that was the real attraction.

I remember these kids from a local white family - it makes me chuckle now to remember how naughty they were - who always used to bang on the door and ask my mum if they could have some buttered chapatis. Buttered chapatis! We would never eat a chapati like that - we would expect to have something with it. But those kids loved the thought of having a chapati on its own. That was so funny. My mum was happy to give the chapatis away because they were left-overs and, otherwise, she would have either fed them to the birds or chucked them in the bin. She much preferred to give them to someone who would enjoy them. And because our kitchen was downstairs and quite cool, the neighbours were always at our home, aware that my mother would be cooking something. She always made plenty.

Then there was my dad's boisterous approach to bringing up his children. As a young man in Pakistan, he had been a heavyweight boxer to quite a good standard for the Air Force, so he was always one for physical sport. He won trophies and cups for his boxing but, unfortunately, he left them back in Pakistan and we no longer have any access to them. I never saw my dad fight, and nor did my mum. She would never go to watch him because she didn't want to see him get hurt.

He did, though, buy me my first pair of boxing gloves when I was six years old and we three youngest boys were always encouraged to spar with one another. In fact, he went so far as to set up a full-scale boxing ring in our front room, much to the dismay of my mother. We were quite a physical bunch and, as there wasn't much of a difference in our ages, we each gave as good as we got. When I could get away with it, I would prefer to scrap our Chinky rather than Tony, who had a bit more size and muscle than I did. Even so, Chinky earned a bit of a reputation around the neighbourhood as a bit of a hardnut, so sometimes I had to back off. We still got on extremely well, though.

My dad used to arm-wrestle too. If ever I came home from school covered in bumps and bruises, he would say: 'Did you give as good as you got?'. In some ways, this sort of thing was quite unusual for an Asian parent. They usually have a reputation for trying to keep their kids away from the rough stuff, not encouraging them to join in with it. Then again, that doesn't account for the ancient sport of kabaddi and, as I have already mentioned, my dad also had a love of that.

For those who have never seen it, there are different styles and variations of kabaddi. This is my argument whenever anyone says that South Asians don't have the physique or mentality to play rugby league. If they would watch a bit of kabaddi, they would have to think twice. And there's plenty of opportunity to do so because we regularly stage events in places like Bradford and Leeds. One of the most popular versions is one-on-one, in which you tig someone and then run to the line. Well, it's not so much a 'tig' as a vicious slap. As sports go, physically kabaddi is extremely tough. And because it's so macho, the players all stand there and see who can take the biggest hit. Then, when they have had enough, they do a runner and defend instead. Basically, it's rugby without the ball.

Yet, despite this liking for rough and tumble, my dad was a placid and laid-back sort of bloke at heart. He had a presence about him because he was bigger than everyone else, but he was not aggressive at all. He had a really even temperament, spoke very well and I used to really look up to him. We all did. Even our mates used to like him. My sister Qudisia's friend, for example, who was a Sikh, once told her that she could talk to our dad in a way that she couldn't with her own.

The most important thing for dad was us, his family. If we were okay, he was okay. Whenever he took us to the park, to play football or rounders or whatever, although he was getting towards his mid-forties by then, as a nine or ten-year-old I used to have trouble keeping up with him. I remember he would eat his dinner and then walk around the room to digest it. Then he would go jogging. Mainly, though, when he wasn't at home with us, or laid quietly on the settee watching *Grandstand*, he would spend his time working, either on the buses or, in the evenings, as head waiter in a friend's local restaurant, all the while providing for both his immediate family in Leeds and the extended family he had left behind in Pakistan. At one point, he had ambitions to be a bus driver - the money was better - but he kept failing the driving test and so had to stick to being a 'clippie'.

\* \* \* \* \*

So, my dad was very much the head of the household but, looking back, the person who really ran it was my mum, Tahira, helped by my sisters. Physically, compared to my dad, mum was short, pretty and quite light-skinned. Although my dad was keen on discipline and would occasionally bend us over and give us a half-hearted clout with his slipper if we'd skipped going to the mosque or something - a bit like Roger the Dodger's dad in *The Beano* - it was my mum who was the strict one.

Mum would always complain about how soft dad was with us and how he always let us get away with things, leaving her to look like the villain. Even when she'd told us off, though, we couldn't stay upset with her for long. For a start, she was such a fantastic cook; she still is. Cooking is mum's speciality. She used to cook at the restaurant too, part-time. Apart from that, she has been a housewife all her adult life and never really worked outside the home at all.

Even so, my mum has a very strong personality. She has had to be strong in her life and she is strong. Even when my father was alive, she took charge. She cooked, cleaned, worked hard and made sure that her children were behaving well and dressed smartly. She always took a lot of pride in our appearance. And whenever guests visited, their needs came first.

The one thing you can say about us Butts is that we like our grub and, at our house, we were always well fed. A typical dish for us was either chicken massala, meat massala, keema (a variation of mince and potatoes) or kofte - meatballs - with eggs. I used to love that last one, especially the way my mum made it. That was our diet. From time to time we also had an 'English dinner', which meant fish and chips from the chip shop up the road, or supermarket fish fingers and chips made by my mother. Now and then, my sisters would make homemade pizza and, as my rugby career took off, I might have spaghetti on toast on matchdays. Otherwise, we pretty much always ate traditional Asian food.

I remember my mum used to grow mint in a little patch of soil in our back yard too, and - along with buttered chapatis (!) - the neighbours would also come around asking for some of that. She was forever handing out ingredients; everyone knew that my mother would have them in her cellar kitchen. Not all the other families were so houseproud; they used to spend their money on other stuff. But my mum and dad always invested in their homelife, keen to ensure that we were self-sufficient. Mum, especially, was a real rock of the community.

Another of the foods that I really enjoy eating is yellow dahl, which is lentils basically. But apart from that, it was meat all the way in our house. As children, if ever there was anything vegetarian in front of us - and my dad was just the same - we would just refuse to let it pass our lips. My mum knew that. So meat was always on the menu. I used to go to friends' houses and they would have a bowl of curry with a few chunks of meat, salad and chapatis. I used to think: 'What's going on here?' At home, the table would be heaving with meat, with maybe just a little bowl of curry to wash it down with. We were well known for that. Our Tony is a decent size, our Chinky is a decent size, and my sisters liked their grub too. We knew how to put it away.

Later on, when I began to play rugby, I became aware of the usefulness of meat and chicken as a provider of protein. Back then, though, we just ate all the time because we liked it. That's one of the things with Asian families; you visit our houses and the first thing we do is put food on the table. That's the way in which we show you our generosity. You risk giving offence if you don't eat. People who know me will tell you that if I've got a chicken leg in my hand I will be satisfied.

Having said that, although I'll eat steak all day, I must admit that, lately, I have slightly gone off meat. Within reason, I could get away with eating whatever I wanted when I was younger and playing rugby. I wasn't still long enough to put any weight on. Also, I was quite selfish and single-minded back then, and people knew that I was a semi-professional sportsman, so I didn't really have any sort of social life, apart from my family. But as soon as I stopped playing regularly, I developed a big problem with my weight, which these days just bounces up and down. I still exercise and play a bit, in charity events and so on, so I've just about got it under control. But what can I say? I like to eat.

Anyway, that's enough about food or I'll be back in the fridge. Let's change the subject. At the top of the road, lived mum's best friend, Auntie Jamila. She wasn't our real auntie but, because she was over at our house all the time, people just assumed that she and my mum were sisters, they were that close. Sadly, Auntie Jamila has passed away now. The thing I most remember about her, was that she was the first in the street to buy a video player - pretty much as soon as they were invented. My mum wouldn't spend money on something like that, although we did get one eventually. We kids liked to spend a lot of time up at Aunt Jamila's house, usually watching rented Bollywood movies, but also one or two martial arts films. Zaman, my eldest brother, is a Bruce Lee fanatic. So, all in all, my mum was a well-known and friendly presence in our neighbourhood. And she had a busy and fulfilling social life, albeit within our own small Headingley community. Yet it wasn't always like that. When she and my brother and sisters first emigrated to England, she found it very difficult to adapt.

Her biggest problem was that she couldn't speak the language. Apart from a programme on the telly - *New Life, New Ways* I think it was called - which she used to watch, English classes weren't easily available at the time. So she put Qudisia and Misbah into playgroups and slowly picked the lingo up that way. Zaman, who is four years older than Qudisia, went into a special class at school for children who didn't speak English too, so it wasn't long before English began to be spoken more regularly at home. As for myself and my other brothers, language was never an issue. Having been born in England, we went through private playgroup, state school nursery and then stayed in the normal school system like everyone else.

Keen to fit in, our parents never forced us to speak our mother tongue, Punjabi, at home either, which is not necessarily a bad thing, although you do lose out culturally in some ways. Apart from our clothing, you couldn't really distinguish us from our neighbours.

The downside of all that is that I only ever learned to speak English. I wasn't bilingual. In our family, my dad could speak English and Punjabi. My mum spoke Urdu fluently and a number of dialects. These days, my sisters and elder brother are fluent; our Tony can speak a bit and our Chinky can now too, but only because he married a girl from Kunjah. My wife is fluent in Urdu, but I'm not. As we grew up, my mum in particular would speak to us in Punjabi and we would reply in English.

## Tries and Prejudice

I can honestly say that I am ashamed that I have never learned to speak the language of my ancestors. I can only blame myself - I would never put any blame on my family whatsoever. I can understand Punjabi - I know every word my mum says - but if I listen to someone else, because it's a different accent, I don't always catch on. I might understand a little, but my response is always in English or broken pidgin Punjabi.

It can be embarrassing. In the old days, if we had old people coming over to the house, or spoke to them on the phone, I couldn't work out what they were saying. Or, if I did know, I couldn't respond. And to think that we used to make fun of mum whenever she spoke in broken English. She does well now but, back then, a lot of what she'd come out with didn't make much sense. But that was because she was trying to learn and we should have known better.

For mum, then, settling into English life was tough. As well as struggling with the language, there were religious and cultural differences to contend with too. She hardly went out. Just going out to the shops to buy a coat was a trial. My dad told her to cool down. There was nothing to be afraid of. But she was still very nervous. When she first arrived, of course, she had the support of the other wives in the house. But when she and dad moved to their own home it became even more difficult.

In Pakistan, outside of the big cities, life is very slow and easy. It's not full-on, like it is in Britain. Women rarely go out and are far more domesticated than women in the west. It is men who do the jobs that are required outside the home - including shopping etc - while wives look after the children and run the household. Adapting to that must have been a huge and traumatic transition. Gradually, though, with the help of my dad and her children - my sisters would take her into town, for example - she got used to it.

# 2

*

# Tragedy Strikes

The death of a parent is a traumatic experience for any child and, when my dad passed away, I was only eleven years old. Yet maybe because I was so young, I don't think that it fully sank in at the time, although the effects were long-lasting.

I loved my dad very much indeed, and still do. He was and is my champion of champions. As kids, whenever we needed him, he was there. He supported me and my brothers in all our sporting endeavours and, as I say, after coming home from work he liked nothing better than to spend time with his family.

That's probably why he didn't go into business like so many other South Asian men. He just wasn't made that way. If you ask me, he had his priorities absolutely right. If any of his children weren't home, he would ask mum where we were. He wouldn't want her to call us in or anything, he just needed to know that we were safe. When I was selected to play in my first big rugby league game for the school, my dad happily made the trip to St. Helens to watch. He was my hero. There's not a day goes by when I don't think about him. My dad was a real inspiration.

On the night he passed away, me and our Tony and Chinky were messing about in our bedroom. Then, suddenly, there was a lot of commotion and noise downstairs, so our Chinky went down to see what was happening. When he came back up, he said: 'Dad's died'. We didn't believe him. We just said: 'Shut up and go to bed'. That was how the news first came to us.

It was a very sad time. The house was full of neighbours. The front room was full of women crying, the other room was full of men, separate, not crying but just sitting there paying their respects. Young as we were, we all raced off downstairs, running about. I can't speak for my brothers but, in my case, it didn't really have an immediate impact. I can't remember the first time I had tears in my eyes. I just couldn't comprehend the enormity of what had happened. That was a blessing, I suppose.

The thing is, he hadn't been poorly beforehand. He had put on a bit of weight by that stage, but my dad had always been a big fellow and he seemed healthy enough. As I understand it, he had been working at the restaurant one night, as usual, and a customer had run off without paying their bill. Always the reliable employee, my dad gave chase and he just suffered an enormous heart attack and collapsed in the street. As a family, we still find the injustice of his fate painful to think about. The restaurant wasn't his but he still felt responsible enough to take action. I am told that someone tried to give him a glass of water as he lay on the pavement. My mum went with him to hospital, but he passed away soon afterwards.

Although, as an eleven-year-old, the pain wasn't there from the start, it wasn't long before I began to notice that there was now a huge gap in my life. Something important was missing. My dad had been larger than life and, as you would expect, my mum was absolutely devastated. For years afterwards, we would find her sitting on her own, crying, just thinking about my dad. She still misses him loads.

After the tragedy, everybody came to our house to pay their respects and read a special prayer. Then they took dad's body back to Pakistan. And that was it. If I am honest, I would have preferred that he was buried here in England. From a purely selfish point of view, it would be nice to be able to go and visit his grave once in a while. But I can understand where my mum was coming from. His own mother was still alive back then and so were all his family. My mum travelled back to Pakistan for the funeral. My sisters and elder brother, who came over from Denmark, stayed with us kids. The rest of the families in the street looked after us too. I am not sure how we got by financially, but I assume that everyone must have chipped in.

Since first coming to England, my dad had only been back to Pakistan once, fourteen years after his arrival, when his own father died. He had six kids to provide for, so, financially, he couldn't justify the cost. Life was tough because he wasn't only looking after his family in Leeds, he was sending money back to Pakistan too. My mum continued to do that after his death.

And that was another reason, perhaps, why we managed to cope better than you might expect. Even at that age, with our dad gone, us boys had to be tough. Our mum was on her own and we had two sisters to protect. So we tried to block it all out, in a way. It made us grow up quicker, without a doubt. We were all quite cocky as kids, all three of us, and that was down to the encouragement my dad gave us. As a result, we all had a lot of ambition. We wanted to look forward and try to make something of ourselves. In time, I did come to realise that I had no dad and thought that unfair, but I think it was him who equipped us to handle it.

In fact, my dad had a massive influence on shaping our characters in a number of ways, particularly when it came to our appreciation of Islam, although it took me a while to catch on to that. Nowadays, my religion is hugely important to me and I try to be as devout a Muslim as I can be. But back then, it was often more a case of doing what you were told without really taking it in. We learned stuff at the mosque but, when I look back now, we often didn't really understand what was being said. We were just saying words and following actions.

Actually, when I talk about going to the mosque, that didn't really happen until later. At first there weren't any recognisable mosques in LS6 - so we tended to pray at home. The exception was Eid prayer, for which we had to walk or catch the bus up to Leeds Met - or Leeds Polytechnic as it was then - in order to join a congregation. I remember my dad had one three-piece suit that he used to wear with the same hat every time. It's strange to think how, these days, my rugby league development work means that I am heavily involved with Leeds Met myself, although they have since moved site and are now known as Leeds Met Carnegie.

Except for on special occasions, then, my dad would kneel and pray at home and he made us kneel and pray with him. I remember we used to position ourselves just behind him and laugh at each other while we did it, especially our Chinky, who was a joker. I only had to look at him and I'd laugh. We didn't really know what we were doing, we were just following dad's movements. Then, as we grew up and one of the terraced houses in the local area was expanded for the job - pretty basic premises and not at all like the beautiful domed buildings you see around today - we would be expected to go to the mosque and pray there too. Certainly, we would go there every fasting period, when the place became packed.

As a rule, us kids used to come home from school and walk down to the mosque, which was about twenty to twenty-five minutes away from where we lived. There were different times you could go. We, the boys, were aged nine, ten and eleven, so I doubt that we would have been allowed to do it these days, what with all the main roads we had to cross. But, as I said before, the traffic was safer back then. The three of us would walk together. My sisters went to the mosque too but they were also self-taught at home by my mum.

I realise that many people will be reading this book who are not all that familiar with Islamic practices and traditions, so I will try to explain aspects of the Muslim faith as they relate to my own life as I go along. In this case, there were different times for different age groups at the mosque, so me and our Chinky would go in first and our Tony would hang around the shops with his mates and go in afterwards. We would then wait for him and walk back home together. Around the mosque, there were loads of takeaways, so we would often be found playing Space Invaders in those too.

The Qur'an - or Koran as it is often spelt in the west - is our central religious text; the sacred word of God. In total, it is made up of 114 chapters of varying lengths, divided into thirty sections or passages. The idea is that you work your way through until you finish them all. As a youngster, the first book you encounter is the Qaaida, which begins as an introduction to the arabic alphabet and basically goes on to teach you about vowel sounds, grammar and so on. How long it takes you to finish the entire Qur'an depends upon you. If you went to the mosque regularly every day, then you could do it in maybe three months or so. During

Ramadan, people have been known to read it in three days. Like a lot of things in life, the younger you are, the easier it is to sink in. In theory, anyhow. My own daughter, for example, is eleven now and she has finished the complete book. I was nowhere near finished when I was eleven.

Part of the reason for that, I think, is that in the past, people used to complain that the imams who had come to Britain from Pakistan couldn't relate easily to those of us born and raised in a parallel British culture. Whenever they were asked to explain anything, they didn't know how to make their advice relevant to our own experience.

Things are far better today. These days you go to a mosque and you find imams who were born in the UK and have studied here. They understand the nature of Western society and its impact on the lives of young people. So when they are asked a set of questions, they don't give an answer that the kids can't interpret, they give them a variety of answers to guide them, all related to their own lives.

Another difference, back then, was the preponderance of mainly Pakistanis at the mosque. Nowadays, on account of all the negative media imagery focussing on militant extremism and the so-called 'War on Terror', a lot of people don't realise that Islam is actually a very inclusive and tolerant religion at heart.

Our teachings say that the Muslim religion must be open to any creed or culture. And if you visit any mosque today you will see folk from all walks of life, including Arabs, black Afro-Caribbeans and white people of all nationalities. In the 'seventies, though, such sights were rare. The mosque was like a classroom, with small tables and they used to get the book out. I remember we used to rock backwards and forwards as we read it. That was just the style, and I am doing it right now just thinking about it. We were required to wear a skull cap - not a scrum cap! - as a mark of respect.

Around this time, I had a mate called 'Frenchy', who lived a couple of streets down from us, near the schoolyard. His dad was black and his mother was a white French woman. He converted to Islam and I remember that, one time, he came to the mosque. People just stared at him and I remember thinking that wasn't nice. He wasn't black, he wasn't white, he had a Mediterranean colour. But people kept looking at him like he was something unusual and that just put him off. He told me that he didn't feel comfortable there. In my opinion, the Pakistani congregation in there was prejudiced towards him. Racism exists in every community.

What I have learned down the years is that, when it comes to Pakistanis, people confuse culture and religion. That's wrong because they are two completely separate things. Some of the stuff to do with the culture is nothing to do with religion, and vice versa. People who don't know about Islam see some of the things going on in its name and think that's part of it, when it's not. What we need is awareness, understanding and a bit of a learning process really.

As I get older, this is something that has become really important to me - getting the message across. I read the biography of Malcolm X recently and saw the film about him, in which, at one time, he was saying that white people are the devil. At the film a lot of white people in the audience walked out, because it really went into them hard. At that time, Malcolm X belonged to the Nation of Islam, a different sect altogether, where they believe that the black man is superior to the white. So that wasn't the true teaching of Islam, that was a sect. And it wasn't until he went on the Hajj, the pilgrimage to Mecca, and had his eyes opened by the sight of Muslims - black and white - sitting and eating together and so on, that he became more moderate in his views.

That, then, is the idea of being guided by the Qur'an. Having read it once, you continue to read it on a continuous basis for the rest of your days, at home and in the mosque, trying always to develop a better understanding. It's a long-term commitment. As kids, we were supposed to go to the mosque every day but, as I said, we did skip it from time to time and if ever my dad found out that was when we got whacked. With my dad gone and my mum home from Pakistan, our Zaman went back to Denmark and his own family, so the job of keeping discipline fell to my mum and sisters more than ever.

Of them all, it was my sister, Qudisia who was the strictest disciplinarian. If she heard about it, she wouldn't let us watch Bruce Lee films because we were still under eighteen. It was like good cop, bad cop. Qudisia would lay the law down, while my mum would be in the background, wading in whenever she was needed with the final word. Qudisia was one of the few girls in our area, for example, who wore the hijaab - a headscarf - while she was growing up. My other sister then followed her example. Even now, I can rely on our Qudisia to tell me off when, in her eyes, I have done something wrong. Usually, it's for shaving off my beard.

Looking back, while I will be forever grateful to my mother and sisters for the way they kept me and my brothers in check, when I think about the death of my father I realise that in losing him I also lost the stabilising male influence that every growing boy needs. In my most impressionable years, rules, limits and boundaries would often go out of the window and occasionally I did come dangerously close to falling in with the wrong crowd. As the years went by and thoughts turned more to teenage thrill-seeking than innocent games of football and cricket in the street, the delinquency, gang culture and anti-social racism that I referred to earlier became an ever-increasing danger for all of us. With no authority father figure waiting for me at home, it was sometimes difficult not to get caught up in all of that.

Then again, it's true to say that, as a youth growing up in Headingley, I did manage to escape being dragged into anything too serious. For one thing, always at the back of my mind was the thought that I didn't want to disappoint my mother; not after everything she had gone through. To this day, she says: 'I have got four sons and not one of you has come out like your dad. Your dad was this, your dad was that, none of you can come near him.' That's my mother for you. I don't mind. To her, no one could ever replace or even come up to the knees of my dad.

# IKRAM WAS ALWAYS RUNNING AND CHASING SOMEONE...
## Mrs. Tahira Butt

Ikram was such a cute baby. He was fair and chubby and very good natured. As children, he, his brothers and all their friends used to play out in the street and Ikram was a very fast runner at that time. He was always running and chasing someone. I'm told that when he began playing rugby league he wasn't the quickest winger compared to some but, as a child, he was very fast indeed.

Everybody liked Ikram. He got on well with everyone. And he had his dad wrapped around his little finger. My other two youngest sons would never ask their father for money, they would send Ikram instead. Ikram would say: 'Dad, give me money, I want to buy chocolate.' And his dad would say: 'Okay', and hand it over. Then Ikram would go off, buy the chocolate, and divide it with the other two. He was very fair like that. He was always concerned that everyone should get their share.

Ikram had a lot admirers, especially among the females. All the women, his aunties, sisters and so on, doted on him.

He wasn't the sort of boy to get into scrapes. Mind you, he did have a close escape once. We used to have a cabinet in our living room and the top part was made of glass. Ikram leaned on it one day and it fell over on top of him, smashing over his head. His sister, Qudisia, ran off in case she got the blame. He survived. He always does.

As with my other boys, his father's unexpected death was a tragedy for Ikram, although he seemed to cope well with it at the time. That was because he was still so young, I suppose. My husband, Mohammad Iqbal, was such a fit man, there was nothing ever wrong with him health-wise. He was big and strong and very energetic and then, one day, he had a heart attack and was gone. As suddenly as that. He was such a good man and I still often sit quietly with a tear and remember him. I miss him terribly every day.

The children loved him too. He seldom got angry and when he did he would turn it into a joke. 'I don't want to punish you, your mum's making me do it...' he would tell them. Being severe was against his nature. Once, when he learned that my oldest boy, Zaman, had begun smoking, he told him that if he was going to smoke he should do it in front of him, not behind his back. On that occasion, I thought he was being too soft. As a result, it was left to me to tell Zaman off and so, to him, I was the bad guy and my husband got away with it. If ever I told their dad that the children had been naughty, nine times out of ten he would let it go.

My biggest regret is that Mohammad didn't live long enough to see the lives that Ikram and his brothers and sisters have gone on to achieve. When I think about that, it makes me so sad. He would have been so pleased to watch Ikram grow into the fine family man and sportsman that he has become. My Ikram is very much his father's son. I am so proud of him.

# 3

\*

# All Our Schooldays

Despite our family tragedy, growing up and finding my feet in such a multicultural Leeds suburb was a lot of fun on the whole, especially with so much sporting activity around. Our circle of friends was very mixed and we Butt brothers had the freedom of the area, from Headingley down to Burley - where Milford amateur rugby league club plays - over to Hyde Park and beyond. We were a happy bunch.

Some friends of ours who deserve a special mention here are the Matharus, the Sikh family who ran a mini-market at the top of our street. My mum used to help out there sometimes and cook for them too. There were four Matharu brothers in all and every single one of them was sport mad. In fact, the lads used to run a football team - Guru Nanak Sports - which our Tony, me and to a lesser extent Chinky used to play for. We would regularly take part in festivals and all sorts. The Matharus were a real inspiration to us; role models in terms of learning the value of sport as a hobby. We were only young kids, with a father who had passed away, and so the bond between our families grew very, very close. We were always in and out of their house. Whenever they went down to the cash and carry at Armley, we would help them out by stacking their shelves and get a free can of pop or bag of crisps for doing so.

The youngest Matharu brother, Amarjit, was our Tony's mate and about four years older than me. Then there was Manjit, who was a smooth guy, liked his clothes and was a good footballer. I got on well with him. Dharam and Mohinder were the oldest two. Between them, the Matharu brothers branched out into lots of different sports. As well as their football side, which toured India at one stage, they also formed a cricket team that played for a while in Bradford. Later on, Amarjit took up golf at the Cookridge Hall club in Leeds, where he broke new ground in playing off a four handicap and became the first Asian Sikh to win a tournament there. Mohinder was big on wrestling and grappling, while Dharam was always more of a coach than a player. Put together, their influence was immense, not only on the Butt family but the community as a whole. Their shop was like the local meeting point - everybody used to go there.

Business must have been good because, eventually, the family moved away to a large £250,000 house in Roundhay. I remember they took all the neighbourhood kids to the house to cut the grass - the garden seemed massive - and gave us all chicken and chips in return. We didn't mind. We thought we were cutting the grass so that we could play football. It was great. We used to call Mrs Matharu 'grandma', that was how close we were.

What's important about this is that it not only shows how Asians can be interested in sport - any sport - if they are given the opportunity, it scotches the idea that Pakistanis can't get on with Indians. That's ridiculous. To us, the

Matharus were like extended family and they still are. I'm really proud, for example, that Manjit's son, Rav, played football to a decent level with Leeds under-19s and that Amarjit's daughter, Kiran, is a well-known professional golfer.

In fact, Kiran is a former winner of the English Ladies' Amateur Championship, has won the Faldo Junior Series twice and represented Great Britain and Ireland in the Curtis Cup. She is one of the best in the country at her age and a real Asian icon, not to mention an ambassador for the Prince's Trust. Kiran Matharu has won sports awards, travelled all over the world and is destined for even greater things. Her brother Haminder, or Froggy as he is called, played cricket for Leeds and Yorkshire and, as a recent Leeds amateur champion, is a very capable golfer himself. So the Matharu family continues to dismantle the barrier that says, for Asians, sport is not a priority. In this, the Matharus were groundbreakers. As a youngster, playing in the tournaments they organised for us when we were kids, I couldn't help but notice that lots and lots of Asians were taking part, from all over the place. The Matharu brothers gave me a taste for challenging the stereotypes.

\* \* \* \* \*

They say that your schooldays are the happiest days of your life and, for sure, although I wasn't too keen on sitting still for many of the lessons, my own schooldays did give me the chance to participate in sport in a more structured and organised way.

As you have seen, Tony, me and Chinky were rarely indoors as kids. We played out all the time, mainly sticking to two favourite places. One was the back street behind our house and the other was the Brudenell Primary School yard opposite which, more often than not, had its gates locked. That didn't stop us. We just climbed over the railings and carried on with what we were doing. The caretaker didn't seem to mind. It was all harmless. We would congregate there and play football or cricket, or just hang about.

One reason the caretaker might not have been fussed was that it was our patch too. We were pupils at the school. I first went into the nursery section at Brudenell when I was around four years old and stayed there - in the school, not the nursery section - until I was nine. After that I moved on to Royal Park Middle School, also nearby in Headingley, and then went to Lawnswood High, where I stayed on into the sixth form because my sister and mother encouraged me to. To be honest, not being the most academic of students, I wasn't much cut out for further education. Sometimes I would think 'this is not for me', but I tried hard and our Qudisia used to make me do extra work at home, but still it didn't really sink in.

All in all, I am very lucky to have lots of sweet memories of my childhood. Especially during my schooldays, it was a time of fun, games, misbehaviour and laughter. And by 'misbehaviour' I mean it was more a case of borrowing apples from trees on the way home, that sort of thing, rather than anything criminal. Although we did get into bother from time to time, we were a decent bunch really and most of our friends were from a similar background. We knew lads who drifted into crime and things like that - this was inner-city Leeds - but for the most part we managed to stay clear of any direct involvement ourselves.

At school, if I had any favourite subjects they would have been history and religious education - RE. As I got older, I began to enjoy hearing stories of the past and learning about other people's belief systems. It is a subject that interests me even now; religion has always been an important focus in my life and always will be. We were taught that Islam, Christianity and even Judaism were very similar, as shown by our prophets - Abraham, Moses and Jesus Christ, among others.

It won't surprise anyone to learn, though, that my favourite subject was physical education - PE. That was the subject I was really passionate about. I remember once arguing with a teacher who gave me a 'B' in it. 'A 'B'!,' I said. 'How can you give me a 'B'?'. Funnily enough, though, despite my future career, the chance to play rugby league didn't come straight away; far from it. Apart from diving about in the snow at playtime, at primary school we played football, rounders and cricket. No rugby. And then, when I first went to middle school, I found I couldn't play rugby there either. Our Tony played rugby league at Royal Park, but he was in the year above me and playing for the year above that, so I had to make do with football instead.

The wait didn't do me any harm. I started to enjoy playing football and, the following year, I played soccer for my own year and, finally, like Tony before me, rugby league for the year above my own. We had a decent side too, as it happened, mainly made up of black Afro-Caribbean lads. We played a team from Hull in our first game and they beat us 6-3 but, after that, we won every single match, so I got used to success quite early on. In fact, we were so good we almost got to Wembley but, because Hull had beaten us in that first game of the season, it was they who ended up playing in the Challenge Cup final curtain-raiser, while we missed out. It would be another fifteen years before I got so close to playing at the old Empire Stadium again and that also ended in disappointment, when Featherstone lost to Leeds, 39-22, at Elland Road in a 1995 Challenge Cup semi-final.

All that, however, was for the future. For now, a number of our Royal Park rugby league team ended up being selected for Leeds City Boys under-11s and I was one of them. As ever, I was following in our Tony's footsteps. As his own career progressed, Tony played for Yorkshire Schoolboys and Leeds under-16s too. But my own highlight from around this time was when we, as Leeds City Boys, played in a curtain-raiser at Knowsley Road, St. Helens, one of the last times my dad ever saw me play.

There was one other Asian kid in the team back then. His name was Matloob Khan and he was a full-back. I played hooker, believe it or not. Packing down opposite me in the scrum was a big fat lad. As soon as the ball came in the tunnel he was all over it. I had no chance and this was still a time when it was vital to win possession (they've got to change the scrums today back to that, they really do). Anyway, at half-time, the coach switched Matloob and I around. It was a good decision. I was never a hooker in a million years. I was quite good on my feet, dodging and weaving and so on. I mean, I knew what to do - strike at the ball as quickly as you can - but I didn't really have any focus on that. And for another thing, I wasn't ugly enough. The Leeds first team that day had stars like the great John Holmes, Les Dyl and John Atkinson in it. They beat Saints and we did too.

And then that appeared to be it. Eleven years old and my rugby league career seemed to be over. Although we still carried on playing rugby in the street, at school it was pretty much back to football. And when I followed our Tony to Lawnswood High, the only rugby being played there was rugby union.

Being a prop, Tony gave the fifteen-a-side code a go and excelled. And anyway, he was spending his weekends playing league for any local amateur club who asked him, leading eventually to his selection for the city's under-16s. As the only Asian player in his age group - and a good one at that - he began to develop quite a reputation as something of an amateur rugby league nomad and, by the late-1980s, he was rewarded with a semi-professional contract under Peter Fox at Leeds.

As for me, it would be four years before I began playing rugby league again but, until then, it was football all the way. I did still watch rugby league. With Headingley just up the road, I used to go there regularly as a kid, usually at half-time when they let me in through the turnstiles without having to pay, because I had no money. People could be kind like that. Once, when I was eleven or twelve and the cricket was on, Pakistan were playing at Headingley. I got on the bus and one of the passengers called me a 'Paki'. The conductor came over and told the guy that if he was going to continue like that he could get off the bus, which I thought was great. He asked me where I was going and I told him: 'the cricket'. 'Okay,' he said. 'Just stand next to me.' And he didn't even charge me the fare.

At school, because my brother was doing so well, they tried to push me into rugby union, but I wasn't having any of that. I had never played rugby union in my life and didn't want to start now. Eventually, though, I was talked into going for school trials, they nagged me that much, but it all felt very odd. I just couldn't get used to having to get rid of the ball whenever you were tackled. My instinct was to go to ground, keep hold and then stand up and play it. And the teachers also had me playing flanker when I was used to playing hooker. All I wanted to do was run with the ball and sidestep. Simple as that. It was rare that I ever passed it.

I couldn't avoid union forever, though, especially as we did it in PE, and in time I started to find it quite good fun. My first rugby teacher at Royal Park Middle had been a laid-back, classy bloke called Mr Baker. He was rugby league through and through. Luckily, when I went on to Lawnswood, my sports teacher there, Mr McCready, was also a great individual and a huge encouragement. At times, when I wasn't doing so well with my school work, he would say that if I didn't start doing better he would stop me playing rugby. That was quite a powerful threat. The other teachers knew that those of us in school team would listen to him, if we wouldn't listen to anyone else. Looking back, Mr McCready was a big influence on my life. He was into basketball, so I ended up playing a bit of that too. He was very supportive.

Even so, at that stage what I really wanted to be was a footballer and, when I was fifteen, I had a trial for Leeds City Boys soccer team. What's more, I got in and played in the same side as the future Leeds United and England midfielder, David Batty. Like David, I was a central midfielder, and in pretty much the same style as I played rugby. On the football field, I was a straight up and down player. A grafter. I got stuck in. My only real weakness was that I couldn't head a ball. I remember I played one game, against Hull, and then went to Nottingham Forest as a travelling reserve. They were a huge club in those days - Brian Clough was still the manager - and it was fantastic going to that ground. Tragically for English football, my round-ball career wasn't destined to last. I got injured soon after and by the time I got myself fit again, the rest of the squad had progressed too far in their training for me to catch up.

Still, every cloud has a silver lining and mine came in the shape of the father of one of my former team-mates in the Leeds City Boys rugby league under-11s. One day, while I was playing for the school football team, this bloke came over from the away school touchline and said: 'Are you Ikram Butt?'. I said I was and he told me that just about all of those lads, including his son, were now playing together at the Stanningley amateur rugby league club, in the under-15s. Would I like to come down? I said, yeah, of course I would. By now, that other Asian kid who played in the under-11s with me, Matloob, had moved from his old school in Kirkstall to Lawnswood and we had become best mates, so he went along to Stanningley too. Nowadays, Matloob was no longer a full-back, he was a hooker and a very strong tackler. He could have gone on to be a professional player himself, but he broke his leg and didn't have the support mechanisms within his family to rehabilitate and come back. That was a real shame. Matloob had huge potential.

Anyway, my next big problem was actually getting across to Gotts Park, where Stanningley trained every week. As I said, the Butt family didn't have much money and I couldn't afford the bus fare. Luckily for me, the manager there, a magnificent fellow called Alan Robinson whose two sons also played for the Leeds City Boys, offered to give me a lift in his car and then bring me home again. That is probably just as well because, without Alan, I would have struggled to make it and may even have soon lost interest. He treated me like a son and his kindness was a crucial lesson in how, when it comes to encouraging kids to take part in sport, it is important to make doing so as easy as possible. We shouldn't put obstacles in their way.

Alan's helper and our coach at Stanningley, meanwhile, was a bloke called Phil Carmichael, who was once a director at Bradford Northern. I think he played a bit too, until he broke his leg. Anyway, the one thing I do remember about Phil is that he used to drive all the way over from Bradford in his milk van. It was that sort of set-up. Everyone was friendly and pleased to see us when Matloob and I arrived. It was smiles all round because we were among old mates. It wasn't long before I had slotted into the side at centre - with Matloob there, my hooking days were long gone - and we had a great little team. Steve Barnett was there, a Bramley lad and stand-off, who signed for Bradford when he was seventeen. I was good friends with Steven. Neil Summers, who also ended up at Bradford, was there too.

At first, we played in the Yorkshire amateur league but that didn't last long because, despite being an under-15s side, we were coming up against seventeen-year-olds and other over-age players every week, which was very tough and a bit silly really. The biggest problem, though, was that the Yorkshire League was prone to very bad discipline and, so far as we could see, not very well run. So Phil and Alan decided to relocate us lock, stock and barrel to Apperley Bridge, where we formed a brand new team and played in the Bradford League instead. More often than not, we were still up against lads older than ourselves but, on this side of the border, it all seemed a bit better organised. We played against West Bowling, Clayton, Queensbury, Dudley Hill, teams like that.

In any case, the move suited us. In our first season, we won practically every trophy going and, in our second year, we actually did - sevens tournaments, the lot. I used to hate playing sevens because, with our team, we were making breaks all the time and you never got the chance to stop for breath. The only real downside to playing in Bradford was that we came in for a bit of stick because, as individuals, most of us were from Leeds.

On the whole, though, those two years at Apperley Bridge were some of my most enjoyable in the game. And although it was sad when the club eventually started to dissolve as a result of players getting older and moving on, by then I had been picked for the Bradford under-17s squad to play in the Yorkshire County Championship, and been voted back of the tournament, with Ian Smales winning best forward. So for me, personally, things were looking up. By now, professional club scouts such as Eric Hawley and Alan Gilfoyle had begun to notice me too. Where's the ambitious and sports mad teenager who wouldn't get excited about that?

# IKRAM IS SOMEONE WHO JUST NATURALLY BREAKS DOWN BARRIERS...
## Greg Mulholland MP

*Vice-Chair, All Party Parliamentary Rugby League Group and member of the All Party Rugby Union Group*

I remember watching Ikram Butt playing for Featherstone Rovers. I never imagined that years later, I would get my rugby boots on and take to the pitch with him at Headingley stadium. Nor did I have any reason to think that Ikram and I would work together promoting rugby and community and become friends, but all those things have happened.

Ikram is someone who naturally breaks down barriers. It used to be defences, now it is inbuilt prejudice and lazy cultural assumptions. A West Yorkshire lad from a Pakistani family, he epitomises the modern West Yorkshire with a strong sense of heritage from both here and from there. From there, a strong sense of community and family; and from here, a love of West Yorkshire and of rugby league.

Ikram went to school at Brudenell Primary School where I am a governor, a wonderful community school that serves very well the diverse population that live around it and he went on, of course, to be the first British Asian rugby star. He made history and people of all backgrounds in Headingley, in my own Leeds North West constituency, are very proud of him as well as him being a role model for British Asians.

Ikram was to be the first of many Asian rugby players, or so we presumed. Alas that has never happened. There are still some barriers that need to be broken down. So not content with his playing career and the achievement that represented, Ikram had seen and lived with the challenges that still exist for integrating our diverse communities on and off the sports field. Thus, as you will later read, the British Asian Rugby Association was born, Ikram's brainchild, to encourage South Asian Brits to play rugby of both codes. This continues to attract players of all ages, but of course is having the biggest impact where it should and needs to, amongst the kids.

When you watch him coaching or refereeing a local schools' tournament, Ikram's passion is just as strong as it was in his playing days. It is inspiring to see the joy on the kid's faces who are trying tag rugby for the first time, and to watch children not only enjoying the thrills of the oval ball game but learning team work and mixing with kids who they might otherwise not have had the chance to meet.

Nor does BARA get enough credit for another bringing down of barriers; it is an association of both codes of rugby. Who could have imagined that a few years ago? Breaking down barriers is what Ikram does. But he does it with a smile and a handshake and makes everyone involved feel they want to help him gently break those barriers down too.

So it has been my pleasure, now as Headingley's MP and both Vice-Chair of the All Party Parliamentary Rugby League Group and a member of the Rugby Union Group, plus occasional threequarter in the Commons and Lords rugby team, to support the work of BARA and to work with the same Ikram Butt who I used to watch all those years ago.

I have even captained an Ikram Butt-coached politicians rugby league side, the first time that such a team has played.

We want to see more - many more - professional rugby players coming from the British Asian communities in our country. But we also want to see people, like me, who just enjoy sport as enthusiastic amateurs and who find that they meet people they would never otherwise meet and learn how to play a part in a team.

There is no better way to break down cultural barriers than through learning and playing sport together. Thanks to Ikram, this is happening the world over, including in West Yorkshire and in South Asia and most of all, inside people's heads and hearts.

# 4

*

# Destination: Leeds

One of the first clubs to make a direct approach for my services was Bradford Northern, now the Bulls. In fact, they said they were interested in three of us; me, Steve Barnett and Neil Summers. We went along to Odsal for a chat and got as far as the boardroom, where they offered us all a contract. It wasn't anything close to decent, though, so we all knocked it back. Later on, the club made an improved bid for Steve and he signed for them when he was seventeen, a record signing for someone of his age.

With Steve gone, Neil and me felt sort of left behind, although Phil Carmichael told us not to worry as he was sure we would get signed eventually. And, as it happened, Neil did end up playing for Bradford. At first he switched codes and went off to Headingley RUFC, where he was selected at one time for the England 'B' team. But amid rumours that his working class background was holding him back from bigger international honours, he came back to league and signed on at Odsal.

As for me, although York were thought to be interested,

the only other firm opportunity came from Hunslet, who offered me, Sonny Nickle (then playing for Leeds amateurs Hunslet Parkside) and another lad £500 each, with £25 for every reserve team appearance and I can't remember the first team terms. It wasn't a lot, I do know that much. Sonny snapped their hand off, while I declined. It turned out to be one of the most sensible moves I ever made.

With no dad to advise me and pound signs in front of my eyes, this was a tricky period for a young lad like me to negotiate, so I will always be grateful to the likes of our Tony, Phil Carmichael and Alan Robinson for the advice and guidance they gave me at this vital point in my career. And just around the corner were two more positive influences in the shape of lifelong rugby league stalwart Harry Jepson and my ultimate coaching mentor, Peter Fox, who were both responsible for giving me what I saw as the opportunity of a lifetime: the chance to sign for my boyhood favourites Leeds in November 1986.

By the time of the move I had most recently played a game or two for Bradford amateur side Dudley Hill, so that was the club I officially left to turn professional at Headingley, rather than Apperley Bridge. More importantly, signing professional forms meant I was forced to pass up on the opportunity of an amateur scholarship in Australia, a decision that its organisers BARLA - the British Amateur Rugby League Association - weren't very happy with, as I recall, seeing as how they were engaged in an ongoing political power struggle with the professional game's ruling body, the Rugby Football League, at the time. And, looking back, it perhaps might have been better if I had travelled down under, if only for the life experience. But when you are an ambitious eighteen-year-old with a club like Leeds in your sights, you tend not to want to hang around, do you?

In all other respects, signing on at Headingley - initially

to play for the Leeds Colts under-19 side - felt like a real no-brainer. For one thing, my brother Tony was there. For another, as one of the biggest rugby clubs in the world in either code, Leeds were just too glamorous to resist. Then there was the fact that I lived just around the corner. I wouldn't have far to travel at all. And, of course, when the time came to sign on the dotted line, there was the money. In what was reported as a £21,000 contract, I received £6,000 in my hand, up front. Then there was £300 a win if I made the first team and £60 for an Alliance or 'A' team appearance. A draw away meant winning pay, a draw at home, losing pay. In the reserves that came in at around £20, but we were still probably the best paid in the game. In any case, we did a lot of winning. Being in the 'A' team at Headingley meant playing in front of big crowds and often alongside star-name players. They used to call us the first team rejects.

Given our family circumstances, to have such a large financial sum coming into the house was very welcome and I remember that my mum took the lot when I signed. She had no use for the brand new Puma boots Leeds gave me, though, and I remember thinking 'this is great'. But, as I later realised, signing was the easy bit. The hardest part was getting anywhere near the first team and, in the end, I only managed to do that once - in my very last game at the club.

In hindsight, the writing was on the wall when Peter Fox was sacked only three weeks after my arrival. I had come to Leeds buzzing with confidence and determined to do well. And at first that is exactly what happened. After impressing with Leeds Colts, I was soon chosen to play for Yorkshire Colts and then, in January and March 1988, was selected to represent Great Britain Colts in two Test matches against France. As it turned out, those would be the last two games that Great Britain Colts would ever play, as the international system had another of its many overhauls shortly afterwards. Anyway, we finished the concept in style. We won the first game, 17-10, in Salon, and followed that up with an 18-6 victory at St. Helens.

Understandably, as a youth international with the bit between his teeth, my next target was to continue my progress with Leeds and go on to make the national under-21 side. Unfortunately, though, that never happened. I was never given the chance. As I became too old for Leeds Colts, it was the Alliance team all the way for Ikram Butt and, some weekends, I even found myself on the substitutes bench.

Now don't get me wrong, I had never thought for one minute that making an impact at Headingley would be easy. As a lifelong Leeds fan, no one knew better than me their reputation for signing top-class players, often from overseas, which made it difficult for young kids like me to be given an extended run. The club was struggling on the field too. But with Peter in charge, I knew I would at least be given a fair crack of the whip.

In fact, by the time of his early departure, Peter had already put me in his first team squad. I am not saying I would have gone on to make the team, but my foot was in the door. I remember David Creasser coming up to me and saying: 'Ikram, are you playing?' I said: 'no, I'm just in the squad'. But that's the sort of thing Peter did for you, to boost your confidence. As a youngster trying to make your way in the game, you can only benefit from the experience of being among talented players and knowing that you are rated by your coach. It's how you improve.

Make no mistake, Peter Fox is a fine coach and an excellent man. He himself, though, would admit that he likes to do things his own way. And that has never been how the Leeds machine works. For a start, the board is constantly under pressure to deliver results. The expectations are so high and, at that stage, Leeds had underachieved for many a season. A one-off individual like Peter was always going to struggle in that environment. He was never one for taking orders, especially from folk who had nowhere near the knowledge of the game that he did.

\* \* \* \* \*

With Peter off to pastures new, that meant a return to Headingley for the equally legendary Maurice Bamford, who had already been in charge of Leeds once, between November 1983 and February 1985, before going on to coach Great Britain.

In writing this book, I have been looking over Maurice's own autobiography, *Bamford: Memoirs of a Blood and Thunder Coach*, and one bit in particular tickled me. In talking about his return to Headingley, Maurice writes: 'In the two and a half years I had been away, the club had gone downhill, not may I add because I was not there, but a general feeling of decline was in evidence.' He continues: 'Although two outstanding centres had been brought over from Australia for a season - Mark McGaw and Andrew Ettingshausen - very little else had been signed to bolster a side that had lost David Ward, John Holmes, Roy Dickinson, Neil Hague, Tony Currie, Ian Wilkinson, Dean Bell and all the good Aussies: Grothe, Hunt, Patterson and Terry Webb. Incoming were Carl Gibson, Andy Mason, Phil Fox, Gary "Slugger" Price, and as it appeared to me, about ten wingers.' And there was me, thinking of myself as a budding centre.

Either way, seeing as how the new coach obviously considered that he had his threequarter line well covered, it's no real wonder that I spent so much of my time under Maurice in the reserves. In fact, Maurice would be the first of three coaches in three years at Headingley, a turnover which meant I was always going to be on the back foot when it came to impressing the man in charge. Our Tony, too, seemed to suffer in this way. It was Peter Fox, after all, who had first brought him to Leeds as well. Around the time of my arrival, Tony looked well on his way to becoming a first-team regular, whether at prop, hooker or even in the second row. But then, after just six appearances - two of them from the bench - with Peter gone he drifted out of first-team contention and had some difficult career choices to make, before making a one-game comeback for the third of those coaches, David Ward, in 1990.

Not that, to begin with, I was unhappy with my lot. The exact opposite, in fact. As my later selection for the GB Colts proves, although first-team opportunities were scarce, I was enjoying myself and doing well. I always got on well with Maurice. He was a local bloke who took a keen interest in the amateur scene, and he knew all about my reputation as a promising junior. And, anyway, I understood the situation. As usual at Leeds, first-team places were in limited supply because of the quality of talent being brought in, and the pressure on the coach for results. As time went on, my only real complaint was that, sometimes, it seemed as if some players were being selected on the basis of reputation rather than form, but that's how it has always been at every club and I was still very young. Nowadays, I do a bit of coaching myself, and I have probably been guilty of doing the same thing. As a coach, there is an understandable tendency to go with experience, rather than take a risk on an unknown quantity.

Either way, with Maurice in charge the first team just about managed to avoid relegation at the end of the 1986-87 season by the skin of its teeth, finishing just above Oldham on points difference. And when the following season began, those of us in the 'A' team went on to win just about every trophy going under the astute coaching of Norman Smith. We won the Yorkshire Cup, the Challenge Cup, the League Cup... you name it. It was wonderful. I was playing in the same side as my brother and we had the best crop of young players in the country. By the end of the season, I had played for Great Britain Colts. What was there not to love?

Meanwhile, in the Leeds first team, Maurice brought in the ultra-talented Garry Schofield and Lee Crooks, both from Hull FC. I knew Schoey of old. A Leeds lad, he had signed on at Hull from the same Hunslet Parkside club that Sonny Nickle played for, much to the disappointment of many in the city who naturally hoped he would gravitate to Headingley. When he opted for Hull instead, the rumour went around that he had done so because they had given him a Ford Cortina.

Anyway, Schoey made his first team debut for the Airlie Birds, as Hull were then known, in September 1983 and I can still remember looking on from the Headingley terraces as he scored a hat-trick of tries against us just a few weeks later. Even though Leeds were my team, Schoey was a hero of mine from that moment on. In his first game after signing for Leeds, he scored two tries against the Auckland tourists in a real bruiser of a match and had to be carried off with a leg injury. By the end of another eventful year, Maurice too was on his way, as Leeds finished fifth in the table and again ended a season without silverware after being pipped 15-14 by St. Helens in the John Player Trophy final.

If Peter Fox and Maurice Bamford arrived at Leeds with big reputations, the next coach to come in, Mal Reilly, was probably the most formidable of the lot. Allan Agar - who had coached Featherstone to a shock Challenge Cup final victory over Hull in 1983 - came with him, too, as Malcolm's assistant, so hopes were high that the mid-eighties trophy drought could be ended. And again, to begin with at least, although I was still playing in the 'A' team, everything was fine. I seemed to be well-liked and part of the bunch, and every year I was offered a new contract. I was still enjoying myself and apparently in Malcolm's plans. I was even named in the extended first team squad now and then. But, as ever at Leeds, for me that was about as far as it went.

Now, more than ever, the pressure was on for success. And, as it happened, Malcolm and Allan delivered in the shape of an exciting 33-12 Yorkshire Cup final victory over Castleford at Elland Road in October 1988. It must have been a sweet moment of personal triumph for Malcolm, who had made his name as a player and coach with Cas. Leeds went on to finish joint-second with St. Helens in that season's Championship, too, hinting that more good times could be just around the corner. Even so, and by his own admission, Malcolm didn't really enjoy the best of times at Headingley. His biggest problem seems to have been that he was spreading himself too thin. Along with also being the coach of Great Britain, he was juggling those roles with a day job at the John Smiths brewery. To make matters worse, he got shot of some popular players, most notably Paul Medley, an exciting runner and real fans' favourite, who he swapped for the hard-working Paul Dixon at Halifax, a decision that didn't go down too well in the South Stand, I can tell you. The end result was that, in September 1989 and just two games into the new season, Malcolm too was on his way, voluntarily in his case. His replacement was one of my boyhood idols at Leeds, the one-time hooker David Ward.

With Mal Reilly gone, it would be another eleven years before Leeds won their next piece of silverware - the Challenge Cup, after beating London Broncos in the last ever rugby league game to be played at the old Wembley Stadium in 1999. As for me, I had more immediate concerns. Well before the end of the 1988-89 season, I had begun to get fed up with the lack of first-team opportunities coming my way. And when, in January 1990, Wardy brought Simon Irving in from local rugby union - a very good centre though he was - I knew that my time at Leeds was all but done. No matter how well I performed, I didn't seem to be getting any closer and the thought was in my mind that I might be better off elsewhere.

Certainly, my earlier target of becoming an under-21 international was well off the radar. Other reserve players had since moved on and my own game wasn't improving. Again, not having a father figure didn't help. Our Tony's rugby career had really slowed down by now because, as the main breadwinner in the house, he felt he had to work and earn some money. So, when it came to my own rugby, I was on my own at Leeds with no one to guide me.

These days, a lot of people tell me that I have a very strong social conscience, and I suppose that's true. But that isn't how it was when I was young. Back then, in my late teens, if folk ever said that I was a bit of a role model - and they often did - I didn't really grasp what they were talking about. At that stage there were so many things that I wanted to do for myself that I hadn't achieved yet. You know how the press are. They build you up when, really, you haven't done anything, but it sweeps you along anyway. All I was interested in was becoming the best rugby league player that I could be.

Young people are naturally selfish and that is certainly how I was. I make no apology for it either because, if you are going to be a good sportsman, a certain amount of selfishness goes with the territory. There is a lot of personal sacrifice involved. A times, it can make you seem quite unsociable, especially among the mates you grew up with. They want to come and see you and so on, but you don't want to do that because it's taking you away from what you want to do. To be single-minded and disciplined is very important if you are going to succeed in your ambitions. I wasn't the most sociable person back then, but I knew what I wanted. If I fell out with a few people because of that, it wasn't intentional.

Nowadays, of course, I recognise the wider importance of being a role model and ambassador only too well. It's how you can make the most positive impact on society. That realisation only came to me in my late twenties, when I went to university and did a diploma in community sports development, after having gone through a traumatic life-changing experience of my own, of which more later. And for sure, when you see some of the real hard core stuff going on in the name of Islam today, it becomes even more important for we Muslims with a public profile to get out and speak on behalf of the community because, if things are left as they are, the situation will only get worse. If we find ourselves in a position to shine a bit of light and understanding, then that is exactly what we should do.

\* \* \* \* \*

Anyway, back to the rugby, and the long and the short of it is that my time at Leeds was nearing its disappointing conclusion.

I remember once playing for the Leeds 'A' team against Featherstone reserves, for example, and telling Peter Fox, who had replaced Paul Daley as the coach of Rovers in May 1987, that I was available if he wanted me, just as a joke, like. At least I think I was joking. But it wasn't until 1990 that Featherstone - through Peter - came back with a firm offer. Later, I discovered that Peter had actually been chasing another winger, Norman Francis, but Norman didn't want to take the jump. We were at different stages in our careers, I suppose. Personally, I couldn't wait to get away. There had been talk about me going on loan to different clubs, but I couldn't drive back then so it was difficult.

Having said that, when it eventually did come to travelling over to Featherstone for my debut with the club, it turned out that I had a fair way to go. Around twelve thousand miles in fact, because I was in Australia when the fax came through. Towards the end of the 1989-90 season at Leeds, Dave Ellis - who was mates with our 'A' team coach Norman Smith and is now the defence coach of the French rugby union team - had come into our changing room after a reserve game and asked if anyone was interested in an off-season stint at a club he would be coaching in Queensland. He told us he was looking for two backs and a forward. The idea of being paid to play in the sunshine and enjoy a different lifestyle appealed to me, so I immediately jumped at the opportunity.

The thing is, although I was, finally, chosen to play in the Leeds first team in the very last league game of the season - I came on for Carl Gibson in a 38-18 away defeat at Castleford - I now had itchy feet big time. I'm not sure how much my selection at Cas had to do with them trying to appease me because I was unsettled, but I do know that I can't have been part of coach David Ward's longer-term plans because I wasn't picked to play in any of the Premiership knock-out games after that. To be honest, back then, David and I didn't really get on. We had a strained relationship to say the least. A few years later, when he came to Featherstone, it was all sunshine again between us; in fact whenever I see him out and about now, we are good mates. Last year, he shook my hand and put his arms around my shoulders at Wembley: 'Now then, Ikram, how are you doing...?'. But at that stage of our careers, for whatever reason, no doubt six of one and half a dozen of the other, he always seemed to rub me up the wrong way. I remember one time, when I was reluctant to come back out of the changing room because I had a dead leg, David exploded with rage and threw a bag of ice in my direction. I suppose that shows a bit of a bad attitude on both sides really, although it all seems quite comical looking back.

At the time, too, I must admit that, as a young player trying to get on in the world, I did suspect that there might be something racial in the way I was being treated. I no longer think that now and am always reluctant to play the race card at the first excuse, but the fact remains that, as an Asian in what was seen to be an essentially white working class game, participation in rugby league wasn't always made easy.

Not that I am suggesting that rugby league is any more racist than other sports, because it isn't. In fact, as the journalist Dave Hadfield wrote in a September 1990 edition of *Rugby League Week* magazine, while interviewing Tony and me after I signed for Featherstone: 'Compared with other major team sports, rugby league has a long and proud record of being close to colour-blind.' On the face of it, that's true. You only have to see the impact on the game of, say, the Lebanese community in Sydney, or the influence of black West Yorkshire-born players such as Sonny Nickle, Henderson Gill and Roy Powell to recognise how important non-white faces have been in the game. And that's without mentioning all-time legends like Clive Sullivan, Billy Boston, Cec Thompson and Ellery Hanley. To pretend that there was no problem at all, though, would be kidding ourselves.

Certainly, the toughest environment in which to operate from that point of view was the amateur game. As you might expect, amateur rugby league was tough enough without any racial nonsense. Once at Apperley Bridge, for example, we played Hunslet Parkside in some cup competition or other, and me and Sonny ended up fighting and eye-balling each other. I'm glad it didn't get serious. He was a hardnut, Sonny. He still is. When you are playing professionally, in front of a big crowd, you know full well that the referee will stop any scrapping after a minute or two, so you can get stuck in without too much worry. But in amateur rugby, it isn't quite so well controlled. In many a game, the kid you were brawling with would offer to carry it on in the showers... no thanks! You can be brave on the pitch but off the pitch is a different matter.

As far as racial abuse goes, most of the stick I took came in the form of insults. I remember watching our Tony play in an amateur cup final once and he got sent off for retaliation after someone called him a Paki. It was so completely out of character for him to do that, I knew straight away that someone must have really annoyed him. And the daft thing is, the bloke who was giving him stick turned out to be one of his mates. But that's how it often is. Most folk say things without realising how obnoxious they are being. They don't see that they are doing anything wrong in acting so superior. You do get your out-and-out racists, obviously, the brainless white supremacists who want to keep Britain for the British, whatever that is supposed to mean. On the whole, though, I believe that most of our racial problems come down to ignorance; a lack of understanding. That's why education is so important, in every culture.

Generally, while I copped a fair amount of racial abuse in the amateur game - and it did sometimes feel strange to be the only Pakistani around - the way you earn respect at any level of rugby league is to play it hard and within the rules. I always tried to do that and became quite popular as a result, especially with the fans at Featherstone. I can honestly say that only on one occasion did I ever hear any negative comments from the crowd - and that was from an away fan, and a black guy at that! The Featherstone supporters were fantastic. All I ever got was encouragement.

And I am being quite open here. If I did hear something derogatory I would definitely say so.

The story was similar away from home too. There was only one club that ever used to give me stick and that was Hull. One particular time, we had just got off the coach and this sweet little girl called me a 'bloody Paki'. She can only have been about eight or nine years old. Unbelievable. Generally, though, I used to enjoy playing away. It lifted me. Warrington was a tough place too, but I did used to enjoy going there. I had played at Wilderspool many times in the reserves so I didn't find it daunting. I enjoyed getting stuck in.

Workington was horrible, and so was Salford. Walking out through those metal grills with the spectators hurling abuse. Again, the obvious question, I suppose, is was any of it racial? My honest answer is that if it was, I didn't hear it. In amateur matches you pick any comments up clearly, but that's not the case when there's a big noisy crowd and you are mentally 'in the zone'. All your concentration is on the game.

Another thing to bear in mind when we are talking about racial abuse is that Martin Offiah used to get stick. Ellery Hanley used to get stick. But they were great players. I was never a great player. I was straight up and down, and an honest toiler. People only ever give stick to brilliant players.

More of a problem for me was the fact that there weren't many Asian faces in the crowd, although that was something I had grown used to, right throughout my junior career. Asian rugby league fans seemed to be rarer than Asian players so, when you did see one, they stood out like a sore thumb. 'Oh, that's nice,' I used to think. Until they started calling me useless or something, obviously.

To be honest, there are complicated reasons why there aren't more Asians in British rugby league. I've got plenty of strong theories and I'll get around to discussing those later in the book. Back in my playing days, like many people, I thought it might have something to do with the fact that many Asian kids aren't particularly well-built, although now I'm not so sure. Undoubtedly, another reason is that, for many kids of a South Asian background, their first sporting love is cricket. Often, they want to make a breakthrough in that, before they go on to other sports.

In that *Rugby League Week* interview I referred to earlier, our Tony thought that rugby league might be suffering indirectly from the way in which local-born Asian cricketers were struggling to get any recognition from Yorkshire CC. At the time, it seemed to many of us that there was a whites-only policy on the other side of the football stand at Headingley. As Tony said: 'They tend to think that if they can't make it at cricket, which is part of our culture, what chance do they have at anything else?'. It was a fair point then, although that can't really be the case anymore.

One thing's for sure, it has certainly never been down to lack of numbers. There are loads of heavily-populated Asian areas in the North of England, where rugby league has traditionally been strongest. Parts of Lancashire and the West Yorkshire region that takes in Leeds, Bradford, Halifax, Huddersfield, Dewsbury and Batley ought to be buzzing with Asian rugby league players and supporters. There's no real reason why that shouldn't be so, if those within the sport in positions of influence have the will to make it happen.

My own oldest brother, Zaman, played all sorts of sports at Moor Grange High School without ever really taking it any further in terms of participation. It's the same story as with most middle-aged blokes, I suppose. Nowadays Zaman is a mad keen Leeds rugby league fan, which has nothing at all to do with the fact that myself and Tony once played for them. He just feels part of the club, that's all. Asian people can be as important a part of the rugby league community as anyone. The key is to ensure that they know they belong to the family.

# IKRAM WAS ONE OF THE LADS AND A GOOD DRESSING ROOM INFLUENCE...
## Harry Jepson OBE

*President of Leeds RLFC*

When Ikram first signed professional forms at Headingley in 1986, during my own tenure as Leeds football chairman, it quickly became apparent that we had found ourselves a very good young player indeed.

For one thing, he was so sturdy and solid, which is obviously a very good thing if you want to make it in big-time rugby league. Ikram was one of the lads but also a very good influence in the dressing room. He quickly played for Yorkshire Colts and then played in the final two games that Great Britain Colts ever played.

Before we took him on, Ikram had already played for the Leeds district junior side as an amateur player. When he joined us, his brother Tony was already at Headingley, and Ikram became a fixture of our own under-19s team. He was a very, very good lad.

If I had to sum up Ikram's qualities as a player, I would say that he wasn't tall but that he was strong as an ox and an excellent tackler. He was particularly dangerous near the line; very much like vaunted winger Alan Smith. Ikram wasn't a long distance try scorer by any means, but if he got the ball ten or fifteen yards out, you knew you were in business.

Put it this way, he was good enough to break into the Leeds 'A' team quite early on and, back then, that was a very good team indeed. The GB Colts side, which I also helped to manage, wasn't bad either.

During his days at Headingley, Ikram was never anything other than a credit to himself, his family and the club. Unfortunately, when the time came to kick on, he just didn't have that extra bit of talent that was needed at Leeds, although he did go on to serve Featherstone well.

Ikram's subsequent achievements in the game are all the more remarkable when you consider how he didn't, like most players, exactly come from a background that was seeped in the sport of rugby league. If we are to attract more British kids like Ikram into our sport, then that is clearly an issue which the game needs to put right.

You look at a town like Batley, for example, which is at the centre of a big Asian community. They have a lovely ground, excellent facilities, but they just cannot seem to get the Asian public interested.

Maybe the answer lies in how the real strength of rugby league lays in its community roots. I am also vice-president of the Oulton amateur club and we have some good young players down there. Even so, it can sometimes be a struggle to attract new players, but relying on amateur clubs to unearth raw talent is a relatively modern phenomenon.

Up until about 1970, when there was a big change in education and it all went to middle schools and so on, in Hunslet we had nineteen schools. Eighteen of them played rugby league. Apart from two or three junior schools, every one of those schools had three rugby league teams - under-

11s, under-13s and a senior team. Every Saturday morning - and this story was repeated right across places like Leeds, Featherstone, Hull, Halifax, Castleford and Wakefield - all the pitches in Hunslet were full of teachers running rugby league teams.

On top of that, all the schools were situated within hundreds of yards of each other, so there was a tremendous rivalry. That's why the Hunslet representative side did so well. While I was secretary of the Hunslet Schools Rugby League, we actually went four years without losing a game. The players all knew each other. Sadly, all that is gone now.

So, really, if there is to be any progress in attracting more South Asians into rugby league, it is going to have to start in schools. I am no expert on race relations but I can see that it would be very difficult to persuade an Asian boy to go out on a limb and join an amateur rugby league club, unless there were other Asian players already there. There are people brave enough to do that, of course; Ikram and his brother are two of them. But if we can help to make that pathway more attractive, then that's what we should do. By increasing the amount of rugby league played in schools - and the RFL are already doing lots of good work in that regard - would make that work much easier.

All of which only goes to underline the strength of character that Ikram has shown in getting to where he is today. Over the past few years he has also served on the Rugby Football League's disciplinary committee at Red Hall; another tremendous achievement. The committee sits just about every week throughout the season and Ikram slotted right in, whether he is seated next to a former referee or a High Court judge. That's just how Ikram is; he can get on with anyone. He is an excellent role model.

# 5

\*

# From Australia to Featherstone

Meanwhile, out in the Australian bush, and I was soon having a whale of a time playing for the Chinchilla Bulldogs in the South West division of the Queensland Rugby League.

After deciding to accept Dave Ellis's offer late in what turned out to be my final season with Leeds, I contacted Steve Barnett, my former amateur team-mate at Stanningley and Apperley Bridge, and we ended up travelling out there together for an off-season in the sun. That suited me down to the ground. Apart from the fact that we were good mates, Steve, now at Bradford, was a classy stand-off and I played at centre. I used to love running off him. Even as a junior, Steve was always a couple of moves ahead of everyone else. He was a heck of a player.

And, when we got there, the rest of the team turned out not to be bad, either. The area in which the club was based, Chinchilla, in Queensland's Western Downs, only had a population of about three and a half thousand, but just about all of them turned out to watch us every week.

## Tries and Prejudice

Although the competition was essentially amateur, it was also very popular. The club president was the former Australian Test player, Jack Gleeson, and he used to tell us many a tale of his former exploits against the likes of Roger Millward. That was how things were at Bulldog Park. Everyone was very friendly and it didn't do any harm that we had a very good side, in which Steve and me were scoring tries for fun.

In fact, during our time there, we got all the way to the Grand Final and won it. Sadly, the lads played that last eighty minutes without me. I was keen to stay on - the Bulldogs certainly wanted me to - but in the lead-up to the game I was faxed a contract by Featherstone and they insisted that, if I wanted the move to go ahead, I would have to return to the UK straight away. I think Peter would have let me stay for another week, but the board insisted that I came back.

The contract Featherstone offered me was a very sizeable one by their standards. That plus the fact that Peter described me in the press as 'a very keen player who was never given his chance at Leeds' made me feel wanted at Post Office Road right from the start. I went there on a three-year contract worth £7,000 a year, including bonuses. I remember that one week we drew at Hull in a cup game and got £400, and then beat them at our place the following week, so that wasn't a bad pay packet. Generally at Rovers, we would get £300 for a win if the team was in the top four, £280 if we were in the top eight and around £250 if our league position was lower than that. Certain individuals had a better deal. Chris Bibb, Paul Newlove, Deryck Fox and overseas signings like 'the baby-faced assassin' Brendon Tuuta, for example, were all on pretty much a full-time wage, although they mostly worked outside the game as well. Match payments, so far as I know, were all the same.

When we lost, we got £50. Less tax, of course. We still had to pay tax. This isn't rugby union we are talking about.

To be honest, I would have gone to Featherstone for nothing. Peter's father-figure support was just what I needed at the time and I never looked back. From languishing in the Leeds reserves, I soon became a respected first team regular, although not without difficulty at first.

After saying goodbye to my mates at the Chinchilla Bulldogs, I flew home on the Friday and was playing against Bramley in the Yorkshire Cup on Sunday afternoon. I met the team and everyone was very welcoming. To be honest, I fancied myself as a centre when I arrived but Peter said he had a place for me on the wing. I asked him: 'Why can't I play centre?'. To which he replied: 'I've got Paul Newlove and Terry Manning at centre, Ikram'. So I said: 'Okay, that'll do.' And it did, too. I scored a try on my debut. During the second half, Terry passed me the ball and I handed-off the one man I had left to beat, which became something of a trademark for me. I scored between the posts after scorching in from, ooh, a good ten or fifteen yards. That was a long way out. I also set up a try for Chris Bibb and we won the game 36-4, so I came away quite pleased.

I had made a good start then but, after that, I didn't score for ten games and the rest of that first year turned out to be quite difficult, in terms of making a successful transition playing-wise. The truth is, I struggled to adapt to the pace of first-team football. Although I had gained years of experience playing among first-team players in the reserves at Leeds, there was still an enormous difference. it was a big jump and I had such a lot to learn. The game was much faster than what I was used to. You had to make quick decisions and those decisions always counted. One slip or lapse of concentration and you had let in a try.

My attacking confidence took a while to build, too,

especially when I wasn't crossing the whitewash. At Headingley, I had scored tries quite regularly, playing alongside the likes of Norman Francis, who would bust tackles all day and make it easy for me. But at Featherstone, for some reason, after that initial game it took me a while to get going. As usual, Peter was very understanding. He kept reassuring me that my all-round contribution to the side was good - and said that tries would be the icing on the cake. I became known as someone who could be relied upon to run the ball strongly from dummy-half or on the first tackle, and so long as I was doing that then everything was fine. And anyway, as time went on, tries just started to happen. I finished my debut season with ten. By the time I left Featherstone, I could boast a rough average of one try scored in every two or three matches played, which isn't a bad record.

As ever in rugby league - and indeed in any team sport - much of my success at Featherstone was down to the quality of the players around me. For a start, there was my centre partner, Terry Manning, signed from Keighley and one of the toughest around. During our time together, Terry outplayed just about every other centre in the competition and we developed quite a rapport. He was a ferocious tackler, which was just as well seeing as how we played on the right-hand side of the field. The natural inclination, for any team, is to pass the ball to the left, which meant we always had lots of defending to do. Occasionally, Terry would shoot out of the line but nine times out of ten he would make the tackle, so it wasn't a problem.

Conversely, when it came to our own attacking play, Terry and I tended not to get the ball in our hands as much as our left centre and winger did. But seeing as how it was Paul Newlove and another signing from Keighley, Owen Simpson, filling those positions, no one was going to complain about that, were they? As I say, Terry was a wonderfully gifted defensive centre, but Newy had to be one of the greatest attacking threequarters in the world; a true force of nature and pretty much unstoppable in full flight. Outside him, Owen continued to be an electric finisher as well. In their first full season together (1991-92), Newy and Owen finished one and two in the try charts after scoring forty-eight tries between them while playing in the same team. With Chris Bibb behind us at fullback, we all had the safety net of knowing that, if ever the ball went over our heads, Chris would be there, on whatever side of the field, covering the danger. There was never any need to worry about chasing back. We were a very solid unit.

In fact, I played alongside loads of great players during my time at Featherstone. As a club, we were never short of strong and talented personalities, that's for sure. The tough-tackling forward Gary Price, known as 'Slugger' to his mates, and my old mate Gary Rose were two such players, while Brendon Tuuta, who would also tackle anything that moved, was another. Brendon was a New Zealander like our other overseas signing, big Clarry Iti from rugby union, and he had arrived at Rovers from Sydney's Western Suburbs with a reputation as a bit of a madman, hence his 'baby-faced assassin' nickname. In fact, it often seemed as if the referees were picking on Brendon because of that. But if ever they left him on the field long enough, he showed that he was a very gifted back-rower. Brendon was as ferocious in his defensive duties on the field as he was friendly off it and he was pretty good with ball in hand too. He darted through many an opening before feeding his supporting player with the killer pass.

Probably the best all-rounder in the team, though, was Deryck Fox, who was an absolute master technician at scrum-half. His coach and namesake Peter once said that if

Deryck hadn't lacked just a little bit of pace, he would have been one of the greatest half-backs ever. And bear in mind that this was at a time when the likes of Andy Gregory and Shaun Edwards were still doing their thing. Peter was right. Whenever Featherstone played Wigan, Andy Gregory was always outplayed by Deryck, who was Mr Consistency and had played over two hundred and fifty matches for the club by the time I arrived.

Also helping me to settle in quickly at Post Office Road was the fact that blokes like Jeff Grayshon and Trevor Clark, who had Leeds connections of their own, were around the place. In that sense, I could never really think of myself as a complete newcomer, because I had built my credibility at Headingley and played against Rovers often in the reserves. Geographically, Featherstone and Leeds aren't all that far apart, either, so it was hard to feel that you were among strangers. On top of that, operating out there on the wing in such a small and homely stadium, I tended to spend a big lump of my time next to the fence, so I was soon able to build a close relationship with the Rovers fans too. As the weeks went by and I became more and more acclimatised to the demands of first-team rugby league, my Leeds disappointment fell away and I began to look towards the future with confidence. Happy days.

\* \* \* \* \*

In fact, over the better part of my first two seasons at Rovers, the only weak link in the chain that I can think of is that we never really had a settled stand-off. And even then, the lad who most often took the role, Ian Smales - a loose forward or second-rower by trade - did a very good job. In fact, Smalesy scored nineteen tries in thirty-two starts during my debut 1990-91 season, while Martin Pearson, who later made the position his own, ran in ten. Brendon Tuuta also filled in well at number six whenever he got the call.

The situation arose as a result of Graham Steadman's close-season move to Castleford in August 1989. It had been a controversial episode. Steady was a very good player, well-respected at the club, and he had forged an excellent partnership with Deryck Fox at half-back. But when Cas came calling, allegedly with a huge offer on the back of an illegal approach, it really turned his head. Rovers, though, were keen that he should stay and they put a massive £185,000 price tag on him, hoping that would frighten Castleford away. The tactic didn't work and after an industrial tribunal finally decided in Steadman's favour, he made the move to Wheldon Road as planned, although Featherstone did end up £175,000 better off, payable over three installments.

In true rugby league style, the first thing the Rovers board did with the money received was go out and spend it - and a fair bit more too - in the biggest cash spree the club had ever seen. Not that I was complaining; I was one of the players they eventually bought! Along with myself from Leeds (£30,000), and Terry (£40,000) and Owen (£50,000) from Keighley, Rovers brought in Leo Casey from Oldham (£100,000), Gary Rose from Keighley (£20,000) and Mark Gibbon from Doncaster (£20,000). It sent a message that as they approached their 70th year as a professional club, Featherstone Rovers were determined finally to join the high-achievers. Until now, they'd had more of a reputation for developing young players and then seeing them snapped up by bigger clubs, so the ambitions of all concerned, including Peter Fox, were obvious.

Despite all the money spent, Featherstone was never going to be a team of glory-boy superstars; not with Peter in charge. If anything, he instilled a pragmatic 'all for one, one for all' mentality into the side. We had an experienced yet mobile pack - no better typified than by our terrific ball-handling prop Leo - and Peter was clearly determined to build a team in his own image. In my first season at the club we pretty much held our own, doggedly picking up an 18-16 away win at Leeds along the way, much to my satisfaction. At the end of it, we scraped eighth in the table, which gave us a first-round Premiership play-off clash at mighty Wigan, a team that no one gave us any hope of beating, seeing as how they were stacked with talent and had lost only four matches all season, amassing forty-two league points to our twenty-five in the process.

Remarkably, though, with Deryck Fox having another of his outstanding games against them, we actually turned Wigan over, 31-26. Not surprisingly, it caused a bit of a sensation. Trevor Clark helped himself to a couple of tries, with the rest coming from Bibb, Manning, Smales and Burton, while Foxy tagged on three goals and a drop-goal. We didn't do too badly in our next game, either, against league runners-up Widnes, until we finally went down 42-28, as John Devereux and Martin Offiah shared five tries between them at Naughton Park.

At the start of the 1991-92 season, my second at the club, we really began to take teams on and beat them. By the end of the first month, we were third in the table having beaten Halifax, Swinton and Warrington and things were looking good. Then there was our victory over Hull in the Yorkshire Cup at the Boulevard. As I said earlier, Hull is a tough place to go at the best of times, and especially when you are two tries down at half-time. Anyway, as we sat in the changing room ready to return and face the infamous Threepenny Standers in the second half, Peter told us that we needed a miracle and asked us to find him one. Terry Manning and I looked at each other, ran back onto the field and scored a try apiece. We drew the game and and then beat Hull in the replay at our place, a week later.

Although Peter had already had a huge influence on my rugby career, it was during our time together at Featherstone that I got the full benefit of his expertise. He had been my first professional coach at Leeds, of course, if only for a very short while. But when he left Headingley our relationship continued. I would ring him up regularly because, in many ways, he was the father that I no longer had. Long after he had gone from Leeds, when I was wondering whether to just go and do something else, Peter would advise me to stay involved in the game, ride out the bad times and see it through. He is the reason why I got involved in the game and the reason why I stayed involved in it. No other coach ever inspired me as much as he did. He was always full of sound advice, and still is to this day.

Peter's philosophy was always that character was the most important attribute in a player. By his own admission, he was never a modern era style coach - first and foremost he was a motivator rather than a clipboard merchant. In other respects, though, he was way ahead of his time. He was professionally trained in industrial management for one thing, and took Featherstone to Wembley twice in successive years when the club gave him his first coaching job in the early 1970s. Peter was always full of ideas and left no stone unturned in looking for ways to get one over on the opposition. He was a great rugby league thinker.

His big problem, if he had one, was that he didn't always have enough players with the ability to put those ideas into practice. Famously, just before I arrived at Post Office Road, he had even tried to sign Wally Lewis, the legendary Australian stand-off and greatest rugby league player in the world at the time, which would have been an amazing coup for a club as unglamorous as Featherstone. He was serious, too, and the signing might well have come off if Wally hadn't then broken his leg and scuppered the deal. At one point, he also made a bid for the Wales and Llannelli rugby union winger Ieuan Evans, who was said to have turned down an offer of £150,000 to stay amateur and was subsequently named captain of his country. Had Peter Fox had been able to call on the sort of players that, say, Dougie Laughton had at his disposal at Widnes, he would have been an even more successful coach, I'm sure.

The thing with Peter was that players wanted to play for him. He inspired loyalty in everyone around him. Well, not quite everyone. As shown by his experience at Leeds, Peter was an individualist who went his own way, which often got up the nose of club officials. Even at Featherstone, his dealings with the board could be strained at times. Peter frequently clashed with the chairman, Eric Gardner, which is obviously going to make things difficult for any coach, and so it was probably inevitable that it would all end in tears at some point.

Even so, when it came, Peter's departure from Post Office Road was sudden and unexpected, particularly seeing as how we had made such a good start to the season. We had only been playing a couple of months when, in October 1991, he was lured away to Bradford Northern by an offer that was obviously too good to refuse. Northern, under the player-coaching of David Hobbs - another former Featherstone favourite - were struggling and looking odds-on favourites for relegation at the end of the season, so no wonder their chairman, Chris Caisley, wanted Peter. After a successful earlier spell at Odsal between 1977 and 1985, he was already a well-respected figure there and, as things turned out, his appointment was inspired because he did manage to keep Bradford up - if only just, on points difference. Looking back, that was a massive achievement and one which I think isn't fully appreciated. It's hard to imagine that Bradford could have gone on to make the impact they did in the summer era as the Bulls if they had been relegated in 1992. Back then, crowds at Odsal weren't very good anyway and they would have dropped even more in the Second Division. Instead, Peter stayed at Bradford for another four years and during that time made them the closest challengers to Wigan. And when Chris Caisley and Co elbowed him out in 1995, new Aussie coach Brian Smith had a solid platform to build upon.

\* \* \* \* \*

Although Peter had left Featherstone, once again I continued to stay in close contact with him. He had helped to get me my day job as a quality control inspector at his own place of work, Yorkshire Copperworks in Leeds, so it would have been hard for me not to have done. That job was an absolute boon and yet another reason why I will be forever grateful to Peter Fox. For one thing, its flexibility meant that I was able to train all the hours under the sun, which made me fit as a butcher's dog. Most of the other lads only used to train at Post Office Road. They were advised to exercise at home too, but seldom did. It was only later, when full-time rugby league came in, that pretty much everyone's fitness became of an equal standard.

Anyway, with another coach on the horizon, we players still at Featherstone faced having to impress the new man in charge. By now, I had established myself as a first-team player and so was confident that I could do that. I was fit and training well and felt that, whoever came in, I should be okay. At the back of your mind, though, you are never quite sure, especially when you are particular sort of player that I was. Solid, reliable, rarely flashy; either you liked the way I played or you didn't. Fortunately, when the new man's name was announced it was Allan Agar, who I knew from his time as assistant coach to Malcolm Reilly at Leeds. Allan was a local lad who had already been coach at Featherstone between December 1982 and October 1985, during which time he led the club to a Challenge Cup final win at Wembley. His son, Richard, nowadays coach at Hull, ended up playing for us too. As a result, nothing much changed. Allan just tried to keep things going as they were and added his own flavour although sadly, by the end of the season, we did end up being relegated. Ironic, really, when you think that we had made such a good start under Peter and that, having left for Odsal, he managed to keep Bradford up.

It was a shame for Allan. Despite finishing second from bottom in the table, under him we ended up on a respectable twenty-two points - level with Northern, Hull and Salford - and only two points away from a top-eight place. We played some good stuff at times. Obviously, the league table says that we lost too many games, but that was nothing to do with Allan's coaching. He coached us very well. We beat everyone over the course of the season - all the big guns, Leeds, Widnes, St. Helens, Hull... you name it. We were on £400 per win and I made more money that year than I ever did. So how come we went down? Beats me. It was a tough year and having beaten Leeds by a Deryck Fox drop-goal in our last home game of the season, we still had a great chance of staying up going into our final away game at Wakefield; we had done all the hard work. But nothing went right for us that day. Trinity beat us and, with so many teams on the same points, that was that.

In hindsight, I suppose that the writing was on the wall from the very first game after Peter left, a 40-12 defeat to Hull, although at that point Allan hadn't yet been appointed. As players, we were all in shock at Peter's departure and feeling a bit rudderless. And it wasn't until a first-round Regal Trophy replay with Bramley in November that we were finally able to get our next win. In the second round, though, we really blew away some of our frustration. Playing Halifax at home, we ran out 64-18 winners and Martin

Pearson scored four tries. Owen Simpson and Paul Newlove ran in five between them, while Chris Bibb and Brendon Tuuta got one apiece. Somehow, I didn't manage to get on the scoresheet - and I can't have had to do too much tackling to do, either! Deryck Fox kicked ten goals, although it was all in vain. In the next round, we were knocked out, 34-22, by Widnes. And just to prove how close the competition was that year, even though Halifax eventually finished seventh in the table above us, we actually beat them three times.

It was the first time that Rovers had been relegated since 1987, but owing to the closeness of the finish - Bradford only just squeaked past an injury-weakened Hull Kingston Rovers, 14-12, in their final game - the Featherstone board seemed ready to stand by Allan, whose efforts in difficult circumstances they appreciated. Our chairman, Eric Gardner, thanked him and the club's supporters for standing by us when things got tough. It wasn't long before Allan himself was talking about winning immediate promotion back to the top-flight and, as it turned out, that is exactly what did happen, although Allan was not to be a part of the following season's successful campaign.

The reason for his departure was tragic. Before the 1992-93 season began, Allan went to the committee and told them he was sorry, but he would have to resign his position, because his wife Liz was suffering from terminal cancer. The club, reluctantly, accepted his decision and Allan left with everyone's good wishes. Sadly, Liz passed away later that same September and her funeral, at Purston church, was packed with people offering their condolences. What an awful way for Allan's second spell at the club to come to a close. Sometimes, admittedly, it was hard to know how to take Allan but, all in all, I had a lot of respect for him. He was a local lad who put his heart and soul into Featherstone and would have done so for nothing.

# IKRAM COULD EAT - MAYBE THAT'S WHERE HE GOT ALL HIS STRENGTH...
## Paul Newlove

*Featherstone Rovers RLFC - 1988-1993*

The one thing you can say about Ikram is that he never let you down. At Featherstone, if we were ever pinned down on our own line, you could rely on Ikram to be in at dummy-half bringing the ball away. Time after time after time.

We had other tactics at Rovers too. Francis Maloney, for example, might kick the ball upfield straight from the scrum on the first tackle and Owen Simpson would chase off after it. Mostly, though, it was a case of Ikram taking the pressure off the forwards, bit by bit. He wasn't the classic speedy winger like Owen was, but he didn't half work hard.

I remember that his mum once made some onion bhajis which he brought to training one Tuesday or Thursday night. Anyway, we all got there early and began stuffing our faces. And then when training came around at half past seven, we were told that we were going on a run. Needless to say, we didn't train very well at all that night. It was worth it, though. They were the best onion bhajis that I have ever had.

He could eat, could Ikram. No wonder, with his mum's cooking. Maybe that's where he got all his strength from. Although he wasn't the paciest of wingers, his body strength was unbelievable. He would push two or three players off before he went to ground.

The way Peter Fox, our coach, had us set up, myself and Owen were the tryscorers, while Ikram and Terry Manning on the other side of the field were known more for their defence. Put it this way, Ikram scored about 60 tries in five years and Terry was a real workhorse as well. And then behind us we had our full-back Chris Bibb, who would join the line at every opportunity. He was a terrific attacking full-back was Chris.

I had some very enjoyable times playing at Post Office Road with Ikram. As a youngster, I had the choice of going to any club but I wanted to play for my local team. It was the best decision I ever made. My family had so much history with Rovers, for one thing, and when Terry came along, and Ikram was there too, I ended up having some of the happiest days of my playing career.

# IKRAM'S FITNESS WORK WAS ABSOLUTELY PHENOMENAL...
## Terry Manning

*Featherstone Rovers RLFC - 1989-1994*

When I first joined Featherstone, I was one of the first to come from outside that area, except maybe for the New Zealanders.

For me, it was great to join a club with so many quality players and when Ikram became my winger that was even better. We were similar in our approach and doubled up at training. We did a lot of running together, fitness work and so on. Ikram's own fitness work was absolutely phenomenal - a little bit better than Newy's!

Ikram was also very consistent. He didn't miss many games in five years and nor did I. Our team was as near as dammit the same every single week. Not just that, we were all best mates and pulled together. There was a small town atmosphere about Featherstone and we all bonded. I go back now and see how small the place is and can't believe how much we achieved. The camaraderie was amazing.

When Ikram arrived, Featherstone were in a bit of a rebuilding process under Peter Fox and he slotted in with no problem at all. The thing is, thanks to the sale of Graham

Steadman and Karl Harrison to Castleford and Hull, it was the first time that Rovers had any money in ages. So Peter was able to blend his own team, rather than just make do with inherited players. Peter is a great man manager so, looking back, it was no wonder that we all gelled.

Being part of a team coached by Peter was very special - he made you feel special. Everything he said and did was for his players. We were the ones that mattered. He understood us and cared about us. His knowledge of rugby league, and his understanding of people was like nothing I've ever known.

Myself, I had been the top tryscorer at Keighley before I arrived, and Gary Rose and Owen Simpson came from Keighley too. So I felt at home straight away. Having said that, the one thing I will say about Ikram is that when I did eventually move on from Featherstone, I expected all the other wingers I played with to be exactly the same as him. At my next club, Hull, for example, my winger was Tevita Vaikona, who went on to play for Bradford. He left after eighteen months and didn't turn out too bad, did he?

Ikram and me developed a really good understanding. A lot of that was down to Rovers being a good family club, and a lot of it was down to our similarities in character. Neither of us were the most skillful players, but we were both hard-workers who were after the same thing. Run the ball in hard and give it one hundred per cent.

Ikram has also taken that attitude into his development work. Like him, I have had racial comments made to me over the years too. But while insults like that are stupid and never comfortable for anyone, you can't let it get you down too much either. In my case, those insults just made me stronger. Handling that kind of behaviour can go towards building your character and, anyway, these days it's nothing like it used to be. At least part of the reason for that is Ikram himself. He's a great example to everyone.

# 6

\*

# Me and Mr. Martin

Death always puts life into perspective, doesn't it? But the world keeps turning and Featherstone once again had to find themselves a new coach. Everyone at Post Office Road knew how important the 1992-93 season was going to be.

In its wisdom the club decided that this time they would go for an Australian. At first, that looked like being John Dorahy, the Newcastle Knights coach, who later ended up at Wigan and Warrington. Everything seemed signed and sealed with Dorahy, terms were agreed, but three times he had to cancel his travel arrangements on account of how the Knights were doing much better than expected in the Winfield Cup play-offs. The Rovers board later said that if they had been told about his reasons from the start, they would have understood and waited for the Australian season to finish. As it was, they lost patience. It just looked to them like he wasn't as committed to coming to Featherstone as he should have been and the deal was scrapped.

In his place, the club approached another Aussie coach

called Steve Martin; no relation to the comedian, although I might have told you different by the time I really got to know him. It was easy to see the attraction. After John Monie's success at Wigan, Aussie coaches were becoming more and more popular with English clubs - it seemed as if many club directors saw them as miracle workers. And it's true that Steve had done a great job in turning North Sydney from the Australian league's rubbing rags into genuine title contenders. If he could work the same magic at Post Office Road, we would be laughing. Or so the theory went.

To be fair, Steve didn't do a half bad job in his first couple of years in charge and the pair of us got on fine to start with. He seemed to like the way I played. My game had matured and developed, so I was scoring a lot more tries on a regular basis. I remember a game at Rochdale, just after he arrived, at which Steve was as an observer. Tex Hudson, the club stalwart, was still temporarily in charge but, at half-time, Steve came into the changing rooms. He patted me on the back and said to continue with what I was doing. As it happened, we lost that game, 26-22, but I found his comments encouraging and, seeing as how we were soon winning most of our matches once he settled in as coach, the rest of the season went along quite comfortably too.

There was one dark cloud - the departure of Deryck Fox to join his namesake, Peter, at Bradford Northern. Deryck had first put in a transfer request during the close-season, which was turned down. I could understand his reasoning. He was getting frustrated with never having won anything of note and, for sure, a player of his ability deserved to be playing in a higher division than the one we were going to have to get ourselves out of. The money on offer wouldn't have done any harm either, of course. Whatever his reasoning, an unsettled player is no use to anyone and, in the end, Rovers were forced, reluctantly, to let him go.

Deryck knocked back good offers from Leeds, Halifax and Hull before the Bradford fans rallied round to raise the required £140,000 transfer fee and he was on his way to Odsal. Again, it was the Peter Fox effect in action. Players just want to play for Peter.

Steve Martin's immediate response was to fill the huge gap left by Deryck with one of his fellow Australians; Brett Daunt. At first, Brett found it difficult to acclimatise. He was a decent scrum-half in his own right, but any player would struggle to follow in the footsteps of Deryck Fox at Featherstone. Steve brought a Kiwi prop over, too, Wayne Takaeta. In time, both Wayne and Brett won the fans around and became important members of our squad. As for the season itself, well, with only eight teams in the division, it meant that each side played the others four times. We were all sick of the sight of each other by the end, let me tell you. Not that it mattered all that much to us. We went on a fifteen-match winning run and finished the campaign eight points clear of Oldham at the top of the table, comfortably fulfilling our objective of promotion at the first attempt. We also appeared in the Divisional Premiership final against Workington, in front of around 36,000 people, at Old Trafford.

Promotion apart, the 1992-93 Division Two season hadn't been all that much to shout about; to be honest we were too good for the division. But that day at the home of Manchester United more than made up for it. In fact, it turned out to be a real career highlight. Until then, our biggest games of the season had been a surprise 18-14 win over Salford in the first round of the Regal Trophy and a Challenge Cup clash with St. Helens that we could have drawn if we had decided to kick a penalty in the closing minutes, rather than take a tap and go for glory. The Premiership final, though, was something else.

Our opponents, Workington, had finished four points behind Keighley Cougars at the top of the Third Division, but they didn't half give us a game. In fact, they led 8-6 at half-time, as we made mistake after mistake and were put off by their, shall we say, rugged tactics. Owen Simpson, for example, was carried off in the first-half, as a result of a horrible high tackle by Tony Kay that should have resulted in a red card, but didn't. By then, the Cumbrians had taken the lead with a converted try by Phil McKenzie off a Dean Marwood kick, before Paul Newlove drove over in the corner from Brendon Tuuta's long pass and Martin Pearson tagged on the extras for us. Marwood's second goal, shortly afterwards, sent Town back up the tunnel in front, and we knew we had a major job on our hands if there wasn't going to be a shock.

We had the players to do it. By now, Brett Daunt had hit his stride, while Gary Price and Tuuta were playing like demons. We had a couple of lads in the side who had arrived in the early part of the season from Leeds, Richard Gunn and Francis Maloney, a stand-off, who had become as disillusioned at Headingley as I was. They were doing well too. Chris Bibb was out for the season after being crunched in an earlier thriller at Oldham, so the goal-kicking Pearson filled in at full-back. And then there was our try-scorer, 'Newy' himself. If anyone could get us out of a tight corner, he was the man.

And so it turned out, although things didn't look like ending so happily when, after both sides had swopped early penalty goals, Newy was felled like a collapsed mill chimney while going for the line. It was a shuddering hit and, for a while, it looked as if his final was over; he was on the ground for what seemed like ages. But after a lengthy period of treatment he somehow got back to his feet and volunteered to play on. A good thing he did, too, because with about fifteen minutes to go, and with us still trailing in one of the tensest matches I have ever played in, Newy took a long pass from Brett and ploughed over to put us in front, despite being absolutely swamped by defenders. It was a really brave effort by Paul and one that his team-mates and all the Featherstone fans appreciated. Three minutes later, he almost crowned it with his hat-trick, but the Town lads just scrambled back in time to deny him. It didn't matter. From the play-the-ball, Neil Roebuck's pass sent Francis in and, with Martin Pearson's conversions, that was pretty much that, although Martin Oglanby did squeeze over for a try near the end, giving the scoreline a more accurate look of Featherstone Rovers 20 - Workington Town 16.

No surprise, then, that when it came time for us players to vote for our Player of the Year, the decision was unanimous. Paul Newlove and his wing partner, Owen, had scored 82 tries between them, with Newy providing an amazing 48 to that total. He scored another four in representative games too and was, without a doubt, the finest attacking centre that I have ever had the privilege of playing alongside. But my own centre partner, Terry Manning, wasn't bad either, and us two had plenty to celebrate also. For one thing, both Terry and myself played in every single game that season - all 37 of them - contributing 27 tries and goodness knows how many tackles of our own. As a team, we scored 243 points more than our nearest rivals and were only four short of scoring 1,000 points over the entire campaign. Martin Pearson's 391 points was a club record.

As for me, well, understandably, I was feeling pretty chuffed. I had been an ever-present in the side, helped the lads to win promotion and then the Divisional Premiership before, finally, and perhaps best of all, being voted Clubman of the Year. That was a huge honour and one of which I was really proud. Featherstone is quite rightly known as a family club and by now I had built a terrific rapport with the supporters, something I treasured very much. 'Ikky, Ikky give us a wave..', they would sing. Or maybe just shout encouragement: 'keep it up, Ikky!', or 'come on Ikky, get them going' when we were a bit flat, because they knew that I had it in me to lift the side. I felt as though I was riding on the crest of an exciting wave. The trouble with waves, though, is that, sooner or later, they all come crashing down.

\* \* \* \* \*

Looking back, the omens for a less successful 1993-94 season were there right from the start. Even before a ball was kicked, in fact. The first problem arose as the season approached, when our preparations suffered a massive blow with the departure of Paul Newlove to Bradford Northern.

Clubs had been sniffing around Newy for ages, which no one should have been surprised about. Paul's reputation was growing fast. He was already an international and seemingly had the world at his feet. In Featherstone's favour, Paul's dad, John Newlove, had also played for Rovers in his day, so there were family ties with Post Office Road. And while, at other perhaps bigger clubs, a young player like Paul might have had to wait forever for an extended chance in the first team - the word 'Leeds' comes to mind - Featherstone was a club that liked to give youth its head and so expected a bit of loyalty in return. In Paul Newlove, they felt that they had hit the jackpot and were sure that a very good side could be moulded around him, if it was given long enough to develop.

Unfortunately, the Rovers directors and fans never had the chance to test whether that was true. It was the Deryck Fox scenario all over again. Although other clubs were interested in Paul and the Featherstone board insisted at first that he was going nowhere, making him all sorts of financial inducements to stay, once it became known that the favourites for his signature were Bradford - where Peter Fox was still coach - there was only ever going to be one outcome. Once Peter had his eye on you he always got his man, and the Paul Newlove transfer saga was no exception. Like Deryck before him, Newy wanted to win things and if his old boss Peter was to be his coach then so much the better. Even so, it cost Bradford a whopping £250,000 transfer fee to complete the deal.

For a club like Rovers, such a sum of money is always going to come in handy, but it has its down side too. For one thing, thanks to the newspapers and the rugby league grapevine, everybody knows there's cash in the bank and so the price of any replacement goes up accordingly. That certainly turned out to be the case when the club decided that Newy's replacement at centre should be another Great Britain international, Andy Currier, from Widnes. High-flyers at the time, Widnes always seemed to feature in the big games, whether it be Challenge Cup finals, Premierships or the World Club Challenge. In reaching the top, though, it turned out that they had massively spent beyond their means and were in a state of financial meltdown. As a result, big-earning Andy could not agree terms and so found himself on the transfer list.

At first, although it had cost Featherstone £150,000 to get him and people were still naturally disappointed that Paul Newlove had left us, there was plenty of excitement over Andy Currier's signing. The fans were looking forward to watching him in action and we, as players, were keen to play alongside him. Andy was a class act who scored and made plenty of tries, along with kicking more than his fair share of goals. After speaking with Steve Martin, he seemed impressed with the progressive plans for the club and, like us, saw no reason why we couldn't finish in the top eight, never mind survive life back in the first division. It would be good to have him in the team.

If we hadn't realised it already, though, this year fate was not to be on our side. And in Andy's case, he didn't even make it to the starting grid. As things turned out, his one and only appearance for Featherstone that season was in a well-attended pre-season home friendly with Dewsbury. After making a break down the main stand side towards the Railway End, he went down awkwardly in a tackle near the 20-metre line and tore a cruciate ligament. As the physios carried him off on a stretcher, you could have heard a pin drop. No one could believe it. At one time, such an injury might have meant the end of Andy's career. As it was, he missed the entire season and recuperated only very slowly. Ironically, he had been relatively injury-free until then.

Whatever our bad luck, we still had a season to get through and so the team building went on regardless. Matt Calland, a strong centre from Oldham, was brought in to replace Andy Currier, and Steve Martin also signed Gavin Hall, a prop from New Zealand. Gavin came with a huge reputation but he was obviously unfit from the start and only lasted four games as a substitute before he went back. A much better signing was my fellow winger, Carl Gibson, from Leeds - a snip at £15,000. Others to arrive during that season included Steve Molloy from Leeds, Gary H. Price from Wakefield Trinity and Graham Southernwood from Castleford, while Iva Ropati, the Kiwi international, came back for a second spell at the club from Parramatta. On the way out, meanwhile, were Ian Smales (to Castleford), Gary Rose (Leeds) and our old reliable full-back Chris Bibb.

Despite our close-season disarray, we began our long-awaited return to the first division in positive style. After beating Leigh and Hull Kingston Rovers, and then losing away at Halifax, we actually turned over no less a side than Wigan, 35-22, at Post Office Road. The rest of September turned out to be a bit of a damp squib, though, and included defeats to Bradford and Sheffield before a visit from Leeds provided us with what turned out, for me anyway, to be one of my favourite games of the season. Martin Pearson, I remember, was buzzing on that day and contributed fourteen points as we beat my old club, 22-20. Best of all, I scored a try - something I always enjoyed doing, especially when Leeds were the opposition. I never felt bitter about my lack of opportunities at Headingley, but it did always give me a big surge of satisfaction to show them just exactly what I could do. I would be lying if I said otherwise.

In fact, those victories over Wigan and Leeds pretty much set the template for what was to come. Mainly, we flattered to deceive. At home, we went okay; it was our away games which usually let us down. Although we were never seriously worried about relegation, by the end of the season we only managed to finish eleventh in a table of sixteen, just outside a Premiership play-off position. Looked at realistically, I suppose that was not too bad an effort given that we had only just returned to the first division, although it did feel quite disappointing at the time. We'd had such high hopes beforehand. We flopped in the Regal Trophy too, losing away to second division London Crusaders, 26-12, in the second round.

We did a little better in the Challenge Cup, raising our supporters' hopes with away wins at London and Hull K.R. (I scored tries in both those games, thought I had better mention that), before going down 32-14 to the eventual winners, Wigan, in a bad-tempered televised clash at Central Park. The most memorable thing about that game was the all-in brawl that led to the RFL giving both teams a

£500 suspended fine afterwards. Steve Molloy and, later, Neil Roebuck were sent off for us, while Andy Platt got his marching orders for Wigan. At one point, Kelvin Skerrett ran in from the other side of the field to join in with the scrap, but somehow the referee didn't notice and he managed to escape any punishment. Lucky boy. Not that I threw any punches myself, of course. Perish the thought. Have you seen the size of Kelvin Skerrett?

If that game was tasty, the best was yet to come. It came on 14th March 1994 at Headingley, when we ended a four-match losing run by completing a league double over Leeds. To be fair, my old team may have had one eye on a Challenge Cup semi-final with St. Helens the following weekend, but their side still had stars like Ellery Hanley, Garry Schofield, Alan Tait and Kevin Iro in it, so they were far from being pushovers. Again, I managed to score a try and generally had an eye-catching game all round, as we unexpectedly took them to the cleaners, 36-10. Apart from myself, there were a number of former Leeds players in our team that day and lads like Steve Molloy, Carl Gibson and Richard Gunn must have all felt they had a point to prove too. As it turned out, however, despite that terrific win, our overall inconsistency cost us in the end. It was Leeds, not ourselves, who featured in the end-of-season top-eight play-offs although, as I later discovered, my own performance that day had not gone unnoticed by one of the men on the receiving end.

\* \* \* \* \*

All in all, then, although it was far from being disastrous, Featherstone's 1993-94 campaign had promised much but delivered little. People were getting itchy for success. We had seen great players like Deryck Fox and Paul Newlove leave the club, while nothing had appeared to come from the money generated by those transfers - in terms of cups or trophies anyhow.

Personally, I ended 1993-94 having played in 32 games and scoring 12 tries. Unspectacular, but steady enough. Like everyone else, though, I knew that if Rovers were going to win anything in season 1994-95, we would all need to lift our game a notch. This was a time when clubs like Wigan were very dominant and they would not be easy to catch.

In the bigger picture, the 1994 close-season saw seeds of enormous change sown in professional rugby league, not just in England but further afield in Australia and New Zealand too. It was then that the idea of a Super League was first put forward, which eventually led to an £87 million deal with Rupert Murdoch's Sky Sports and a switch to summer for the British clubs too. The most controversial idea of the time, though, was that a number of famous old clubs should merge.

Originally, for us, that meant Featherstone would join forces with local rivals Castleford and Wakefield to form a new 'superclub' named Calder. Elsewhere, Warrington and Widnes would become Cheshire; Barrow, Carlisle, Whitehaven and Workington would be known as Cumbria; Hull and Hull Kingston Rovers would form Humberside; while Oldham and Salford would be Manchester, amongst others. As the thing panned out and thousands of marching fans made clear their disgust over the direction in which the game was heading, the proposed Super League was whittled down to more sensible proportions. I didn't know it at the time, but the revolution that followed would still have major implications for my own future career.

Anyway, more about that later. Once the 1994-95 season got underway, for Featherstone events didn't get any less chaotic on the field than they were off it. We made a terrible start to the campaign and straight away our coach, Steve Martin, really began to sweat under the pressure. The more the team struggled, the less he seemed to want to change the game plan and it wasn't long before he was looking for a scapegoat. Unfortunately, that turned out to be me.

To be fair to Steve - which is showing him a little more support than he gave me - a lot of the things that went wrong early on that season weren't really anyone's fault. Our leading pointscorer Martin Pearson, for example, got injured pretty much at the start and only managed to play five games all year, although Mark Nixon, the Kiwi international, came in from Rochdale Hornets as cover and did very well. Owen Simpson was another who missed a big lump of the season with injury. But one of the biggest issues was with our scrum-half, Mark Aston, who Steve Martin had signed from Sheffield Eagles for £100,000 during the summer. A lot was expected of Mark, or 'Tubby' as everyone calls him. At Sheffield, Mark was a great player who had fitted in well but he couldn't quite slot in at Post Office Road. We couldn't get the best out of Mark and vice versa, as I am sure he would admit himself. It wasn't his fault, we just played to a different system, that's all. On the plus side, the club notched a first when it signed two Frenchmen, Daniel Divet and Freddie Banquet, who both went on to become crowd favourites.

As for me, well it all started to go wrong when, after three or four games, Steve announced that the next person who made a mistake in a game would be dropped. At first, I wasn't too worried. I felt that, despite our struggles, I was still playing okay. Then, during a game at Wilderspool, Warrington ran a move, scored a try and I took the blame for it. It would be true to say that I got caught in no man's land, but whether it was all my fault, I'm not so sure. Anyway, Steve hauled me off there and then, even though I had been having a good game until that moment. Even the referee couldn't believe it. 'Where are you going, Ikram?' he asked me. 'He's taking me off,' I told him. And that was that.

I didn't get back on again, either. Then, after the game, he told me he was dropping me. I said: 'What? After one mistake? But I am one of your best performers.' And he said: 'Yeah, I know. But I've said I would do it, so I will'. In other words, I was the fall guy and our relationship deteriorated from there. In the end, he wouldn't even talk to me and I had to conduct any negotiations with him through the captain. There were even rumours that he was trying to swap me for Dean Sampson at Castleford, which Steve denied but Dean later confirmed to me were true. I lost trust in him completely after that. Even the Featherstone chairman, Steve Wagner, was apologetic at my treatment.

In total, I missed one game and had to train and play for the reserves. No one could believe I had been dropped - my team-mates, the fans, no one. I had been playing well! In my first reserve game against St. Helens reserves at home, I scored a hat-trick. Then I scored a try against Castleford reserves at Wheldon Road.

Steve didn't really have much choice after that. 'Right, Ikram,' he said, 'you're back in the first team.' I was glad to return to the side, of course, but things were never the same between us again. No player likes to be dropped and I am no different. I had made it clear that I wasn't happy and that was the start of him falling out with me, basically. He didn't like the fact that I had challenged him. Also, he wasn't being up front with me and he knew that I knew that. When he picked me again, I asked him how come he was selecting me now when I had scored a hat-trick against Saints, who were a very good side, the week before. 'Oh,' he said, 'that one try against Cas was a lot better than those three against Saints.' I wouldn't mind but I actually dropped the ball over the line at Castleford but none of the officials spotted it - it wasn't even a fair try!

Anyway, even after I had got my first team shirt back, the atmosphere continued to be poor. Steve's attitude towards me just grew worse. Before and after every match he would go around the changing room talking to each player in turn, but he wouldn't come and talk to me. I was just ignored. It's no wonder, then, that I wasn't being inspired and had no motivation whatsoever. I felt really disappointed and low. It might not have been so bad had my brother, Tony, been there for a bit of moral support, but he had drifted away from rugby league for good by now, after having been brought to Featherstone by Peter Fox who, true to form, had given him the chance to resurrect his career. When Peter left, Allan Agar continued to give our Tony a go, but then his hamstring went and what with that and all the other factors, his mind was made up to retire.

I've got to admit that when things got really bad with Steve Martin, I contemplated doing something similar myself. Or maybe I could just stay away from the club, I thought, and move on. I'm glad I didn't. You can get a bad reputation doing stuff like that. It's best to just grit your teeth and take it like a man.

# IKRAM WAS AN ALL-ACTION PLAYER WHO NEVER KNEW WHEN HE WAS BEATEN...
## Terry Mullaney

*Featherstone Rovers RLFC*

What a great honour it is to contribute to the autobiography of Ikram Butt, a great rugby league player of his era and a genuine all round nice lad.

I have been involved at Featherstone Rovers in an official capacity for more years than I care to remember, something like thirty-four, all told. A substantial proportion of that time was spent as either football chairman or football secretary, dealing primarily with the needs and welfare of the players; a wide spectrum of duties ranging from contract negotiations to health care issues and generally looking after the boys as well as a club with our limited resources could.

At any small town club with inherent financial limitations it is always difficult to give players what they feel they deserve. What we could offer at Featherstone, though, and in abundance, was an atmosphere of warmth and togetherness which few of the more 'illustrious' clubs could emulate. As these were also attributes to which Ikram was accustomed in his family life, he settled immediately at Post Office Road.

I first saw Ikram in action when he played as a young centre against Rovers in an 'A' team game for Leeds. The match was at Featherstone in the 1989-1990 season and he scored four cracking tries through the elusive running and power which defied his physical stature at that time.

His performance that night was certainly the main talking point amongst the fans in Rovers' new clubhouse after the game. From then on the club duly monitored his progress. As always, the Leeds club was saturated with great players. It was said that they used to sign all of the area's young talent just to prevent other clubs from doing so. As a result, many youngsters never reached their potential. Richard Gunn was another who eventually ended up at Featherstone, the club which tried to sign him as a junior but lost out to the financial muscle of the Loiners.

The 1990-1991 season saw Rovers with money to spare after the controversial but profitable departure of Graham Steadman to Castleford. Rovers officials hadn't forgotten about that night at Featherstone when the young Asian kid had destroyed their reserve side almost single-handed and, with the blessing of coach Peter Fox, asked about his availability. Leeds were prepared to let Ikram go and Rovers were elated. He scored a try on his debut against Bramley in the Yorkshire Cup on August 26, 1990.

Ikram was soon to make his mark on the club and he quickly became a favourite with the discerning Rovers faithful. The Post Office Road fans were a knowledgeable lot and, indeed, still are. If a player wasn't 'up to it' they'd sure as hell let him know!

Ikram was an all-action player who never knew when he was beaten. His robust style combined with an uncanny ability to beat man after man with nifty footwork was a joy to behold. He had many great games in the blue and white, but the one I remember most was a Yorkshire Cup tie at the

115

Boulevard in 1991-1992, when Rovers were 16-4 down with time running out. Suddenly, Ikram made an astonishing run, knocking off several attempted tackles and mesmerising others before putting his centre partner Terry Manning in between the posts. Almost from the restart, he then took a pass at full tilt, evaded two defenders and left the full-back for dead, before scoring under the posts to give Rovers an unlikely draw. We won the replay at Post Office Road by three points, with Ikram contributing a try. I still have the video of that game at Hull.

Ikram won Second Division Championship and Premiership medals with Rovers in the 1992-1993 season under Australian coach, Steve Martin. And he went on to his highest honour of representing England against Wales in 1995. A few weeks later, he scored his final try for Rovers at Elland Road before a crowd of almost 23,000 in a Challenge Cup semi against his old club, Leeds. Rovers, unfortunately, lost and were infamously told, just a couple of weeks later, that they would have to consider merging with neighbours, Castleford and Wakefield. The rest is history and life at the famous old club has never been the same since.

But they can't take away our memories and Ikram Butt will always be in the hearts of those Rovers fans who are fortunate to have witnessed his exploits in the famous hooped shirt. Along with his playing ability, I will remember Ikram Butt as one of the most genuine young men ever to come into the Featherstone club. It doesn't surprise me at all to learn about his continued loyalty to the sport and his wonderful efforts to encourage more involvement from our South Asian community in the joys of rugby league.

I wish Ikram well in all that he does. He made a big impression at Featherstone and it is certain that, at some time in the future, his on-going influence and impact on the game as a whole will be equally recognised.

# 7

\*

# A Question of Culture

I suppose that, considering the title of this book, the question might be asked: did the issue of race have anything to do with Steve Martin's treatment of me at Featherstone?

Well, my answer to that is no, I don't think so. I would never accuse Steve of that, but his behaviour was certainly very disappointing because I had been so happy at Rovers until then. Ultimately, I am not sure what motivation he had for singling me out and I don't see how I can ever know. But to be fine with me at first and then totally blank me out was not very mature, that's for sure. It would also be true to say that most of the people around us were on my side, which was another thing he didn't like. I always got on well with our chairman, Steve Wagner, for example, who used to put his arm around me and say he couldn't believe the way I was being treated. Maybe Steve Martin just felt insecure and was trying to demonstrate his authority. I'm in charge, that sort of thing. As I said, we'll never really know.

Generally, throughout my playing career, the attitudes of coaches and my fellow players to the question of race and religion has varied, although few of them could ever have been described as out-and-out racists. Usually, if there have been any difficulties they have come about through ignorance, or lack of education, which is why I am so keen these days to ensure that everyone understands just what being a rugby-playing Muslim Asian in Great Britain actually means. If we want more Asians to play a role in British sport, it's important that everyone feels that they belong.

I have never been what you might call backward in coming forward when it comes to correcting misconceptions of the Muslim faith. Thankfully, the situation is a little different in this day and age; there is a new, open-minded breed of rugby player in both codes who want to understand the world around them. There are encouraging signs at the administrative level too. Of the new breed of coaches, for example, the England and Warrington boss Tony Smith is really keen to have a deeper understanding of the different communities who watch and play the game within the UK. If there's something Tony doesn't know, then he goes out of his way to find an answer. Within the 13-a-side code's ruling body, the Rugby Football League, there is a greater emphasis on encouraging equity and diversity; certain elements of the RFL do extremely well within that area and are very supportive. That's good and something to be encouraged but it hasn't always been like that; we shouldn't be complacent. In my experience, there are still plenty within sport in this country who don't get it at all.

Throughout my own playing days, it would be true to say that, as a rule, rugby league players weren't all that intelligent (well, the forwards anyway!). Or maybe that's wrong and they were just very good at hiding it. I don't mean to be insulting - that's just how it was back then. For most working class people, going to university or anything like it was never really an option. Everything you learned, you learned through experience. As a result, I found myself giving lessons on Islam and what that really means in many a changing room. Often, the questions I was asked included statements that had nothing to do with Islam or being a Muslim. I didn't mind putting them right. The fact that I was able to answer the questions and put my team-mates' minds at ease made them more comfortable towards me in their perceptions. I suppose I was raising awareness, which is what I still try to do to this day.

One obvious way in which my religion impacted on my rugby playing was in the area of diet - particularly around the Muslim observance of Ramadan. And if we are looking for an area where I didn't get much in the way of leniency from my coaches, then this would be it, with one clear exception. If ever there was a coach who couldn't care less about your creed and colour, only how well you played the game, it was Peter Fox. Nevertheless, Peter was also very sensitive and supportive when it came to understanding your needs as an individual. He always said that family, work and religion were very important things and that they should always come first, before sport. He didn't only say it, he meant it, and always accommodated me when necessary.

As for the others, well, let's just say that none of them really had an understanding of the implications of my Muslim faith and how important it was to me. I wouldn't pick on any one coach in particular, with the exceptions of Peter and Allan they were all that way. I struggled sometimes with coaches who wouldn't give me any leniency, especially when it came to training. I was always expected to turn up on time and train just as hard as everyone else, even though I was fasting and, therefore, shorter on energy. It was a real struggle sometimes. I suppose it's easy to say that they should have had more understanding of my situation, and no doubt they should.

119

But it does all boil down to a lack of awareness and, more importantly I think, the failure to understand an important aspect of my culture. I never felt like an outcast - far from it - but a little more understanding would have made the nature of my life in rugby league that bit easier and, just possibly, attracted more of my fellow Asians into the game.

Of course, as far as my coaches were concerned it was simply a case of 'when in Rome, do as the Romans do..'. David Ward is a classic example. An absolute legend, a terrific player and one of my heroes, Dave lived and breathed rugby league. That was pretty much all that interested him. So, to expect someone like him to get to grips with different religions and cultures was a big ask. Within the competitive nature of the game, as a coach, you just want the best results regardless. You want people there on board, on time and fully committed to the cause. So I do understand the issues. But, as a sport, we did have to move forward. There were times, particularly when I was at Featherstone when, because of the timing of fasting, I was actually rushing to the ground, having a quick sandwich and then going out to train. That brought a few raised eyebrows. But on the whole we had a good bond as a team. Although the lads did used to make fun and have a joke at my expense, they did that with everyone and it was all done in good taste.

I suppose that, since I am in educational mode, now might be a good time to explain just exactly what Ramadan entails. If you already know, you might want to skip the rest of this chapter!

Basically, as I have already partly explained, Ramadan is a period of intense religious observance which includes a month of fasting, otherwise known as Sawm, one of the five pillars of Islam. The other four pillars are Shahada (sincerely reciting the Muslim profession of faith), Salat (praying five times a day), Zakat (giving money to the poor and needy) and Hajj (a once-in-a-lifetime pilgrimage to Mecca). The time for fasting begins at sunrise and ends at sunset, while the month in which Ramadan falls varies annually. In 2008 Ramadan was in September, in 2009 August and so on; it moves back a calendar month every year.

Not surprisingly, the summer months are particularly difficult because of the long days but - and this might surprise a few people - I have to say that, no matter when it is, Ramadan is a time of year that I always look forward to. Fasting, you see, is not just about the intake of food. Although scientifically it has been proven that it is a great way of replenishing the body - de-toxing if you like - it also has its physical, spiritual and mental benefits. For one thing, fasting encourages self-discipline which, in turn, goes a long way to shaping positive personal character traits. And sport is all about discipline, isn't it? As I said earlier, though, it is also a fact that during this time, your performance is not as high as it might otherwise be. You can't sip water or have any intake of food before a game, which can drain your strength and add to mental fatigue.

Another benefit of summer fasting is that you get more time to reflect upon what you're doing in life and why. In the shorter winter months, you wake up later, have something to eat, go to work and then, before you know it, you are back at the table eating. In an average working day, sometimes you don't get the chance to eat anything anyway, so a lot of people fast without much effort. When the longer days arrive, if you do get hungry you have to make a conscious decision to stay on track. As I write this, we are in the middle of Ramadan and it's only eleven o'clock in the morning. I'm famished. But mentally, it's not really a problem. Naturally, I am a lot more tired than I generally would be. But I am satisfied with the reason I am fasting and the importance of doing so.

Think about it. I could quite easily have a cup of tea or a bite to eat, what's stopping me? No one need ever know. But the thing is that Ramadan helps me to enjoy the hunger, in a way. It's a bit like rugby league, where you learn to enjoy the pain. And keeping strong is the only way to reap the benefits.

Ramadan, then, is the ultimate Holy month in which we Muslims cleanse our bodies, both physically and spiritually. It is a time when, religiously, everything is scaled to the hilt. Muslims are encouraged to give more to charity, for example. The more good things we do, the more blessings we receive. The onus is on us to go out and grasp them.

And not only are there personal benefits for ourselves, there are social ones too. In most Islamic countries, for example, crime is greatly reduced during Ramadan. At the end of the day, the Muslim community is just like any other - you get your black sheep everywhere. But even the black sheep - most of them anyway - will go without food during Ramadan. The ones who do so will think twice about mugging an old lady or committing some other crime because of the severity of the punishment and the amount of blessings that will be lost.

I still haven't told you exactly how all of this directly affects my own life, though, have I? Well, the Islamic calendar is slightly different to the British calendar. As I write, sunrise is officially at 6.00am. For Muslims, however, sunrise - or Tashreeq to use the arabic term related to it - took place today at 4.20am. So, this morning, I got out of bed at 3.30am, relaxed and performed my ablutions - which is to prepare for prayer by washing your hands, your mouth, your nose and your face; a general cleansing not only of the body, but also of the sins. As the five pillars of Islam state, whether it's Ramadan or not, we must pray five times a day.

Today, I went downstairs and cooked my own breakfast,

because my missus didn't get up. There are a number of instances when, in Islamic law, you don't have to fast. Women who are breast-feeding, pregnant or on their menstrual cycle, don't fast. An infant doesn't fast, an old person doesn't fast, nor does anyone who is undergoing medical treatment. The widespread perception of Islam being rigid and unbending is just totally wrong. Really, it's all about common sense. If you are old and it is going to cause difficulty, then you don't fast, it's as simple as that. Maybe give to charity instead.

Anyway, my breakfast. Today I had egg on toast and a bit of Weetabix. No special reason for the Weetabix, that's just the cereal we were brought up on. Had I been at my mother's house, she would have made me paratha, which is like a buttered chapati, one of my favourites. Not the sort of buttered chapati that the kids in our street used to ask for - that was just a chapati with butter on! This one is fried, with the butter within. Actually, no she wouldn't. I have stopped eating paratha these days because I am trying to watch my weight. When you are younger, you don't really understand any of this routine, but as you get older you ponder what it's all about.

Essentially, the idea is not to indulge in lots and lots of breakfast, as that goes against the grain of what you are trying to do. The more money I save this month, the more I can give to charity. So egg on toast and Weetabix it is. Plus a cup of tea and quite a few glasses of water, just to make sure that my water supplies are replenished for the day.

What I try to do nowadays, which I had fallen away from since I stopped playing rugby, is to eat correctly before the fasting season begins. Doing so boosts your energy reserves once Ramadan is underway. Again, in my younger playing days, I didn't have the greatest advice in that area and pretty much had to work it out for myself. Still, I got by. Now that

I am not so energetic as I used to be, it's even more important that I eat a proper diet.

Mouth washed, teeth brushed and breakfast done, with the arrival of sunrise at 4.20am, you would have found me in front of the Islamic channel on television, listening to their advice, watching interviews and so on. Then it's time for the first prayer of the day. As I said, there are five daily prayers - Fajar (morning prayer - two rakats, or parts); Zohar (afternoon prayer - only on a Friday it is called Jumaa, where you do two rakats instead of four, but only at the mosque); then Asr (twilight prayer, early afternoon, four rakats); Magrib (as the lights come on and sun begins to set - three rakats); then Isha (evening prayer, four rakats).

For all of these prayers, we are encouraged to go to a mosque or, if that is not possible, pray in a congregation, which derives more blessings. We don't have a mosque near to our house so, in the mornings, I tend to pray with my wife, because two people are considered to be a congregation. Today, as I was downstairs by myself, I prayed alone. There is a time limit in which to pray, however. If you are the forgetful type, you are reminded by the Azan, our call to prayer, which can also be heard on television. Its message is basically 'be prompt', which is another act of self-discipline, of course.

For Muslims, the act of praying consists of standing up, bowing down and kneeling to the ground. We do that for each prayer. For the morning prayer, we bow twice. In the afternoon and mid-evening, we bow four times. Twilight is three, and the last prayer of the day is four. There are other prayers which act as attachments too, but those five are the compulsory ones.

Once I have prayed I sit down, read some teachings from the Qur'an and then have a nap before waking up again for work, this morning at about nine o'clock. What can I say? I had a lie-in. Bear in mind that the kids can be running riot by then. My eldest, for example, is eleven and she has just started a new school. We encourage her to fast as often as possible. So things can get a little noisy. That's how my day starts during Ramadan.

As the day progresses, it continues to go along in a similar way. At work yesterday, for example, we had an away day with a couple of breaks for coffee and biscuits and lunch. I was worried that I might struggle but, in the end, I was quite comfortable. I think a lot of it is down to lifestyle. Ramadan is a blessed month and I want to reap the rewards that derive from it. But I also welcome the structure it brings to your life. I know who I am, I know where I have been and where I want to go and what I want to do. This puts me in place. It might be a psychological thing, but I feel comfortable.

I have mentioned in one or two newspaper interviews about how my religion puts things into context. At one stage, rugby league was my life. But now, if you believe in the hereafter, the important thing is to be a good individual, a valuable member of society and someone who tries to do the right things. It is important to reach for the after-life, too, because along with many other religions, Muslims believe that this life is just a journey to a greater end. Ramadan allows you to reflect on all that and, hopefully, gives you the inner-strength to build throughout the year until the next fasting comes along.

Of all the days of the week, Friday is the most important, although we don't have a Sabbath or Holy day as such. We are encouraged pray in congregations all the time but on Friday even more so, especially in the afternoon at around half past one or two o'clock. I'll go to the mosque around two o'clock, pray and then come away. In Islamic countries, shopkeepers don't even lock their shops, they just go and pray. Then it's back to doing the usual things until six, which is time for the mid-afternoon prayer. Outside the fasting month, people may not go to a mosque, they might just pray at home or work. But during Ramadan they will go because their blessings are increased. Eventually, we reach sunset - which is when we open fast.

The ideal way to do that is to eat dates, because that is the way that our Prophet Mohammad, peace be upon him, opened his fast. To us, the Prophet was the walking Qur'an, a model character. The Qur'anic revelations were revealed to Him in stages over twenty-three years. The Qur'an itself, therefore, contains the sacred word of God, and corrects any distortions in previous holy books, such as the Old and New Testaments. As a result, we follow the example of the Prophet Muhammad (pbuh). He led that life in order that we would follow it too and derive the benefits.

Having said all that, it is also a fact that dates are absolutely full of nutrients. So, again, it's not just a case of saying that this is how we act because we have always done things that way; our traditions have a scientific or logical basis. This is a really important point, particularly when you are trying to explain Islam to a non-believer or someone who is simply interested in the way our religion works. We do not just follow these traditions on heresay; the practical advantages are proven. This is why we believe that our religion can be useful to the whole of humankind. The benefits of Islam are universal.

So, we open our fast with a date and then maybe have a starter. As I said, it's important not to indulge in too much food; just a few dates, a bit of fruit and a glass or two of water. Last night, the missus wasn't fasting and the kids had already eaten their meal around six o'clock, which meant that they were all watching *EastEnders* while I sat on my own at the table. After that, the telly went off and we all said a prayer. I suppose that I could have gone and done that upstairs but the whole idea is to be in sight of the kids, so that they see their dad praying and develop an understanding. After prayer, I indulged in a light meal - chicken massala, two naan bread and a bit of salad, oh, and a low fat strawberry trifle (but we won't mention that) - had a cup of tea and then went training.

Luckily for me, the Fitness First gym is just around the corner from our house and it opens until midnight. The area around the gym is predominantly Asian, so the owners have accommodated that community knowing full well that many of their customers probably wouldn't fancy lifting weights in the daytime during Ramadan, which is great, I think. Very forward thinking. As it was, I did twenty minutes on the running machine and nearly killed myself, plus some light weights just to keep on top of what I wanted to do. I am trying to get back some sort of physique and this is the ideal time to help that along.

At about nine-thirty there is our final prayer of the day and that is pretty much that, although the more conscientious types will perform another, non-compulsory, night prayer too. All in all, it is really interesting how Ramadan helps you to treat your day, from a psychological point of view. Occasionally, you might think about getting up to something that you are not supposed to in the middle of the morning, but then have to think twice because you know that you have afternoon prayer coming. It's like a good timetable. It keeps you in check and you focus your life around it. Ramadan helps you always to stay organised and on top of things, and the act of praying ensures you don't take your spiritual health for granted.

Mind you, having explained all that, it is also important to remember that just because you are a Muslim, it doesn't necessarily follow that you will be fasting during Ramadan.

As in any religion, some are more devout than others. One of my present-day work colleagues doesn't fast, for example, and that's his prerogative. Nor would I claim to be perfect, myself. At work the other day, I actually asked if we could plan our away days before or after the fasting period. A Muslim colleague replied: 'Well, isn't that the whole point of fasting, Ikram, just to go through it?' He was right, of course. But given the choice I would far rather do that sort of thing outside Ramadan, so that I can indulge in tea, biscuits and lunch at work's expense too. I am the first to admit that I am no saint, particularly when I was younger. I don't always manage to pray five times a day for instance; although I try to as much as I can. Fasting is different. You don't want to miss out on that, because you know full well that if you do, you have missed out on a good opportunity.

On the whole, there is an awful lot of misunderstanding about what it means to be a Muslim in this country. And, to be honest, I can understand why. Some of the more zealous Pakistani Muslims can come across as being a bit crackers. But what people should know is that there are distinct differences within our community when it comes to things like culture, religion and tradition. A lot of those differences get lost or confused when people over-generalise. A lot of Pakistani culture, for example, carries strains of Hinduism within it because, way back when the area was all one geographically, Hindu was the majority religion. So a lot of Pakistanis still have that inherited culture in them.

If you ask me, too often religion boils down to: 'Our fathers did it, so we will do it'. Culturally, we need to move away from that and just try and do what is right. As long as that has no negative impact on our religion, then I don't see any problem. Some of us need to take a more progressive attitude because, in Islam, it shouldn't matter if you are black or white. Racism doesn't just exist in the white

*Family album*: (Clockwise) Me as a baby; Mum, Khurshid (Tony), Misbah & me on the front step in Leeds; The three musketeers - Tony, Chinky & myself (nice threads!); Three lads and our dad - our hero then, and our hero now

*Round ball game*: Injury cut short my promising schoolboy career in football - but things haven't turned out too bad, have they?

*Family celebration*: Any excuse for a cake - me on my eighteenth birthday & in my Yorkshire jumpe

*Wedding day*: My lovely wife Bushra and I get hitched - we *were* happy, honest!

*Brotherly love*:
Our Tony and me go
for an unscheduled
run for the cameras
in our home streets
of Headingley
*PICS: ANDREW VARLEY*

*Youth representative*: My selections
for the Yorkshire County Junior
side and Great Britain Colts,
*below*, gave my career a big boost

*Huge influence*: The great
Peter Fox - my mentor

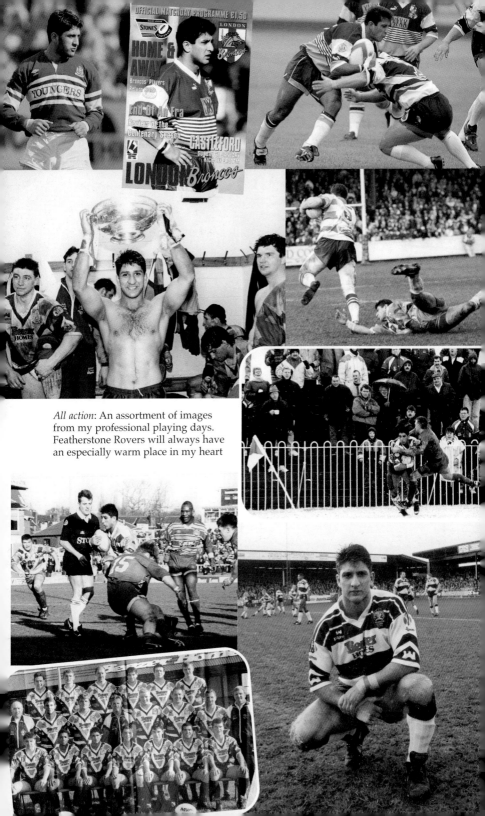

*All action*: An assortment of images from my professional playing days. Featherstone Rovers will always have an especially warm place in my heart

*1995 & all that*: Ikram Butt becomes England's first Muslim rugby international in either code - my proudest sporting moment - but unfortunately I missed the next game against France in Gateshead. *Below*: Grass roots - rugby in the park with Victoria Rangers

ENGLAND PHOTO COURTESY OF LEAGUE PUBLICATIONS LTD

*Going global:* BARA & South Asia Bulls are active across the world

*Front row:* MPs Neil Turner & Greg Mulholland

*Above:* Dave Braham, *left,* & Dave Jackson (both Leeds Met Carnegie) with the All India trophy

*True star:* Rahul Bose is a huge rugby fan

*A world of progress:* BARA's Pakistan players fly the flag while, *below,* Peter Rodgers of Leeds Met Carnegie, England coach Tony Smith & RLEF officer Kevin Rudd are fully committed to international RL development

*Big night*: I am inducted into the Asian Power 100

*British Zions:* Jewish & Muslim team-mates
*Below:* The BARA Celebrity side at the Stoop

*Playing politics:* BARA's relationship with the All Party Parliamentary Rugby League & Union Groups is beginning to pay rich dividends. *Below:* I line up alongside Rob Andrew, Government Sports Minister Gerry Sutcliffe MP & others for the Commons & Lords side at Twickenham

community, unfortunately it can be a problem in all communities and that is a shame. As a Muslim, you need to embrace everyone.

As far as I am concerned, my heritage is Muslim first, then British Pakistani. Pakistan comes at the end, because I was born in Britain. My mum would argue that it should be British first but I say, yes, I am a British Muslim, but I like to have Muslim first, as that is my faith. The bottom line, though, is that if you are prejudiced against other nationalities, how can you call yourself a true Muslim? And once again it all comes down to education.

The fact is, all the world's major religions influence each other. Along with my interest in reading the *Rugby Leaguer*, or example, I have a keen interest in Judaism and the early books of the Torah - Moses, David, the Book of Psalms. Muslims also believe in the second coming of Jesus Christ, peace be upon him, or Isa to use his Arabic name, amongst lots of other shared beliefs.

In the Qur'an, we have a full chapter about the miraculous birth of Jesus and his mother, Mary, who is among the four highest women we regard in the world. The only belief we don't share is that Jesus is the son of God. But just about everything else, his healing of the blind, lepers and other miracles such as raising the dead by God's permission, we believe. Islam and Christianity are very, very close - a lot closer than many people imagine.

# 8

\*

# Pride of England

On the whole then, while my experiences with rugby league coaches weren't always straightforward, it could have been a lot worse.

Peter Fox went out of his way to ensure that my needs were met and Allan Agar was a very family-orientated man who believed in looking after his players too. At Leeds, not being in the first team, I never saw much of Maurice Bamford - although you have to admire his achievements in the game - while I was in absolute awe of Malcolm Reilly. Malcolm was a true gentleman who always treated me with respect.

No, if I had a major problem with any coach it was Steve Martin and, later, Tony Currie, neither of whom had any sensitivity towards my situation at all. I put it down to ignorance really. Steve Martin even went so far as to stop me attending my brother Tony's wedding. I asked him for some time off from training so that I could attend and he said no. I couldn't believe it. If anything cheesed me off, that did. Although, to be honest, by then he had lost the plot completely.

After our disastrous start to the 1994-95 season and with big changes on the way for the sport in general, it wasn't long before the Featherstone board began to grow restless. In the end, Steve said he was prepared to move on as long as Rovers paid up the remainder of his three-year contract. Happily for everyone - and especially me - the club agreed to his demands and off he toddled, never to return, which left me more relieved than anything. His replacement was yet again my old coach at Leeds, David Ward, who arrived in October 1994.

Now, being no stranger to the occasional run-in with David at Headingley, at first his appointment put a bit of worry in the back of my mind. At Leeds, our relationship had been awkward and I had sometimes found him lacking in empathy. For example, he was keen on bonding sessions out on the town with the rest of the squad, something that, for obvious reasons, I wasn't so happy about. To be fair, David wasn't on his own in that. For me, after away games, it was usually a case of sitting on the coach alone or going to the bar. I didn't have a problem with that. You couldn't expect everyone to change their routine just for my benefit. So just to be sociable I would drink orange juice, while my team-mates tried to persuade me to 'have a pint' because 'nobody will know'.

Thankfully, with the passing of the years, both David and I had mellowed a little - not a lot! - and at Featherstone all turned out fine. At heart, David Ward was a players' man who was very close to his lads and we came to a mutual understanding. The main thing was that he knew me and didn't question my ability. With him in charge I could get on with my rugby league and, later that season, I was called up to play for England, which says it all really.

All that, though, was still to come and even after David Ward's arrival we continued to flap about at the wrong end of the table. David said at the time that he had never seen a dressing room in such low spirits and it was clear that he had a major rebuilding job to do if he was ever going to turn us around. As a team, our confidence was shattered. In any sport, when a new coach comes in it often has an immediate positive effect, but that wasn't how it was with us. We lost nine games on the bounce, although the margins were narrower than they had been and the signs were that it wouldn't be long before we turned the corner. In the end, it took us until the new year to do that when we beat Doncaster, 34-16, at home on 22 January. After that, we never looked back. An away defeat at Workington apart, for the next ten matches it was pretty much victory all the way. Even a late-season stumble couldn't stop us finishing a safe eleventh again in the table.

One of the best decisions David made was in appointing Steve Molloy as our captain, allowing Mark Aston to concentrate on his own game instead. That worked a treat, particularly in the Challenge Cup, where we ended up only eighty minutes away from Wembley after victories over Barrow, Salford and Whitehaven, away, in the quarter-finals.

If you remember, I had been close to going to Wembley once before; back when I was at Royal Park school and our appearance in the curtain-raiser was only denied by an early season defeat to a team from Hull. This, though, was something else again. It is surely every rugby league player's dream to walk out at Wembley and I honestly thought we had a great chance. In the previous season, the final had been between Leeds and Wigan and, this year, those clubs were kept apart at the semi-final stage again. As it turned out, Wigan drew Oldham while Leeds got us, with our match set to be staged at Elland Road, the home of Leeds United football club.

The reason for my confidence was because, as we have

seen, Featherstone always seemed to go well against Leeds, and I usually put in a good performance. This time, though, it was not to be. Maybe the big match nerves got to us, I don't know. But as a team we made too many mistakes and, after Garry Schofield's interception try in the second minute, we never really looked like recovering. A final scoreline of 39-22 shows how well we competed and, along with Danny Divet, Matt Calland and Roy Southernwood, I managed to go in for a try. I didn't realise it at the time, of course, but it would be the last four-pointer I ever scored for Rovers.

\* \* \* \* \*

One man who did get to Wembley in April 1995 was Ellery Hanley. As Leeds captain, he scored two tries against us in the semi-final to equal the record of 40 in a season set by another former Leeds man, Bob Haigh, in 1970-71.

Before then, in February, Ellery had impressed me even more when, as national team coach, he chose me for his England side to play in what was undoubtedly the highlight of my career - the opening game of that year's European Championship against Wales.

It would be fair to say that my international call-up came right out of the blue. I hadn't expected it at all. In fact, aside from my pleasure at being selected, one of the first things I thought was: '... I didn't get that put in my contract.' So I went to the club and asked if there was any chance of some extra money. They said they would 'look at it' but I never heard anything. That's how naive I was when it came to agreeing playing terms. But, really, I never seriously expected to play for England. There were so many great wingers out there at the time. Martin Offiah, Jason Robinson and so on. Jason was still a young kid then but outstanding anyway. You thought you had him lined up and then -

whoosh - he was gone. Billy Whizz. Then there was Anthony Sullivan. Anthony and I played together with Great Britain Colts - he is the same age as me but with pace to burn. I was never that type of winger. And another solid international winger was Paul 'Barney' Eastwood of Hull. So to find myself in such company was a massive surprise.

Even though I was pleased to be included, I never kidded myself that the absence of quite a few established international stars hadn't helped my cause. Although the three-team European Championship had a rich tradition in rugby league, it was staged at quite an awkward time for England and suffered a little in comparison to the 1995 World Cup, which was scheduled for later in the year.

Then there were the selection problems brought about by Great Britain playing in an almost simultaneous World Sevens event, sponsored by Coca Cola, in Sydney. Most of the ten players who went to that were English, while the first Euro Championship game in Cardiff coincided with their return flight back from Australia. So, while we still had a strong squad to choose from, England had to manage without the likes of Denis Betts, Chris Joynt, Lee Jackson and Martin Offiah, although Martin later pulled out of the Aussie trip with injury. Injured Wigan pair Shaun Edwards and Gary Connolly missed the Cardiff game too, while Alan Tait of Leeds turned down the chance to play for England as he had already represented Scotland at rugby union.

Our opponents, on the other hand, were buzzing. Since the European Championship was re-formed in October 1991, Wales had only ever selected Welsh-born players or lads whose parents were Welsh. This time, because the World Cup was on the horizon, they had been given the thumbs up to use the grandparent qualification rule. The result was that they had a stronger squad than usual and were much more dangerous.

All that being said, I felt at the time - and still do feel - that I deserved my international selection, mainly for the good and steady form I had shown in the seasons leading up to it. On top of that, as well as being grateful to my brother Tony for the sacrifices he made which allowed me to come so far, I also wrote in a matchday programme at the time of how, in many respects, my selection for England was as much down to Peter Fox as myself. I meant it too. I owe Peter so much, not just because of the fact that he signed me (twice!), but because he always had faith in my ability even when things weren't going so well. I continue to ring him for advice to this day.

It was also a thrill to realise that one of my all-time rugby league idols, Ellery Hanley, rated me as a player to such an extent. Maybe that was because every time I played against him I ended up being a bit of a handful. I remember once playing against Wigan when he was in his prime there and I had just signed for Featherstone, and it was men against boys. Andy Gregory at scrum-half, Shaun Edwards alongside and then Ellery Hanley - that triangle just controlled everything. Unbelievable. But when we went back to Wigan about a year later in the play-offs, as I described earlier, we beat them. And then there were the times I always seemed to score against Leeds - on one occasion going past about seven men on my way to the tryline. Put it this way, it can't have done me any harm.

The first time I trained with the squad I had a strange mixture of confidence and nerves. I was confident in my own ability but nervous about being in the company of so many players with big reputations - household rugby league names in many cases. I knew some of the lads - Deryck Fox, for example - and had played against just about all of them at one point or other. But being in the same England team was something else entirely. Sonny Nickle, Richard Gay, Garry Schofield...

## Tries and Prejudice

Ellery made me feel very welcome. He has such an aura about him and can leave a lot of people feeling over-awed. And we shouldn't forget that when he was first appointed coach of Great Britain during the Ashes series of 1994, he became the first black person to coach or manage a major national team in this country. I bumped into him again recently, when Leeds Met played Doncaster in the Challenge Cup at Headingley. I tried to get him to play for my team in a charity match against the Members of Parliament, but he wasn't having any of it. That's Ellery for you. He does have that stubborn, single-minded side to him. But the fact is that he is a legend of rugby league and a true superstar of British sport, so how can you not respect his achievements?

My own first meeting with Ellery came when I was eighteen or nineteen and he came jogging past Lawnswood School in Headingley. I ran with him for a while and then, on a later occasion, I visited his home. He knew I played rugby and told me to come to Wigan. I said I would love to but pointed out that I had just signed professional forms with Leeds. Anyway, after we had sat there drinking tea and chatting, Ellery very kindly lent me some of his rugby league video tapes. Being young and irresponsible, I then passed them on to a friend and the daft so-and-so taped over them! Can you imagine? I couldn't believe it. After that, if ever I bumped into Ellery he would have a go at me: 'Ikram, where's my tapes?'. For a while, I tried to keep out of his way. Happily, as time went on, he began to treat it as a joke, thank goodness. Even so, just telling this story makes me burn with shame. So Ellery, if you are reading, please accept this public apology. It maybe wouldn't have been so bad if my friend had taped some decent films over them or something, but he didn't. Just random bits of 'eighties telly.

Anyway, back to my England training and, although the actual exercises and routines were not that far different from my usual three nights a week training at Featherstone, the handling errors were fewer and the tempo was quicker - that was the thing. That became especially obvious when it came to skill drills. Every single player was fully switched on and focussed, no one messed about and there were no mistakes, so it felt like a big step up from what I was used to. I had just begun to carry a groin injury, too, which was a bit of a hindrance.

All in all, though, I felt that I slotted in well. It was a good mix. As a coach, Ellery was quite relaxed but then, Ellery being Ellery, he didn't really have to say much to get your attention, such was the respect he commanded. If I remember rightly, he flew to the Cardiff match by helicopter after going to see the Queen, and who else in rugby league could have done so well in *Celebrity Dancing On Ice*? The thing about Ellery, though, is that it is never just about glamour and charisma. He is always on the park with you leading up to the game, and even when he isn't full of praise, which is rare, any criticism he makes is always constructive. Ellery is a great one for encouraging players and so, when he speaks, you listen.

One thing is for sure, his approach contrasted sharply with the motivational tactics of certain other coaches who just used to shout at players rather than treat us as intelligent, rational adults.

With that sort of coach, it was often as if, when it came to the crunch, they were feeling the pressure themselves and that always transmits to the team. No such problem for England in the 1995 European Championship, though. Although we were a bit thrown together and a largely new side, every one of us could now claim to be a top quality rugby league international.

## Tries and Prejudice

\* \* \* \* \*

The big match, when it arrived, came as a bit of a relief. In the days and weeks leading up to it, I had never seemed to be out the media. The interest in the first Asian ever to represent England in either code of rugby was amazing. Everyone seemed to want to interview me; the newspapers, television, radio... you name it.

Not surprisingly, most of it portrayed me as some sort of 'role model' - a person who might have advice on how rugby league could attract more kids into the game from the Asian community. On one level, that was fine. I had been irritated for ages at the way Asians were always described as being, in some way, unsuitable for a rough, tough sport like rugby. As I said at the time: 'All young kids need encouragement and a pat on the head sometimes. I don't think young Asian players get enough encouragement. I don't believe that coaches in general think they are truly bothered about the game. It's a load of rubbish that Asians don't like physical contact sports. My religion is Islam, which I still follow, it's there in my heart. But there is nothing in my faith to prevent me from playing rugby league.' If my England call-up could help correct those misconceptions, then great.

On the other hand, like most other young professional sportspeople, all I was really interested in at that stage of my career was playing the game to the best of my ability and seeing what developed from that. Or to put it another way: how many white English players are aware of their Christianity, if that is their religion, when they are out there on the field? As I told the *Rugby Leaguer* newspaper: 'When I'm playing, the fact that I'm Asian is erased from my mind, just as it is with most other activities. I'm obviously proud of my background, I want to stress that, but it's a long way from being at the front of my mind when I'm out on the pitch.'

By and large, that was the truth. Although I can admit now that there was one aspect of my selection that did make me a bit uncomfortable. It was to do the shirt itself. Not only were we sponsored by John Smith's - a brewery - it of course had the red cross of St. George on the front.

Now, as well as being the English flag, the cross of St. George is also a heavily loaded symbol of Christianity - and I am a Muslim. For me, it carries all sorts of historical connotations reaching right back to the medieval Crusades. It is sometimes difficult, I think, for many in the west to appreciate just how offensive the word 'crusade' can be to Islamic sensibilities. And for many Muslims, the implications of Christian Europe brutally recapturing Jerusalem and the Holy Land from Muslim rule back in the eleventh and twelfth centuries, are still a relevant issue today. Hopefully, now that we have Barack Obama as President of the United States, progress towards greater understanding can finally be made. But for many in the Muslim community, over the past decade or so the Crusades have had a worrying parallel with America's so-called 'War on Terror'.

Even in 1995, six years before George W. Bush came to power, the cross on that England jersey gave me real food for thought. In the end, though, I stuck to the principle of compromise. No one was more proud to play for England than I was. England is my country and I would do anything for my country; fight for it, defend it, die for it even. My religion is very important to me, though, so how could that quandary not be in the back of my mind? It would have to be, wouldn't it? Even so, and I'll say it again, in the end I was proud to wear that England shirt because of all the other great things it stood for. And I respected the fact that I was wearing the same uniform as my team-mates and fellow countrymen.

This, then, is another example of an area in which a little give and take is needed - on this occasion from me - and it just goes to show that cultural and religious compromise does not only go in one direction, as some of the more extreme political elements in this country would have us believe. Let's face it, England is never going to change its flag or its patron saint, is it? So if I wanted to represent my country - and I very much did - then I had no choice but to put my own personal discomfort into perspective. Compromise is not a dirty word or a sign of weakness. In fact, it's the opposite - a sign of spiritual strength. If being mindful of other folk's feelings helps us to live together in peace and harmony, then what's wrong with that? In such a civilised society, we can still put our own point of view forward and have a rational and intelligent debate.

Let me give you a couple more examples of religious compromise and tolerance. The second time I visited Pakistan, I represented that country in a rugby union tournament. Before one of the games, our team gathered around for a Muslim prayer and it suddenly occurred to me that one of the boys, André, was a Christian. As it happens, he has converted to Islam since but, back then, that wasn't the case. Even so, he joined in the prayer with us, no problem. That really opened my eyes. In Pakistan, everyone is not necessarily a Muslim; there are Christians and all sorts of other faiths. As a younger man, that was news to me and something I hadn't realised.

Well before then, in the days when I played at Headingley, the Leeds shirt sponsors were Youngers, another well-known brewery. Again, as a Muslim, that could have been a problem for me, but I wore the logo without making a fuss, knowing that the sponsorship money was needed by the club. In fact, I am wearing it on the front cover of this book! Interestingly, though, I was delighted to read a news story more recently in which the South African cricket star Hashim Amla was faced with a similar problem. The kit of the South Africa Test team has a beer brand plastered all over it and, after Amla made his debut in 2004, he wrote to the United Cricket Board to ask politely if he could be exempted from wearing it. After consultation with the sponsors, who were very accommodating, the authorities agreed to his request. Isn't that great? And if any country has had difficulties with racial prejudice it is South Africa.

In the end, whatever our own religious and cultural needs, we must never stop looking for the common ground. For any society to work correctly, it needs awareness and reason from every sector of the community. It is all about dialogue.

# IKRAM WASN'T THE SORT WHO WOULD WAIT PATIENTLY ON THE WING...
## Peter Fox

*Former Great Britain RL coach*

I have great admiration for Ikram's achievement and the way he has got as far as he has in the game. After all, with a background like his, although he grew up near to Headingley, in lots of other ways the odds were stacked against him.

Ikram wasn't steeped in the traditions of the game and didn't have many of the support mechanisms enjoyed by most other kids who end up playing professional rugby league football. Anything he achieved had to come from within himself, which is true, in the end, for any professional sportsperson, but especially for Ikram.

To show you what I mean, myself, I was born and bred in Sharlston, a mining village in between Wakefield and Featherstone. Everyone there was rugby league through and through. We played rugby from being tots to adults and lived and breathed the game.

My council school didn't play rugby, but when I left I went to Wakefield Junior Tech at the age of 13. We started a rugby team there and I was mainly responsible for it. The metalwork master said to me: 'Fox, you come from Sharlston.' I says: 'Yes.' He says: 'You love playing rugby.' I says: 'Yes.' He says: 'Right, well, I want to get Wakefield Junior Tech into the Wakefield junior schools' rugby league. You can coach the team for me and pick it, and I'll make sure your marks are all right in metalwork.' And I did, at the age of 13, so you can see how I was steeped in rugby.

The following year I got picked in the second row for Yorkshire schoolboys. I always wanted to be a loose forward. All my childhood heroes, players like Harry Street and Ken Traill and so on, were all loose forwards. And then I became a loose forward for Featherstone Rovers, so that was an ambition fulfilled. Later, when I went to play at Batley, I could tell my team-mates all about the opposition, player-by-player. I used to study rugby, properly study it.

The thing is, having a background like that, rugby league was in the blood. With all that encouragement from such a young age, how could it not be? Seven or eight of my mates at Sharlston went to Wakefield Junior Tech, so we had a nucleus of a team right there and a good team too. We won the Wakefield Schools' league in our first year. We had grown up together and now we played together.

By the time I left school at 15, I had played for Yorkshire at 14 and even Sharlston Rovers amateur open-age side. I was 15 and they put me in the second row with a lad called Georgie Green, who played a bit with Halifax. It was a tough education but, in our family, it felt like a natural progression. Our Don and Neil, my brothers, were blessed with huge talent and went on to be superstars of the game, although neither of them acted that way off the field. Neil, in particular, was one of the greatest players rugby league has ever seen. There will never be another Neil Fox.

My dad actually captained Sharlston when they knocked

the professionals of Workington out of the first round of the Challenge Cup. He was the steward of Sharlston Working Men's Club and came out of retirement at 37 to play, because the club was demoralised for some reason or other that season. He was on the committee and three or four of his mates, all big rugby men, also volunteered to help the team out. They got through to the first round of the Challenge Cup proper - all the amateur teams used to play off first in those days - after beating Batley Carr and Buslingthorpe Vale, in Leeds. I remember that me and my mate, because our fathers played, were allowed to sit in the aisle on the team bus.

So we were brought up to play and watch rugby league and that was that. It was our birthright and I'm sure there were very similar stories all the way across the north of England. But for Ikram, that wasn't really the case. For an Asian to play rugby league seemed, to a lot of people, to be a very strange thing. Not for Ikram individually. He had the urge to play rugby league, wanted to play rugby league and had the ability to play rugby league. But in the family home and among the Asian community generally at that time, to want to play rugby league must have been quite unusual. The kid was a pioneer.

The first time I met Ikram was when he came to sign on at Leeds. I had heard about his exploits in the amateur County Championships alongside Ian Smales, who also went on the play for Featherstone, but hadn't seen him in action yet myself.

Ikram was in a meeting with Harry Jepson and Eric Hawley, and I came into the room. I thought I knew what to expect of him because I was already coaching his brother, Tony, who was a big strong lad who could really play rugby. Tony Butt was a great tackler and a very physical, but a bit limited with ball in hand. He was a smashing competitor but didn't have the other skills that would have made him stand out as a great player.

Anyway, when Ikram came in, I liked what I saw and put him into the first team squad straight away - not to play, I just wanted him to experience what being a professional was all about and help with his development. I wrote him a list that told him what I expected from a threequarter. Unfortunately, Ikram and me were only at Leeds together for about three weeks after that. Who knows, maybe I would have given him his chance sooner rather than later because, through necessity, I was having to rely very heavily on young 'uns at the time; it was me who brought in the likes of Roy Powell and Paul Medley for example. I had to build from the bottom at Leeds because they wouldn't spend any money.

The year before I came to Headingley, Leeds had thirteen overseas players. But when I arrived, eleven of them had gone home. Only Terry Webb and Tony Currie were left and they weren't at their best. In fact, I told Tony he could go back to Australia at Christmas because he wasn't pulling his weight, but he pleaded with me to let him stay. From then until the end of the season he played much better, so I offered him a new contract. But he turned it down and said: 'I'm going back, boss, because you've shown me how I can win a green and gold jersey.' He did as well.

So, three weeks after he signed at Leeds, I left and Ikram had to fend for himself. The thing is, as any player will tell you, if a coach brings you to a club then he has an interest in you and will be keen to give you opportunities. If you are already there when the coach arrives, then there often isn't that same bond and sometimes it can be difficult for both player and coach alike. I think Ikram suffered from that scenario on a number of occasions in his playing career. As a result, he struggled to make any serious impact and it must have been a very frustrating time for him.

## Tries and Prejudice

My memory of Ikram is that he was a very steady, reliable player who put everything into a game but who, like his brother, was limited skill-wise. He was game, he wanted to succeed and he could tackle. He wasn't afraid of anyone or anything. If he didn't quite have the skills that would have made him stand out as a top-class player it didn't matter. He worked hard at his fitness and was as strong as a bull. He wasn't the sort of player who would wait patiently on the wing for the ball because he didn't have the pace to beat anyone on the outside if it did come his way. Ikram's game was straight up and down, coming inside to take the pressure off the forwards, putting in hit-up after hit-up.

I told him once: 'Ikram, you are never going to make a lot of money out of this game, but you will do okay.' And I think we can safely say that he did okay.

I was delighted to have the chance to bring him to Featherstone because I was in need of players and Rovers seldom had the money to sign lots of big name stars. I knew Ikram would do a job for me and I remember I gave another career lifeline to his brother, Tony, too. Both were big-hearted lads who I was confident would go well. When he first arrived from Australia, after scoring in his first game against Bramley, Ikram went another ten games without scoring but I wasn't much bothered. As long he had a good work-rate and was contributing to the team, which he was, then that was okay with me. He was a solid player who I could rely upon.

Throughout my coaching career I have always taken the personal approach with my players. I have never let a player down in my life. If he wasn't good enough for me then I would find him a club where he could still continue. I used to put all my effort into building a personal relationship and it worked, because they would all then play like demons for me. Ikram is a classic example of that.

As far as I was concerned, his race had nothing to do with it. I wanted Ikram in my side because he was a very good player and what I always call 'a reet lad'. If you were a 'reet lad' then you could work with me. If you were deceitful, or a bit crafty or sneaky then, sorry. All my players knew me for that. If they did something wrong and I got to know, they were in bother.

Ikram slotted in very well at Featherstone. And although I wouldn't describe our back-line then as the very best that I ever coached, it had a good balance and was certainly very talented, especially at that level.

With the reliable Chris Bibb at full-back, Ikram never had to field a high ball, something which, even he would admit, he later got found out for once Chris and he had moved on. On the other wing, the speedy Owen Simpson from Keighley was a good contrast to Ikram and, in the centres, we had Paul Newlove and Ikram's partner, Terry Manning. Terry was dynamite, a very formidable and tenacious player. As for Paul, well ... I brought him into the side aged 17 after just one 'A' team match and I knew he was something special from the start. Sure enough, he developed into the finest British centre of all time, even if I did have to tell him off from time to time for closing his eyes in the tackle!

You could never say either of those things about Ikram. Tackling was his bread and butter. If I had to find one word to sum him up, I would say 'determination'. Ikram might not have been the most skillful winger in the world but, with an attitude like his, there was never any doubt in my mind that he was going to succeed. As I said before, I value players on whether or not they are a 'reet lad.'

And the one thing you can say about Ikram Butt is that he is very definitely a 'reet lad'.

# 9

\*

# London Calling

As big a fan of 'dialogue' as I am, there is not much room for talking in the middle of a rugby league match - any rugby league match, and especially when that game is your international debut.

What do I remember about it? Well, the date - February 1, 1995 - and the fact that the atmosphere was tremendous. Mainly, though, everything happened at, like, one hundred and ten miles per hour. I was very quickly out of breath because I just wasn't used to intensity like that. I can't remember exactly the first time I touched the ball, although I do know that it wasn't long after the kick-off.

Anyway, the teamsheets that day read as follows. Wales: Paul Atcheson (Wigan); Phil Ford (Salford), Allan Bateman (Warrington), Iestyn Harris (Warrington), Anthony Sullivan (St. Helens); Jonathan Davies (Warrington - captain), Kevin Ellis (Workington Town); Kelvin Skerrett (Wigan), Martin Hall (Wigan), David Young (Salford), Paul Moriarty (Halifax), Mark Perrett (Halifax), Richie Eyres (Leeds). The Welsh subs were Adrian Hadley (Widnes), Daio Powell

(Wakefield Trinity), Neil Cowie (Wigan) and Rowland Phillips (Workington Town). The England side lined up: Richard Gay (Hull); Jason Robinson (Wigan), Daryl Powell (Sheffield Eagles), Paul Newlove (Bradford Northern), Ikram Butt (Featherstone Rovers); Garry Schofield (Leeds), Deryck Fox (Bradford Northern); Karl Harrison (Halifax), Richard Russell (Castleford), Harvey Howard (Leeds), Anthony Farrell (Sheffield Eagles), Sonny Nickle (St. Helens), Phil Clarke (Wigan - captain). England subs: Simon Baldwin (Halifax), Mick Cassidy (Wigan), Steve McNamara (Hull) and Steve McCurrie (Widnes). The referee was Russell Smith of Castleford.

I decided from the start that if I was going to impress, it would be through playing my own usual type of game - running the ball out of defence and taking the pressure off our props. I knew that the best thing I had going for me was a high work rate, so I got myself in the mix straight away which, of course, meant that I got tired straight away. Looking back, I put that down to the intensity of the game and also the nervous energy wasted during the build-up. But that couldn't be helped. It was my international debut and I didn't know what to expect.

As the game wore on, I realised that although the speed was greater, the knocks weren't all that more intense. Usually, anyway. What do they say - pride comes before a fall? There was one occasion, towards the end of the first quarter, when I ran it in and got smashed by Kelvin Skerrett and Neil Cowie. That was my running style for you. Sometimes I didn't even look where I was going. Go forward. Head down. That was me. In this particular collision the ball fell out of my hands and Wales got possession. Towards the end of the following set of six tackles, the Welsh hooker Martin Hall fired a pass to his scrum-half, Kevin Ellis, who shot in unchallenged under the posts for the first of his two tries on the night.

Potentially, that might have got me down and, on other occasions, probably would have. But not in this game. I was still quite confident. I had enjoyed some good runs before then and was, I thought, playing quite well. I told myself it was just one of those things. The other players were very supportive and told me to keep my head up and it wasn't long before we were level. My fellow England new boy, Richard Gay, was the scorer, making the most of a superb pass from Garry Schofield. Richard's try, converted by Deryck Fox, meant we trailed just 8-6 at half-time, seeing as how Jonathan Davies had already kicked his conversion and added a penalty goal shortly before the break.

We began the second half very brightly and were first to cross for a try, after eight minutes. This time, it was my old Featherstone mate 'Newy' who did the initial damage, with one of his trademark length-of-the-field runs. The Welsh defence scrambled back well to cover, but when Deryck's huge bomb was then fumbled by Paul Atcheson, under pressure from Sonny Nickle, 'Foxy' was on hand to touch down. Four minutes later, we went further ahead when Steve McCurrie's perfect pass created a try for Jason Robinson in the corner. One conversion in two from Deryck and it was 16-8 to England.

Then, later in the game, I lost the ball again when Phil Ford, my opposite number and a far more experienced international winger, reefed it from my grasp. The television pictures confirmed that it had clearly been stolen, but Russell Smith, the referee, didn't see it that way and he ruled a knock-on. It was disappointing to see Paul Cullen on Sky television the next day blaming me for the mistake. Those were the only two errors I made - if you can call that second one an error.

Unfortunately, though, as the match moved into its final quarter, Wales steadily began to grow in confidence. In fairness, they had played a conservative game and defended brilliantly, meaning that when Kevin Ellis went in for his second try on 67 minutes - after a classy move involving Atcheson and Allan Bateman - which was goaled by Davies, they only trailed by two points. And when Davies then added another penalty, with less than ten minutes to go it was all square. I can honestly say that the closing stages of that game were some of the most tense I have played in. Jonathan Davies, though, sailed through it like the quality individual he is. On 71 minutes, he kicked a drop-goal that really set the cat among the pigeons and then, two minutes before time, sealed the match, 18-16, with another one-pointer. Although we had scored three tries to two, Wales had hung on for their first victory over England in seven matches, the last win coming at Headingley in January 1977. They made the most of it, too, going on to beat France at a muddy Carcassonne, 22-10, to secure the 1995 European Championship.

Me? Well, I was gutted to be on the losing side, obviously, but also quietly pleased with my own performance, as I sat there in that Ninian Park dressing room. You know yourself whether you have played well. Ellery came to me after the game, patted me on the back and said 'well done', which meant a lot to me too. I was knackered. I couldn't have given any more and just prayed that I would get a second chance when the next match came around, two weeks later, against France at Gateshead. And as things turned out, that is exactly what did happen - I won my second selection for England's international rugby league team. Sadly, though, this time it was all destined to end in frustration and crushing disappointment.

The reason I was to be given another run owed as much to good fortune - on my part, at least - as anything else. For the France game, a fair number of the Great Britain sevens squad were once again available, including the likes of

Halifax winger John Bentley, soon to create an even bigger name for himself with rugby union's British Lions. On the other hand, Jason Robinson and Martin Offiah were both now out with injury, which left a gap to be filled by yours truly. Or at least that was the plan. Unfortunately, on the day, I suddenly went down with flu.

It was all just sheer bad luck. Before then, I had never missed a game with illness in my life. In fact, in the previous five years with Featherstone I had only ever missed two club games - once with a dead leg for Peter Fox and once when I was dropped by Steve Martin. My temperature rose to over one hundred, after the doctor at our team hotel gave me an injection. They wouldn't let me out of my room, because they were frightened I would give the flu to everyone else. Even then 1 wanted to play, but Ellery and assistant coach Gary Hetherington ordered me not to. I was very disappointed. Instead, my place went to Francis Cummins of Leeds, who lined up on the left wing in my absence and scored a try in a side that beat the French, 19-16.

And for Ikram Butt, England rugby league winger, that turned out to be that. My one and only cap had come a fortnight before, in Cardiff. There would be no more. In May, Ellery Hanley was offered a big-money contract in Australia and quit his jobs both as coach of the national side and Leeds. Into the England set-up came Phil Larder, a man who seemed to know exactly what he wanted - and it wasn't me. Larder picked a train-on squad of 40 ahead of the 1995 World Cup, and when I wasn't even named in that it was obvious that my brief international career was over. Even so, I will always be grateful that I got the chance to play for my country. It may have ended unsatisfactorily, but I am glad that I was given the opportunity.

Not that I was ever actually given the cap itself, mind you. I am told that you have to play two games for that.

\* \* \* \* \*

As a passionate supporter of the idea that rugby league needs to grow its appeal everywhere in the UK and beyond - not just in Yorkshire, Lancashire and Cumbria - I was chuffed to see the Bridgend-based Celtic Crusaders enter Super League in 2009.

Having said that, bearing my earlier comments on the red flag of St. George in mind, I do think that the owners would have been better advised not to have used 'Crusaders' as a nickname. After all, there are plenty more names they could have chosen, aren't there? I'm sure they don't intend any offence, but if the club is trying to appeal to everyone within the South Wales community, it might not have been the most sensible idea.

Still, all in all, taking rugby league to Wales is a fantastic thing. When it comes to rugby league I am a dyed-in-the-wool traditionalist, but I am also aware of the need for modernisation. We have to expand rugby league and get into as many parts of the world as possible. Just think of all the great Welshmen who have lit up the thirteen-a-side code down the years - Billy Boston, Lewis Jones, Jonathan Davies and many, many others. Why wouldn't we want to develop some more?

When I was at Wembley recently, for the Challenge Cup final, I ran into a lot of the old Welsh players. John Devereux was on my table and so was Kevin Ellis, who I played against in Cardiff and who is involved with the new Celtic club. It was great to see them. Paul Moriarty was there too. We talked about old times and, of course, that Test match in 1995.

Back then, with that day over, I had some serious personal decisions to make regarding my own, domestic, future. And I mean 'domestic' in both senses of the word, because not only was I about to move on from my beloved Featherstone Rovers, I was also about to settle down and get married.

First things first, though. I wasn't the only crowd favourite to have left Featherstone by the end of the 1994-95 season. Iva Ropati went back to New Zealand after only nine games, while my old centre partner Terry Manning joined Doncaster. Away from the field, it was a time of turmoil too. As the season wound down, many of our supporters became more and more wound up, as the proposed new summer Super League loomed ever closer. At Featherstone, it all came to a head on April 17, the date of our home game with deadly local rivals Castleford. Not surprisingly, given all the plans for club mergers and so on, our fans were worried that this could be the last such derby match they would ever see.

Before the game, the fans staged a protest march from Pontefract to Post Office Road, waving banners and chanting against the plans all the way. And then, at half-time, there was a peaceful demonstration on the pitch, in front of the main stand, although no one could hear the respective club chairmen because of all the noise. At that stage, we players were inside getting our half-time team talk, of course. But when I later read that Featherstone and Castleford fans - sworn enemies usually - were standing with their arms around each other, promising undying love, it was hard not to smile. This really was a crazy time for British rugby league; a time when, one way or another, common sense went out of the window and just about everyone involved in the game seemed to be in danger of losing their marbles.

In hindsight, Super League's original merger plans were never going to last. They were way too ambitious to be pushed through all at once and, eventually, something closer to sanity did prevail. Even so, the fall-out from those days still rankles with plenty of people in rugby league - particularly the ones who follow those lower division clubs that missed out on the big time when supporter pressure stopped the mergers from going through, such as Featherstone. I can understand why people still get upset; it is often hard to bounce back after a knock like that. But, let's be honest, it was almost fifteen years ago now. Personally, I always try to look forward rather than back.

Having said that, it's hard to write an autobiography if you don't look back, isn't it? So much for that theory, then! And after my final try for Featherstone in that Challenge Cup semi-final with Leeds - and six more league games which ended with a 36-14 win against Oldham - the season and my days at Post Office Road were over. The 1994-95 campaign finished in April and, in May 1995, I signed for London Broncos.

Why did I want to leave Featherstone? I didn't really, not to begin with anyway.

If I hadn't got the call from London, I might well have stayed where I was. In fact, I'll go so far as to say that if Peter Fox had still been coach, I would have stayed at Featherstone. After all, I was now an established first-team player and going okay. I didn't put in a transfer request or anything like that, but if something came up, well, that was different. Ultimately, what made my mind up to leave was that I didn't really have all that strong a connection with David Ward. And with the Steve Martin debacle still fresh in my mind, I was never quite settled again. Also, I had always secretly doubted that I was David's ideal winger. Once London got in touch, I thought maybe it was best to move on.

Another tempting reason to leave, of course, was that the new Super League offered every player who was good enough the chance to go full-time. To be fair, David Ward and Howard Cartwright, Rovers' assistant coach, had made good plans for moving ahead. They wanted to retain all their players and told everyone so. As for the club itself, the board had invested quite a lot into getting Featherstone into Super League in their own right. When they were knocked back, they put the club forward as first reserves, just in case anyone dropped out. But whatever happened, Rovers were determined to win instant promotion back into the top flight; that was the plan.

Deep down inside, though, I wasn't really convinced that the club would be able to fulfill those ambitions. It wasn't that I got wind on the grapevine that Featherstone were going to miss out or anything like that. I was just reading between the lines of what I saw in the press; that for one reason or another Featherstone would not be on the list to go into Super League.

Neither did it have anything to do with having my head turned by having just played for England. Yes, I had seen how a move from Rovers to Bradford had helped Paul Newlove and Deryck Fox to win international recognition, but at the end of the day I am a realistic man. I may have done some daft things in my life, but I'm not simple. I realised then, as I do now, that my England cap was a reward for my efforts in previous years rather than my form in the season just gone. I was fully aware of that and wasn't about to get carried away.

My experience in Cardiff had definitely been a couple of steps above what I was used to and I doubted that, internationally, I would ever be able to hold my own on a regular basis. In any case, going to a bigger set-up does not necessarily mean you are moving forward - you might just be a small fish in a big pond, whereas Featherstone had always been a great club for me.

\* \* \* \* \*

London's approach came out of the blue. I got a phonecall one day from their coach, Gary Grienke. He rang me up. 'Ikram,' he said, 'we would like to give you £40,000 a season.' Just like that. Straight out with it, over the phone. I thought: 'Flippin' 'eck'.

If all this felt too good to be true that's probably because, as things turned out, it was. Let me say right away that none of the blame for the troubled times ahead had anything to do with the London club. Far from it. Leaving aside some later problems I had with Grienke's eventual replacement, Tony Currie, under their chairman, Barry Maranta, the Broncos were never anything other than supportive right from the start. They even signed me knowing that I had just had a groin operation.

My groin had been nagging me for a while and, unbeknown to anyone, I had been trying to ignore it even on the night I played for England. The medical experts always say that the best thing for a groin injury is rest and so, once my international prospects came to a halt, that's what I tried to do. I played for Featherstone on the weekend, and gave it everything I had as usual. But I didn't train anywhere near as often or as hard as I used to.

That didn't go down too well with David Ward, who told me: 'Since you played for England, Ikram, you are hardly training'. Maybe he thought I was getting a big-headed. I wasn't, but in a way, he was right to be narked. I was saving myself, but it was my groin and rugby league clubs tended to treat their players like cattle back then. In any case, thanks to cortisone injections and so on, I played through the pain barrier until the end of the season, when it was finally decided that I had to get the problem seen to. Steve Molloy,

Gary Price and me all went down to Harley Street, London, for the same operation.

The surgeon we were under was well known for operating on sportsmen and he had a very good reputation. His name was Doctor Gilmore and, over the following years, he also went on to treat the likes of Alan Shearer and Jonny Wilkinson. As I said, London knew all about the situation. I wasn't hiding anything. The club doctor, 'Doc De' Jennings, who works for the RFL nowadays I believe, knew I was in good hands. Literally, more often than not! I will never forget how Doctor Gilmore made his diagnosis. He just sat you on a bench and put his finger under your nuts. If you screamed, he said: 'Right, you need it doing.'

Anyway, when Gary Grienke rang me, once we had finished speaking I got straight back on the telephone to Peter Fox, who I knew would help me to do the deal. As a sign that they were serious, the Broncos invited Peter and me to join them at the Wembley Challenge Cup final that year and they provided us with five-star accommodation. At the time, I wasn't yet married, so I took a mate down with me to share my twin room. They left the club credit card open for my use in the hotel and I couldn't believe it. Free room service, cable television, the lot. At the game itself, London had a box and Barry Maranta was there. Peter did all the talking, as usual. I said to him: 'Don't mess this up, will you? I'm on a right do.' He just laughed.

As things turned out, I needn't have worried. Peter did his usual first class job.

To take account of the switch to summer from March 1996, a shorter winter season was scheduled from August 1995, featuring every Super League club except Paris.

Peter negotiated a fee of £15,000 for that, £50,000 for the first season of Super League and then £70,000 the season after that. Effectively, he was acting as my agent but - and this is the sort of bloke he is - he never took a penny for it.

Not surprisingly, then, I was rubbing my hands together, thinking 'I can't go wrong here'. And, as things turned out, on the rugby league front anyway, I did make a pretty good start. As expected, I got over my groin operation through the pre-season and then did quite well for London throughout the whole of the shortened one-off 1995-1996 campaign. In August, nine days before that season began with an away tie at Warrington, I had my married my lovely wife, Bushra, and we were soon settled in a smashing two-bedroomed apartment five minutes from the Copthall Stadium, Barnet.

In many ways, then, life really could not have been any better. Bushra and me were still young, living in London, and the world was at our feet. Yet what ought to have been a time of great fun and optimism was instead threatened by dark clouds gathering overhead. My past was about to come back and haunt me.

# 10

*

# Wedding Bells and Car Trouble

December 22, 1966. I know that date off by heart. 22.12.66. How can I forget it? For one thing, it is our Tony's date of birth, three days before Christmas, so it's not a difficult one to remember. Secondly, repeating it to a police officer landed me with a six-month prison sentence.

To be honest, I find this whole episode very shameful. There was a time when I would have preferred to keep quiet about it. But, given the job that I now do, occasionally working with kids who have had similar problems, I have since come to realise that it's healthier to have these things out in the open. Being sent to prison is not something of which I am in any way proud. On the contrary, remembering my time inside makes me feel deeply ashamed. If I could go back in time and change things, I would. Not only did I hurt myself, I hurt many of the people - family and friends - around me who deserved better. If it is possible to take something positive out of such a negative experience then that is what I am determined to do.

In any case, whichever you way look at it, it is a fact that I broke the law and was punished for it. I did my time and those days are now behind me. Nor is there any doubt that prison turned out to be a major test of my character. It brought me up with a shock and made me question my own selfish attitudes and lack of any sense of social responsibility. Ultimately, I feel it gave me a greater insight into the difficulties which young people in all communities face. Maybe it gives some of the advice I can give more empathy and clout. I hope so. I realise the dangers young people face because I have faced them and suffered the consequences myself.

For me, the nightmare began during my last season at Featherstone. I was driving up Victoria Road early one Saturday afternoon, about five minutes from our house in Headingley. The car was a red Cavalier hatchback, which had originally belonged to Brendon Tuuta as part of a sponsorship deal. When Brendon had finished with it, I bought it off the company.

Anyway, driving up Victoria Road was nothing new to me. I had done it loads of times with no problem, I knew the road well. Unfortunately, on this particular occasion, there were two police officers by the side of the road on a spot check, pointing a speed gun. As I drove by, I saw it pointing at me and, suddenly, everything went into slow motion. I could see the gun, but it was too late to do anything about it.

My first thought was: 'Oh, no'. My heart stopped, my stomach dropped and I went into a sort of trance. My main thought was: 'What am I going to do?' I hadn't gone far up the road when the policemen waved me down and signalled me to pull over.

They began to ask questions ... whether I had been stopped before ... where was I going ... was I aware that I had been speeding ... that sort of thing. Then I was asked to get out of my vehicle and sit in the back of theirs, where they pointed out that I had been doing 37mph in a 30mph zone and continued to ask questions. I knew that there was no point in denying that I had been going too fast, it was all cut and dried.

My real problems began, though, when they asked me for my name and date of birth. The thing is, to my eternal shame, I was driving without any insurance. I thought, I'd better not give them my details or I will be in trouble. So I gave them our Tony's instead. It was a stupid thing to do, but when the policeman asked for my name, I was thinking: 'Shall I give mine or our kid's'. On impulse I gave our kid's - the biggest mistake I ever made. Then they asked me to sign a producers form, to be taken to the police station with all my other bits and pieces, insurance, MOT, drivers licence and so on, which is where I really did trip myself up. I didn't only give our Tony's name, I also tried to copy his signature.

To be honest, this wasn't the first time I had lived life dangerously around cars. Right from the start of my motoring 'career', I had shown irresponsibility. How I didn't get caught, I'll never know. In my late teens, after failing my first driving test, I took it again immediately afterwards and failed for a second time. Soon, I was sick of the whole situation because, in my arrogance, I thought I could drive perfectly well. I didn't own a car of my own, but from time to time I would just drive any that was available. Our Tony wasn't happy about it, but if ever he left the keys to his car at home, often I would just take his.

As time went on, I suppose I became complacent. I had no accidents or anything like that, so I just stopped worrying. Plus there was the fact that, with my rugby career just getting off the ground, I had to rely so much on others for transport. When I first went to Featherstone, for example, I used to get a bus into town to the Smith's Arms pub, which is knocked down now, and get picked up by Gary Rose. Gary would then give me a lift to Featherstone and back. Sometimes, if I was late, he would drive off without me. So you can imagine the frustration of wanting to drive and feeling hard done by.

Eventually, I went so far as to buy my own Mini. It was another example, I suppose, of the lack of a father's guidance. Looking back, it must have been a particularly difficult time for my mum, who having lost her husband didn't want to lose any of her sons too. Now, I feel deeply sorry for what I put her through. All three of us lads must have have been difficult to control at times, and there's no doubt that I put her and my sisters in an awkward position.

My first serious brush with the law came when I bought a Vauxhall Astra off one of my team-mates at Featherstone. Unknown to him or anyone else at the club, I still hadn't passed my test but I thought I was driving quite comfortably. Anyway, this car was a right dud. It spent most of its time in the garage at Yorkshire Copperworks. Every month there was something wrong with it and I probably spent more money trying to fix the thing than I paid for it in the first place. I was once stopped in that too and got into trouble for having the wrong date on my MOT certificate although, in my defence, it was like that when I was given it and I hadn't noticed.

Luckily for me, on that occasion I managed to get away with it. A mate of mine owned a takeaway, one of the best in Leeds, down by the university, near Hyde Park. The traffic police used to wait there all the time. They also used to go in for free curries, so you could say that my pal and them had a good relationship. Anyway, when I reported to the station as ordered, I told them about our mutual friend. I filled in a form, the desk sergeant turned a blind eye and that was that.

Now, you might think that I would be happy about this

and, it's true, I was at the time. But nowadays, and especially with later events in mind, it leaves a bitter taste in my mouth. Too often, it seems, there is one law for police officers and one law for everyone else, especially when it comes to driving offences. Is that really the way to build trust with any community, whatever its culture or religion?

But back to the incident on Victoria Road and the irony of what followed is that I knew exactly how my brother wrote his signature, the way it went up at certain points and so on, because I had copied it many times before, when we were just messing about at home. However for some reason, on this particular day, I panicked and did it wrong. Looking back, I think it was just a case of scrawling something - here, there you are - and getting away from the situation quickly.

And perhaps the silliest thing of all is that, although I was pretending to be someone else, I was actually sitting there with my tracksuit and Featherstone drill top on. What if they had been rugby league fans? That five or ten minute interview was one of the longest of my life. Obviously, I wasn't thinking clearly. The only thing on my mind was: 'I'm not insured'. But, as I drove away, I did think: 'What have I done?' I knew then that I should have given my own name and taken the rap myself. I also knew that the repercussions could end up being quite severe.

So for the rest of that day and a couple of weeks following, my conscience was in turmoil. At first, I didn't tell anyone. Eventually, though, I had to tell our Tony who, reluctant but loyal as ever, went along to the police station in my place to provide the expected papers. Otherwise, I just kept what had happened to myself and, after a period of not hearing anything more about it, let the incident slip quietly to the back of my mind.

\* \* \* \* \*

Along with the move to London, another big reason why I was able to forget all about the Victoria Road incident in the months ahead was that, in between training and trying to get over my groin operation, I was looking forward to my marriage to Bushra.

Eventually, our wedding took place over the weekend of 11 August 1995. My proposal, though, had been made over a year before. Sensibly, because she was still in Spain and France gaining work experience as a teacher of European languages back then and, after that, went on to do her PGSE or teacher training, her parents insisted that she should finish her degree before getting married. You might have guessed by now that Bushra is the bright one in our relationship! That ought to get me in the good books.

By the time I proposed marriage, I had known Bushra for most of my life, our families had been friends for years and only lived about ten minutes away from us in Headingley. She had four sisters and one brother, who was a lot older than us, more our Zaman's age. Two of the sisters, though, were very close to my sisters.

Our families were never in each other's pockets but we knew them well and Bushra's father was a very well respected man in the community - he still is. My father-in-law is a very old school religious man, well educated - he went to university with the Labour politician Jack Straw - but quite a forward thinker, unlike many of the imams I referred to earlier who used to come over from Pakistan. In fact, he used to teach Islam at his house and our Chinky at one time went to be taught by him. He also taught Bushra, which is why she is so brainy, and the bonus is that she can now teach our kids in turn. All of them can either speak Arabic or are learning it.

For all that he is a religious man, my father-in-law is also a very relaxed individual and we have always got on well.

## Tries and Prejudice

Everyone has ups and downs in their marriage and Bushra and I were no exception. If ever my wife stormed off home to her mothers after an argument or something, her mum would sit there giving me filthy looks when I went around to try and patch things up. I can't say I blame her - I would have done too! Her dad, though, always used to welcome me with a smile.

Bushra and I went to the same nursery, primary and middle schools. Then, as we grew older, she and my sisters went to West Park Girls High School. In our youth, there was never any romance between us or anything. I was with my friends and she was with hers. We would say hello and that was about it. Then, when she changed school, I didn't really see her at all until sixth form, when she came back to our school to study French.

Even then, though, we didn't have what you might call a close relationship. Bushra is far too decent to talk about it, but I dread to think what she must have thought of me at that point in my life. I cringe about it now but, like many teenage boys, there were times when I acted like Jack the Lad and ran a bit wild, although nothing too serious. Outside of sport, it got to the point where I struggled to apply myself to anything sensible at all and so it came as no surprise when my days in the sixth form were brought to a premature end. Perhaps my misbehaviour was down to hormones or the lack of a father's discipline, who can say? But whatever was going on inside my head, Bushra was a good Muslim girl and I wouldn't have cut the most attractive marriage prospect, that's for sure.

As we moved into our early twenties, Bushra and I would occasionally find ourselves at the same family do or something, but you must remember that at Muslim events the women and men don't intermingle. So we didn't really meet there properly, either. And once my rugby league career began to take off and I began to be a little more focussed and (sometimes!) mature, I became devoted to training and playing. I didn't have enough time to be messing about on the streets or think about marriage. It was work, training and home.

Then, one day in 1994, me and our Tony were driving home and I saw Bushra again, for the first time in years, walking along the road with her friends. Although the rest of my brothers and sisters were fixed up with marriage partners, me and our Tony weren't. When I got back to the house I said to my mum: 'What do you think of Bushra? I've just seen her and she looks really nice.' Even though I was in my mid-twenties by now, I was still in no real rush to get wed - or so I thought - but something inside me had clicked. Not surprisingly, my mum and sisters were delighted. The wheels were set in motion.

Now because I am aware that a lot of the readers of this book won't be all that familiar with the Muslim faith, and because there is a huge amount of confusion when it comes to arranged and forced marriages, this would probably be a good point to explain the difference. Our marriage, like the vast majority of Muslim weddings, was arranged, not forced. In a forced marriage situation, the parents do not consult their children. They have other agendas, not necessarily that their children should just be happy and blessed. Those parents can coerce or emotionally blackmail the children, sometimes with the support of other family members.

In the past, back in India and Pakistan, this area was more ambiguous because families knew each other well enough to know what each child's strengths and weaknesses were, so it wasn't such a gamble in wondering how their son or daughter would fare. That meant everyone was in agreement, so there were very few disputes and proposals were rarely turned down. You had an agreement because, Islamically, you have to consent and agree to a marriage, so it wasn't considered to be forced, it was arranged. In the female's case, traditionally she was supposed to be shy anyway, although, again, that is changing now. Her modesty would be seen as acceptance of the proposal.

Nowadays, the difference is a lot more straightforward. For example, when my niece got married recently, she did so after having had a number of proposals. My sister, her mum, told friends that if they knew of anyone who was a suitable match, these were her interests, this was her level of education and so on. The result was that we had meetings with each of the prospective husbands and my brothers and I were invited so that we would have a chance to speak to them ourselves. In each case, the lads' parents came too and that allowed us to meet their families. We had a dinner. My niece and the boys had chance to have a chat. It was a nice arrangement. Ultimately, though, it was up to my niece to say whether she wanted to go any further with it or not. Once or twice she said no. And then, on one occasion, she accepted. His family came to our house, we went to his, we had our discussions and they ended up getting married. Whatever you are doing in life, it is always good to hear another opinion. At the end of the day, the decision was made by my niece, but she valued the rest of her family's thoughts.

In the case of Bushra and myself, my mother and our Tony - who was also busy organising his own marriage at this time - went to see her family and came back saying that her parents were okay with the idea if their daughter was too. Maybe, because of my prior reputation, they thought they had better take some time to mull it over, I don't know. But whatever the reason she then made me wait six months for her answer!

Partly the delay was due to her being out of the country, gaining teaching experience, as I already said. But I do know that she also had a number of other marriage offers to consider, from both here and in Pakistan, which is normal for a Muslim girl. Some of those guys had good financial prospects too, with businesses in America to inherit and all sorts. But when it came to the crunch she turned them all down and accepted my proposal instead. I told you she was bright.

When she came back from abroad we then had another year or so to wait before the actual wedding. We had planned to get married in July 1995 but someone close to one of our families died, so we postponed it for forty days as a mark of respect. By this time, I was down south, getting over my operation and training with the Broncos, when I wasn't travelling backwards and forwards to and from Yorkshire, that is, for reasons that will soon become apparent. I was in London and Bushra was in Leeds. They say that separation makes the heart grow fonder but, so far, we hadn't had the best of starts.

Fortunately, the wedding day itself was a much happier affair. In Islam, the actual marriage - or Nikaah as it is known, preceded by a ceremony called the Baraat - is usually organised by the bride's family. That's followed, a couple of days later, by a Valimah, or special dinner, organised by the groom's side. Obviously, the marriage comes first and ours was held on a Friday night in a local school, Bedford Field, nowadays known as the City of Leeds School. In fact, my sister Qudisia teaches there every Saturday morning.

As usual in orthodox Muslim communities, at our wedding the men were in one hall and the women in another. As the ceremony progresses, the Imam collects the groom's signature and that of the bride's father, before going next door to see the bride herself. Although she is then asked the same questions as her future husband, she answers nothing which, in the Muslim tradition, is taken as an acknowledgement that she agrees. Technically, once the contract - or Nikaahnama - is signed in the presence of witnesses, you are then married, although at that stage still in separate rooms. Then you eat a lavish dinner and right at the end of the event when most of the guests have departed and there is only close family left, the husband goes to see his bride and they sit on the same sofa, although still without touching. It is then that more prayers are spoken, the cake is cut, photographs are taken and so on. The bride's father gives his daughter's hand to her new husband, tells him to protect and take good care of her, and the couple depart to their first home together.

For us, that meant a semi-detached house in the Holt Park area of Leeds, although we didn't spend too much time in it at first because, by then, I already had that two-bedroomed flat in London. The morning after our wedding, though, we got up late - as you do - and spent the first day of our married life together before going to visit my mum in Headingley. And then, on the Sunday, it was time for the Valimah, which took place up Chapeltown Road in Leeds, at the Bangladesh Centre. Our Tony organised it and a super time was had by all. With that done, we went back to my mum's house to pick up some stuff and - in another old rust bucket of a car arranged at short notice by a mate - headed south.

When she first learned that I was taking her daughter to live in London, my mother-in-law, Safdar, was not happy about it at all. She was worried she would never see Bushra again. But, as usual, my father-in-law came good and told her just to be thankful that I wasn't going off to Australia! And I think that, nowadays, even she would admit that our marriage turned out to be a blessing. For one thing, we ended up giving her three lovely grandchildren. My eldest daughter, Aamina, was born in 1996 and is named after the mother of the prophet Mohammad (peace be upon him). In 2000 came Ruqayya, who is named after Bushra's grandmother and my son, Hayan, was born in 2002. My sister-in-law chose his name. I wanted to call him Yusuf (Joseph).

Anyway, it wasn't as if Bushra wasn't used to travelling and working away from the north of England. My new wife found herself a teaching job at a school in Barnet and the pair of us were very happy. Back then, the Broncos played at Copthall Stadium, which was literally five minutes away from our flat. Bushra's school was twenty minutes away, so she took the car and I walked. Although we didn't go on a honeymoon due to a death in the family, we used to get out all the time into London so it was great. Bushra had family and friends living in the capital. I was on decent money and she was on decent money.

At last we were together. Life was good. Had it not been for the repercussions of my earlier misdemeanour in Leeds, it might even have been perfect.

\* \* \* \* \*

The one nagging problem during those, on the face of it, happy days was that the driving fiasco I had hoped was done and dusted suddenly came back to bite me in the backside.

In fact, it wasn't until six or seven months after the initial incident that I heard anything more about it. I had gone down to London and, as time passed, let it go from my mind. Then, one day, I had a phonecall from my brother, Tony. He told me that a couple of police officers had been to see him at the Post Office where he worked as a manager, in Armley.

They said to our Tony: 'We've got the producer form here

and your signatures are different.' Had my signature been the same as his, who knows, maybe I would have got away with it. But when the two different signatures were noticed at the police station, they came straight out to see him and realised straight away that this wasn't the same person they had stopped. He was left with no choice but to admit everything.

We had a right set-to about it at all on the phone. Our Tony said that I was always getting him into trouble and gave me a right doing. He said I had embarrassed him at work. He also told me that the police had said I should just come down to the station and they would caution me. That's all they said that would happen; it would be a caution. I wasn't keen to come back because I was down in London, but our Tony insisted that I should.

So that's what I did. I travelled back up north and went to the police station. But instead of cautioning me as they had said they would, the policeman on duty immediately said: 'Right, Mr Butt,' and read me my rights. I said: 'I thought I was getting a caution?' But they just ignored me.

Anyway, I was arrested and in the cells for a few hours while they questioned me. And then they let me out, just like that, although it took a good few months again before the whole thing went to court. The waiting seemed to drag on for ages. And even when it did come to court, every time I went there it seemed to be adjourned. I wasn't very happy with my solicitor. He kept going on about the all the big cases he had been involved in before. I thought: 'Yes, but what about mine?'. He was talking about doing deals and all sorts, while I struggled to keep my mind on more positive things, such as my forthcoming marriage and pre-season training.

In hindsight, it's amazing that I managed to have as solid a season as I did in that first year with the Broncos. The club knew about my predicament and were amazingly supportive, especially Barry Maranta who made a wisecrack to the press about how Australians were used to having convicts around, or something like that. I really appreciated their backing. I can admit now, though, that personally I felt under a huge amount of pressure. I tried to put it to one side when the season got underway, but it was always in the back of my mind, even when I was playing.

To be honest, that shortened eleven-team 1995-96 Stones Bitter Championship was a bit of a strange old season anyway. Everything in professional British rugby league had split into three divisions ahead of Super League and, as I said earlier, our first game was an away fixture at Warrington on Sunday 20 August. We followed that up with a midweek home game against Halifax the following Wednesday night. My old club Featherstone, meanwhile, dropped into a reshaped First Division and played Hull, away, on their opening Sunday.

When the campaign came to a close on Sunday 21 January 1996, with a home game against Castleford, London were tenth in the table with only Workington Town below them. We did, though, have the same points as Warrington (14) and were only two behind Bradford and Oldham, who had 16 points each, so things looked pretty promising for the club's future. Wigan were that season's short-lived champions, eight points clear of Leeds at the top, with 36 points.

As for Super League itself, that exciting new summer competition was now only two months away from kicking off in style, with a match between Paris and Sheffield in France. London's first game, meanwhile, would be an away fixture at the slightly less glamorous Halifax, which we won, 24-22, under our new coach, Tony Currie. Not that any of that concerned me. I would have loved to have been lining up in London colours myself, but my mind was now fixed on more pressing matters. Word had come through that I was wanted back in court - and this time looked like being the real McCoy.

# 11

*

# A Harsh Lesson

As soon as it became obvious that D-Day was approaching, the first thing our Tony and me did was change our firm of solicitors. The last bloke had organised a barrister to represent us, but the costs would have been astronomical so we decided to go down the Legal Aid route instead. The signs, though, still weren't promising. One of the Legal Aid junior barristers sat us down and said: 'You guys have had it. This judge, Hoffman, does everybody. First-timers, everyone. It doesn't matter who you are.'

Funded by Legal Aid, our new solicitor was a very nice bloke, Jewish, and he too warned us that Hoffman - who was also Jewish - was notorious for being tough. He said: 'The fact of the matter is, he's going to do you.' Our solicitor put us in contact with a barrister who was another super guy. When the case did finally come to court, he represented us very well. Even Judge Hoffman said: 'That was an excellent mitigation. However...'

As soon as I heard the word 'however', I knew that we

had had it. The rest of Judge Hoffman's summing-up didn't really sink in. 'Blah blah blah ... there's no excuse for what you did ... blah blah blah ...' and so on. I heard the next bit, though. He said we could both go away for a month and get ourselves a probation officer's report, before adding that when we came back he was seriously considering a custodial sentence.

It was the most worrying time of my life. All sorts of things go through your head. Although you know, deep down, what is coming, there is always this glimmer of hope that you might be let off. I kept thinking: 'Please, please don't let me go down. I won't do anything bad ever again.'

Anyway, everything in that report was glowing. The references were top class, as even the judge admitted. 'But,' he said, 'I can't let you go for what you have done.' He gave me a six-month sentence, but with half of it running concurrently, so I did three months in the end, basically. Our Tony was given two months and ended up serving one. By now, my wife, Bushra, was pregnant with our first child, Aamina, which the judge knew all about, but it didn't make any difference. My mum had told me to go to court in a suit, to create a good impression. But the omens were that I wouldn't be coming back.

Waiting to be sentenced was terrible and I wouldn't wish it on anyone. Will they send me to prison? Won't they? Awful. So much so that when I was finally sent down, in a funny sort of a way it came as a relief. At last, I thought, I will finally be on my own and can just get through it and suffer the consequences.

It wasn't long, though, before the reality of losing my freedom began to sink in. Straight after sentencing, they take you downstairs in the courthouse and you are officially in custody. I remember that there was a little old fellow serving sandwiches and tea. He said: 'Ikram, what are you doing here?' I thought: 'Oh, no'. That was when it really hit home. Maybe that bloke was a Featherstone fan, I don't know. And then, when I went inside, I used to get it from the other prisoners, too. 'What are you doing here?' It's hard not to ask yourself the same question when you are hearing it all the time.

Over the following twelve weeks, I served around a month or so in Armley and then went to Wealstun open prison near Wetherby, until my release at the end of May 1996. The worst thing about that was that, at the start of the sentence, me and our Tony were in Armley together. He was furious about what had happened and wouldn't talk to me. Once or twice I asked him if he wanted to go into the yard for a walk and he said: 'I'm not going out there. It's full of convicts. I'm only in here because of you.' Eventually, he did begin to thaw, but to begin with it was terrible. The whole situation was a disaster. My mother was crying and so was my wife. At one stage, she came up from London to see me, with my younger brother, Chinky. I said: 'What are you doing here? This is no place for you.' I didn't want Bushra to be exposed to a place like that.

I suppose that when you first get put inside, it's natural to be depressed and embarrassed, especially when you are far from being a hardened criminal. As well as losing your freedom, you know that you have let everyone down, but once you get through that you realise that you have no choice but to get on with it. Fortunately, I am a positive-minded individual and that didn't change just because I was in prison. When the doors clanged shut on my cell, I thought I am going to have to make the most of this. I even managed to look on the bright side. I was in a room on my own. I was being fed and watered. I even got my meals on time. At home, with my missus being a hard-working teacher, that wasn't always the case.

If anything, passing the time was the biggest problem, especially in Armley. That was difficult, especially over the first seven days, when they lock you up for twenty-three hours a day, with just an hour for a stroll around the prison yard. During that time, you just walk round and round in circles, with your hands in your pockets, talking or thinking. It's a one-way system. You can't vary things and go in the opposite direction for a change, because then you would bump into everyone coming the other way. You have to go with the flow.

Worst of all, in that first week there were no trips allowed to the toilet. You had to use a bucket. How horrible that was. But then, with the first seven days out of the way, if you wanted to go to the toilet you just pressed a buzzer. Another way of passing the time was to get a job. There were several jobs of offer, most of them menial and which you had to accept. The first one I did was rolling up plastic bags. I can't remember why, I just know that I did it for eight hours a day. Later, I was lucky enough to be allowed into the prison gym. Everyone knew why I was in and most of them thought that I had been hard done by.

On one occasion I even got to watch the 1996 Challenge Cup final between St. Helens and Bradford on the telly. There were these two physical training instructors who were also involved with the Bradford Bulls supporters club, in fact it was them who allowed me in. Because they were rugby fans, they were very friendly and understanding towards my situation. In any case, I was only a category 'E' prisoner, which isn't too bad. They don't put high-risk offenders in category 'E'. These two lads managed the gym and, when I got talking to them, they started to let me go training there, sometimes on my own, which was very useful as by now I had a second groin injury. Anyway, on this particular Saturday in April they also let me watch the

Cup final at Wembley. I was sitting there with my feet up eating tuna sandwiches.

All in all, though, I spent most of my time in Armley locked up in the cell. Which was fine at first. As I said, you just wanted to close the door and stay away from everybody. But then, when I was moved to the open prison at Wealstun, I couldn't help but notice a huge difference. From being in a place where everyone was locked up all day long, I went to a place where everyone was free to wander around. My room at Wealstun - it wasn't really a cell - was like a big dormitory, containing four or five people, who I became quite good mates with. You had your own key and everything. Then there was the canteen food.

As you will know by now, I like to eat and at Armley you were only given so much food and no more. If you wanted any extra you had to get friendly with one or two people who worked in the kitchen, which I'm not ashamed to say I did. At Wealstun, though, when you had your dinner you could then have seconds or even thirds. I was just eating non-stop for the first few days. I also got friendly with some Asian lads, which was a good move because they all stuck together. I would go to their room and they had a big box of food, drinks and valuable phone cards galore. 'Ikram,' they told me, 'don't worry about anything. Just help yourself to food.' So I thought: 'Life's not too bad after all!'

My Broncos team-mate Steve Rosolen paid me a visit once, when London were playing a game up north, which was nice. And we used to have an Imam who came in on a Friday and we Muslims would all pray together. When Eid came around, he brought in some food. Some of the other lads, who weren't Muslims, came to sit with us anyway, because it was such good grub. I also used to receive regular letters from Featherstone Rovers fans, and I had a letter from a lady in Wigan which was particularly lovely. After all, I had always had the knack of playing well against Wigan, I tended to raise my game, so maybe she remembered me from that. I will never forget her kindness.

There was a gym at Wealstun too - which was just as well considering the groin injury. I spent a lot of my time there trying to get fit and rehabilitating. But it was difficult to fully get over it because I wasn't getting any proper physiotherapy, which is important after an injury. The result was that, as a player, I was never really right again. Apart from the gym, I spent the rest of my time watching television in a communal room. The video of that George Michael song, *A Different Corner*, was on all the time. Even now I can't hear it without being reminded of my days behind bars.

It was a bizarre time, in many ways. Once, I was talking to a guy from Northumbria, super chap, just chatting, and he asked me what I was in for. I said driving without insurance and then asked him the same question. 'Oh,' he said, 'for shooting a guy in the legs.' As casual as that. I thought, flippin' 'eck. But everyone in Wealstun had almost served their time and were being eased back into the community. A few of the prisoners had jobs on the outside and were then coming back into the prison on a night. Most of them were being reintegrated into society.

As for myself, when I went out I could have brought anything back in, but apart from the odd carton of cigs and a few phone cards I resisted the temptation. That's the whole point of an open prison - they are trusting you to have changed your ways. If they happened to search you and found something serious, you would be sent back to a closed prison. Even so, lads used to take the risk and were in and out with stuff all night.

Occasionally, you would see the guards wearing night goggles, looking out and trying to catch them in the act. And there were stories that some of the wardens were turning a blind eye in return for a few favours, although I don't know for sure how true that was. There were certainly more drugs available inside prison than outside it, though, that much I can tell you. Cigars, drink - you name it. I didn't want to get involved in anything heavy like that. All I was interested in was doing my time and getting out.

Although it was definitely an experience, I have never been proud of my time behind bars. Far from it, the memory fills me with embarrassment and regret. But it is important for me to recognise that what happened, happened. Tony and me served our time and I honestly think we are both bigger men for it. And, in the bigger picture, it showed me how a simple mistake can put a blemish on a whole life. Would I now be able to go to America, or start a new life in Australia if that's what I wanted to do, for example? I don't know. Most of all, I will always regret dragging my brother down with me.

One thing I do know, though, is that the entire experience changed me for the better. When it got to a point where my family were getting hurt and the police were involved, I had to make a decision either to continue along a dangerous road or get out and make something of myself. It was at this point, too, that I remembered what my father was about, when I was too young to really appreciate it.

Being in prison made me take a good hard look at my life, and weigh up the direction in which it was heading. In many ways, I was blessed with a God-given talent and, other than turning up to play rugby league week after week, not doing anything really useful with it. That is not the case anymore. If I can take something positive from such a negative experience and use it to help others, then that is exactly what I will do. I feel I was really lucky because I also saw what happened to people who did not get out in time.

In short, my experiences have left me able to empathise with kids who may have departed from the straight and narrow. I can see things from their point of view. I also know now how wrong it is to judge people on the basis of one stupid mistake.

\* \* \* \* \*

Over the years, from time to time, I have been sent a form in the post asking me to become a member of the London fomer-players association. I have always resisted doing that because it would bring back too many unhappy memories.

Recently, though, my one-time London team-mate Ady Spencer asked me to join again and this time I agreed to play in a fund-raising game for them. One of the questions on the form was: 'What was the highlight of your time at London?' As you can imagine, I had a struggle to think of anything!

In the end, I settled on our away game against Wigan on 9 June 1996, the first Super League match I played in after my release from jail. Understandably, after what I had been through, I was chuffed to bits simply to be chosen in the side. London were going through a bit of an injury crisis, so our coach, Tony Currie, had little choice but to pick me.

My last couple of weeks inside had been tough because I knew the release date was coming, but not exactly when it would be. In the end, I finished up serving a day extra in order to avoid having to pay off the original fine. I had already been inside for three months so what was another twenty-four hours? Once that was over, I went to see my mother in Leeds and then headed south, back down to London.

Having returned to the Broncos, things didn't exactly get off to a flier. For one thing, despite having spent so long out of the game, my groin was still bothering me. It had gone again in the close season before Super League, while I was busy training with London and travelling backwards and forwards to Leeds for the court cases. The doctors told me that I had weakened it during the short 1995-96 season, by over-compensating for it the first time around. As a result, I underwent my second groin operation while I was at Wealstun.

As before, it was my specialist, Dr Gilmore, who gave that operation the go-ahead. I got a pass-out from prison and went to see him in Harley Street. One old lag told me not to bother asking because I had no chance and if I'd have listened to him that would have been that. But, keen to get fit, I pursued it anyway and ended up getting a day release. I got a taxi to York station and then caught the train down to the capital. Knowing that I was still in prison, Dr Gilmore, bless him, made his diagnosis quickly and I was then able to nip across London and visit the wife. Afterwards, I got the train back north and limped back into Wealstun.

But now, a few weeks later, I was back among my team-mates, with prison and the operation both behind me. And after two half-games and a full match for the reserves against Wakefield, I was selected to face Wigan in a game that, against all expectations, we actually managed to draw, 18-18.

Despite those injury problems and no one giving us a chance, confidence at the Broncos was high. After beating Halifax without me in their opening game, the lads followed it up with a 38-22 victory over Paris on Easter Thursday, in front of 9,638 fans at our new ground, the Valley, at Charlton. What wouldn't the present day London club, Harlequins, give for regular crowds like that? By the end of the season, the Broncos were fourth in the table, just in front of Warrington and behind champions St. Helens, Wigan and Bradford. And if any game showed that the London club were serious contenders, it was my return to first-team action at Central Park.

As we have seen, whenever I played against Wigan in the past I had always seemed to pull a good game out of the hat and this was no different. Afterwards, our opponents and their fans were adamant that we had deliberately used slowing tactics, but so what? It got the job done. We were 18-4 down at one stage after having scored first. While I was walking back from the tryline, a woman in the crowd - maybe it was the lady who sent me the letter while I was inside - shouted: 'Oh, Ikram ... scoring first was the worst thing you could do'. And for a while it looked as though she might be right.

Thanks mainly to outstanding work by our pack, though, who made more yardage than the Wigan six all night, we soon managed to fight our way back. Duncan McRae, our full-back, was absolutely super, while our stand-off, Tulsen Tollett, had a great game too. To be honest, it was only through the efforts of big Va'aiga Tuigamala in the centres that we didn't completely steamroller Wigan in the second half. The man who stole the headlines for us was the current Castleford coach, Terry Matterson, whose penalty in the last minute levelled the game. And we might have come away with more than that if Shaun Edwards hadn't charged down McRae's drop-goal attempt in the dying seconds.

Make no mistake, London was buzzing big-time back then. And the excitement went up another notch when, in August 1996, Martin Offiah signed for the club. Unfortunately for me, however, once that initial buzz at Wigan was over, the first season of summer rugby league settled down into one of disappointment and frustration. I didn't score a try all year. Partly that was down to my nagging groin injury, but mainly it was down to my not getting on at all with Tony Currie.

When I first heard that Tony was coming in as coach of London, I thought 'fantastic'. In my days as a supporter of

Leeds, Tony Currie had been one of my favourite players. Peter Fox always spoke highly of him too but sadly, once he was actually in charge, it didn't work out. Tony hadn't brought me to the club himself, he had inherited me. And when he came into the set-up after being a specialist defensive coach at Brisbane Broncos, he did so with a lot of arrogance. I wasn't the only one to think so. Tony was too big for his boots with everyone - whether it be the players or even Barry Maranta, who paid his wages.

Once, he even ended up brawling with one of his players, Justin Bryant, or 'Dog' as he was known. Justin was rock hard; not quite the finished article but a good solid player, and a real Aussie country boy. I can't remember who won that fight, but I'm pretty sure it wasn't Tony.

Despite the team's encouraging on-field form, for me it was an unhappy period behind the scenes. Most of the London squad were Aussies in those days and doing their own thing. And even though I was one of the most senior players, I never seemed to have the confidence of the coaches. It didn't feel like a settled environment. I also struggled with being a full-time player. With more time on my hands, I began to eat and put on weight. It was all a bit new and disorientating.

True to form, while I was struggling on the field Peter Fox actually came down to London to talk to Tony Currie, who he had coached at Leeds a decade or so before. I was grateful but it didn't do any good. I couldn't seem to play to the way that Tony wanted me to. The coach didn't rate me so that was that.

Gary Grienke had largely played me out of position and so did Tony. Every time I came in off the wing I would get told off - but that was my game. So the writing was on the wall and I can't say I was surprised when I found out that he wanted to sell me. I wasn't performing, true, but that was no real surprise was it? Not with everything that I had recently been through. Not only was I carrying a groin injury, I had begun the season later than everyone else and so needed encouragement rather than being shut out.

Still, when a coach says you've got to go, you've got to go. And given that I was on decent money, I can understand why the Broncos went along with his wishes.

As I had just under two years left on my contract, at first Tony tried to do a swap-deal for me with Wakefield, but it didn't come off. For one thing, I didn't want to go to Wakefield. I was on £50,000 a year in London, rising to £70,000 in 1997. Why would I want to leave? That didn't exactly endear me any further to Tony Currie, but I decided to hang around anyway and wait for my chance.

In the end, it never came. I only made five appearances in all for London in 1996, one of them as substitute. And when things didn't get any better the following season, after the Broncos moved to the Stoop and were taken over by Richard Branson's Virgin group in February 1997, it was clear that there was never going to be a future for me in the capital. After not making a single appearance, I negotiated a £30,000 pay-off and left, in May, for Huddersfield.

# IKRAM IS JOVIAL AND EASY-GOING, BUT HE IS ALSO EXTREMELY COMMITTED...
## Khurshid 'Tony' Butt

*Ikram's rugby league playing brother*

When we were youngsters, my brothers and me were always close. We all took an interest in sport, for a start. And until we reached our teens and then went off to different schools, me and our Ikram used to hang around together all the time.

As a little brother, Ikram was a really jovial character who always had a big smile on his face; he was no bother at all. Everyone has their troubles and we were no different but, even though ours ended up being a single parent family, I have more fond memories than anything else.

Ikram's two front teeth were quite prominent when he was a kid; if you look at the photo albums they really stand out. As he has grown older his face has balanced out but, back then, we all called him 'Bugsy' after Bugs Bunny. And wherever he went he was always smiling.

Our father used to box in the Pakistani Air Force and from a really young age he would spend his Saturday afternoons watching *Grandstand*, so we had sport in our house right from the start. On Saturday's, my mother would just have to work around him, vacuuming around his legs and so on. Sport was a big part of our lives and us boys took to it like ducks to water.

The obvious difference between Ikram and myself was that he was more of an all-rounder. He was short and stocky but also very quick; he had a lot of pace in those days. I wasn't as quick and he was probably fitter than me too.

At school, Ikram always seemed to be at the top of his year in games, whether it be football, athletics or cricket. He was a natural athlete and actually made it into the school's athletics relay team. That might surprise some people nowadays, because he was never known as a flying winger in his professional career. As he admits himself, he was no Martin Offiah.

People were also often surprised at just how strong Ikram was. I remember when we were at Featherstone Rovers together and we did this fitness exercise. He was as strong, if not stronger, than the forwards when it came to weightlifting, even though he was nowhere near as heavy as them.

In his amateur days he was quick enough but, when we turned professional, that was when you realised how fast some of the other wingers were. But what balanced that out was Ikram's strength and the ability to break the first or second tackle. That's priceless for a team whenever you are near the line and Peter Fox knew enough to capitalise on that.

One time I was in the crowd at Post Office Road, when he was against playing Wigan. I was with a group of Pakistanis, so we stood out like a sore thumb. I overheard one of the Featherstone fans saying: 'That young lad is as strong as Kevin Iro.' That was some compliment because Kevin Iro wasn't elusive either, his game was built on his physique.

# Tries and Prejudice

Like most kids, when we started playing rugby we did it for fun; it was a recreational thing. We used to play touch and pass in the road and even used to tackle on concrete. Whenever there was a football match everybody in the street played.

But once Ikram began to get involved with the school team nobody could touch him. He was the sort of lad who could run around teams on his own. And when I started to be recognised as a decent player, that must have motivated him even more.

In our house, there was no parental pressure at all - for us, playing rugby league was always about going out and enjoying ourselves. And I think that Ikram has always kept that spirit in his play.

Our friends used to say that if Ikram would have had as much aggression as me on the field, he could have gone even further than he did. But the thing about my brother is that he is very placid. I am quite placid myself, but he certainly is. He is very happy go lucky.

Even on the pitch, he just switches off. You can have a right argument with him but, within seconds of falling out, he will just crack up laughing. That has always been his philosophy throughout life. Sometimes I used to tell him he needed to be a bit more tenacious, but you can't really change people's personalities, can you? They are who they are.

We have had many proud moments with Ikram, but when he was selected for England that was the icing on the cake. By then, he had already played for Great Britain amateurs. And even though he was my younger brother, there were times when even I had to stand back and be impressed by his ability. The way he sidestepped - everything. I realised quite early on that he could go a lot further so long as he stayed focussed.

And when he played for England, well, that was it. He has made English sporting history, hasn't he? Once Asians become more active in rugby league, no matter where you go, the name of Ikram Butt will be mentioned. That is nothing to sneeze at.

So it was very pleasing when he was selected to play for his country; not only for me but for the entire family. When you put a lot of effort into something and get a result there is no better feeling. We were very proud.

In a way, it validated my own decision to retire from the game, although I didn't really see it that way at the time. It was just the sensible thing to do.

Because of our family situation, becoming a full-time professional rugby league player was a big ask. And although I say Ikram is jovial and laid back, he is also extremely committed when it comes to getting what he wants. Back then, he was fitness mad and competitive. He used to cycle all the way to Featherstone!

In those days, there was me, Ikram and my younger brother, Chinky, at home with my mum. Ikram would be out at training or playing three or four times a week and so would I. There was no man about the house.

I had a decent full-time job at that time, and it was round about then that Leeds said they were going fully professional. Contracts were being renegotiated and it was something that everyone had to think about. I remember Roy Powell was a self -employed plasterer and he wasn't too keen on the idea either. How long was it going to last? How much money would you be paid? I was the manager of a Post Office and knew that if I stuck to that, it would give Ikram free reign to concentrate on his rugby career and become as good as he could be.

If anything, he deserved more. If certain things had gone right for him at Headingley he would have gone a lot further. If you ask me, he signed too soon for Leeds, where they could have turned out three or four good teams. His talents were wasted and he lost confidence. He bounced back at Featherstone when the great Peter Fox gave him a lifeline. Young lads like Ikram need to be nurtured.

When the prison episode came along, I think I handled it better than he did - and I was the one who had to stay in the cell for twenty-three hours while he went off to the gym! I was actually pretty angry about it all at the time, not only with Ikram, but also the fact that he was in there at all.

Ikram himself would never offer excuses but, in my opinion, the fact that he was sent down was ridiculous. And, although there were some inside who gave him plenty of support, there were some who seemed determined to make his life difficult.

After we had been sentenced and taken downstairs under the court, they were taking all our details, doing the paperwork and so on, and one police officer said: 'Ah, Ikram Butt, professional rugby league player - he must have got a right packet moving to London...', so you can see what was going on there.

In fact, the copper who first arrested him when he got pulled up in the car, I didn't like him at all, either. If you ask me, he saw Ikram as a scalp. In court, our barrister tried to make a comparison with Eric Cantona - when he kicked the fan in the crowd at Crystal Palace and got away with community service. But the judge just said: 'That wouldn't have happened in my court.'

It's easy to forget that it was only a driving offence. And, after all, perverting the course of justice is as broad as you want to make it. Nobody could believe that we had both been sent down and if you look at what certain sports stars - in football and rugby - get away with today, it all seems even more harsh.

Still, the one thing you can say about Ikram is that he is optimistic by nature and can turn any negative into a positive. The way he has since been able to turn that experience around and use it in his work to help others is pretty inspirational, I think.

All in all, our Ikram works hard, whether it be for himself, his family, the game of rugby, or the British Asian community in general. He should be proud of his achievements. I know that I am very proud to call him my brother.

# 12

\*

# From Currie to Curry...

Leaving London Broncos meant the end of my Super League playing career, which was a sad and frustrating way to bring the curtain down on my time in rugby league's top-flight.

Yet although the Broncos as a club had stood by me, I never really felt that I was being played to my best advantage and it was hard to enjoy myself and get on a roll, especially with all the interruptions of prison and injury. To be honest, by the time it was all sorted, I was glad to get away and come back north.

As time went on, I found it more and more of a struggle to fit in. One of my biggest problems was that the club had such a strong drinking culture, especially on the Monday after a game on Sunday. It was then that they would have these big booze-ups at which every player was expected to turn up. To put it bluntly, I didn't want to go. 'Just come along, Ikram,' they said. 'You don't have to drink.' But that would have been ridiculous.

Also, for most of that first Super League season, I was training with the reserves rather than the first team, which left me hanging about on the edge of things and not really feeling like I was part of the gang. I realise that I had made my own mistakes too, such as getting sent down and so on. But the club had also now moved from Barnet Copthall to the Valley at Charlton and my missus still worked in Barnet at the school. I went with the team, while she stayed there on her own. Often, people who don't live in London underestimate how big the distances are across the capital, travelling can be a nightmare. True, I was still being well paid as a professional sportsperson. But when you don't have the passion or desire for your sport anymore, things do get very difficult. And at London, for one reason or another, all that was gone.

Fortunately, just when everything seemed to be at its gloomiest, my old mentor Peter Fox once again came to my rescue. As I said, when I was having my problems with the Broncos coach, Tony Currie, it was Peter who came down to talk to him and try to smooth things over between us. When even that didn't work, it was quite clear that I was no longer in the picture at London and we began to discuss my other options.

One of those options was the swap deal at Wakefield I mentioned earlier, which never came off. I was also reported to be going to Paris St. Germain and Hull at one point - it was all over the Hull papers that chairman Tim Wilby wanted to sign me, but that never materialised either. In the end, Peter spoke to Steve Ferres who was the head coach of Huddersfield at the time. Steve said that I would be welcome at Huddersfield, so I took Peter's advice and went there in May 1997. Okay, I was no longer playing in Super League because Huddersfield were in the level below, Division One. But they had put an experienced squad together, including players like Garry Schofield, Phil Veivers and Paul Dixon which, together with a decent backline, ended up winning promotion, albeit through the back door.

I fancied going to Huddersfield as soon as Peter told me about it. I met up with the managing director and we agreed terms. I was very pleased. They gave me a £1000 retainer and I would be on £400 every time I played, win or lose. I was still a full-time professional. Away from the club, I lived with our Tony in Leeds. My missus left her job in London and moved back north with my new baby daughter, Aamina. So for all of us, it was like making a fresh start.

Soon, though, it became obvious that, rugby-wise, things were never going to be the same again. Having lost my desire for the game in London, I struggled to get it back. In hindsight, I can see now that this was where my career effectively ended. Any player will tell you that when they are doing well it is because they have the desire and hunger. I thought that I could get that back at Huddersfield but, instead, I just continued to struggle.

Partly, that was down to the injury that I still hadn't quite recovered from. Partly, it was down to the atmosphere at the club and, partly, it was down to my own frame of mind. On the whole, things were fine. I didn't mind training and was glad to be back home with local people. I wasn't in my comfort zone exactly, but I was playing rugby league how I used to - it wasn't an Australian influenced set-up, like in London. But even so, at the back of my mind, I just wasn't enjoying it anymore. And also in the back of my mind I was thinking: 'What next?'.

Looking back, it must have been a very difficult season for Steve Ferres. He was in a strange situation. He was the coach but he had all these wise old heads underneath him. It was very difficult for Steve to exert any real authority over the likes of Schoey, Phil Veivers or Paul Dixon. On the field, Schoey was completely in charge - until we lost, that is. Then, suddenly, Steve was to blame again! As far as I was concerned, although Steve did strike me as being a bit odd at times, that was harsh.

We had loads of experience in the side and most of us knew what we were doing. So if things didn't go well, we only had ourselves to blame, not the coach. On top of that, we won most of our games anyway, finishing second in the table behind Hull, who had beaten us four times through the year and went up automatically. We did manage to turn them over, 18-0, in the Divisional Premiership Final at Old Trafford, though. Afterwards, with the collapse of Paris St. Germain, Huddersfield went up into Super League by default.

Not any of that had much to do with me. By the time Old Trafford came around, I was no longer playing regularly in the side and so missed out on the big match. In fact, I had only made ten appearances all season, but still managed to score five tries. Even so, at the end of the season the club asked me to sign for another year. But by now I had other plans. My brain was still active but this old body of mine wasn't getting any younger, so I told them that I didn't want to be full-time anymore. And if I wanted to go part-time, that meant I had to leave, which I did, for Hunslet, in October 1997. As it happened, if I had stayed Steve Ferres wouldn't have been there anyway. Despite winning the Premiership Final and taking the team to promotion, he was fired and replaced by Garry Schofield a month after my departure.

\* \* \* \* \*

As for the future of Ikram Butt, well, for now my mind was more on chips, burgers and curries rather than rugby balls. Several of our friends ran takeaway restaurants, so my brothers and me thought it would be a good idea if we gave it a go too. We decided to set up our own business.

The takeaway we bought was in Bramley, near Leeds, and we did pizzas, burgers, kebabs, curry, the usual thing. We called the place Bugsy's after my childhood nickname and two front teeth, although the logo was a buggy rather than a rabbit. Our younger brother, Chinky, would be the nucleus of the business (in other words do most of the work!) while Tony and myself, who had other jobs, came in to help when necessary, which was quite often to begin with. We worked hard to make Bugsy's a success

As for rugby league, when I told Peter of my situation with Huddersfield he had become involved again and organised some talks for me with Hunslet. The Hunslet player coach at the time was David Plange, and his assistant was the late St. John Ellis, known to friends and foes alike as 'Singe'. Given our business plans and my experience at Huddersfield and London, I took some persuading to give the game another go. But Singe persuaded me that he and Plangey had big plans for the team so, eventually, I said okay.

I knew it was a mistake almost from the start. St. John Ellis was a fantastic bloke who Plangey used as a go-between for the players and the coach. He was always cracking jokes and having a laugh, dancing and so on. Singe was a joker and that brought everyone together, which was important seeing as how it was very much a new squad when I arrived. We gelled very quickly as a team and Singe was responsible for that. For me, personally, though, I found it very difficult to concentrate on the new business and rugby league as well, especially when Plangey started playing mind games. The players, particularly the younger lads, would look to him for advice and direction, but David could be very moody and not say a word to anyone.

I was quite disappointed by his attitude. As a coach, you have to earn respect, not just expect it, especially when you are also playing in the side, as David was. I had also played against Plangey several times - like me, he was a decent if hardly spectacular winger - and so I found respect for his authority hard to come by. Mainly, though, I just didn't agree with his methods. It was hard to know what he expected - but I assumed that, in my case, it was too much. I thought he had fully understood where I was coming from when I agreed to sign, I hadn't hidden the fact that I was now getting on a bit, but obviously that wasn't the case.

Ultimately, though, I can't blame David Plange for my failure to set Hunslet on fire, can I? The fault was my own. I shouldn't have gone to Hunslet in the first place. I had hoped that I still had enough commitment and enthusiasm to play the game, but should have known better. Now and then, when I needed to pull my finger out on the field, instead I found my mind wandering. The Hunslet supporters were great - as they were at London and Huddersfield. At all three of those clubs, there weren't all that many of them, but the few who did turn up, week after week, were extremely enthusiastic. Nevertheless, I quickly began to wonder what I was doing there. Unless I could put in loads of big defensive hits and take the pressure off the forwards, I was not really contributing to the game. My time had been and gone. I was past it really.

In the end, I made nine appearances in the 1998 season, and one as sub, scoring a single try in the fourth round of the Challenge Cup at Cumbrian amateurs Ellenborough, where we actually lost, 14-12. And at the end of the season we were sixth in Division One, just outside the play-off positions. As at Huddersfield, though, my own season fizzled out long before the season came to a close. And it would be another three years after that before I pulled on a pair of rugby boots again, for Victoria Rangers, an amateur club in Bradford.

\* \* \* \* \*

So there I was; part-time rugby league player, part-time takeaway owner with Bugsy's.

The premises in Bramley had been a chip shop before we

bought it. And to train me up I spent a fair while going up to Ripon in North Yorkshire, where one of our Tony's mates, Bally, owned a fish and chip shop himself. While there, I learned how to fillet and fry fish, make proper chips and so on. That was my main job for a while; chief potato peeler. So even though I was now playing at Hunslet, most of my concentration was on the new business.

At first, we just opened Bugsy's at lunchtimes and early evenings. But business was slow and we quickly realised that if we really wanted to get things going we would need to have a rethink. So we closed the place down for a while and absolutely transformed it, bringing in pizza ovens and so on. We dumped the fish and chips and introduced pizzas, curries, burgers and kebabs, that type of stuff.

To be honest, although our Tony and me were heavily involved with the business, our Chinky was the one doing most of the actual hard work, preparing the food etc, and a few of our mates mucked in too. A couple of my old schoolfriends worked for us for a month without pay, just to get us up and running. I used to help out myself when needed but, at first, I was mainly an observer because I wasn't used to working in that trade.

On top of my playing and takeaway commitments, I was also now doing a bit of work for Andy Harland, who was the rugby league development officer in Bradford at the time. Later, in March 1999, I would take over from Andy full-time.

Initially, Andy just rang me up and asked if I would like to get involved with a three-day free coaching clinic he was about to hold at Green Lane Recreation Centre in Manningham. I had known him since my days in amateur rugby league. It was Andy who briefly took me to Dudley Hill, when he was coach there and I was playing at Apperley Bridge. Although, if you remember, I only ended up playing a couple of games before signing for Leeds.

Anyway, I had been a friend of Andy's ever since. To be honest, over the years ahead, him and me would have a few issues workwise but, at heart, I still think Andy is a top bloke. We may not see eye to eye on the best way forward in certain regards, but he is a genuine person who knows exactly what he thinks and has a deep commitment to what he is doing. I have a lot of respect for Andy Harland.

The best thing he ever did for me, though, was leave his job! Six months before he was due to go, Andy told me that he was about to take on a similar role at Red Hall for the Rugby Football League, so I knew that there was a vacancy on the horizon and was well prepared for the interview when it came along. In fact, I had already met the council officer in charge of the process, as he had actually watched me coaching some Asian kids himself at those Green Lane training sessions. Andy told me that there might be a role for me, if I was interested. I said: 'Of course, I would love to be involved.'

In those days, Andy's role was jointly-funded by the council and Bradford Bulls RLFC, where Andy worked virtually full-time. The former Kiwi player, Darrel Shelford, was also part of the development department, although mainly with the Academy - i.e. under 18s - team. I paid a visit to the Odsal Stadium to see Darrel, who I knew as a player and had a lot of respect for, with Andy. When we first met, Darrel was quite keen for me to come on board. I was excited by the idea too. Bradford were a terrifically well-oiled set-up; the envy of both codes of rugby.

I still had the interview to get through, though. And while, by this time, I had already retired from Hunslet, there was still our takeaway to think about. Happily, my brothers both said that I should go for it. After all, professional sport was where I wanted my future to be, not selling pizzas, chips and chicken madras. In any case, I had always intended to start a business, earn some money, learn about paperwork and then move on.

As things turned out, I did get the job despite there being more than forty other applicants for the position. And at first I tried to combine it with working at Bugsy's, which was a total disaster. I would work through the day and then go to the takeaway in the evening and it all became too much. It caught up with me. We had issues with the business, such as drivers not turning up on time and so on, and were struggling to cope because our Tony was busy with his day job too. We began to rely too much on the mates who were only there to help us out and that wasn't fair on them. It was inevitable that something had to change so, eventually, we decided to sell up and, from then on, I was able to devote all my attention to my new role.

I was now Bradford Council's rugby league development officer and, happily, things started off really well. Andy had done a great job before me and built up a strong relationship with the Bulls which, at first, I was able to take advantage of. It wasn't long, though, before problems began to surface.

To begin with, the council had been successful in obtaining a large social regeneration budget for the Manningham and Girlington areas of Bradford, both heavily-populated by the Asian community. So a large part of my job was helping to use those funds wisely. This is where a lot of people went wrong at the time, misunderstanding what I was actually there to do.

True, my job title was rugby league development officer, which left some - particularly at Odsal - assuming that my full focus should be on promoting the sport of rugby league in the region for its own sake. But, as I said, I was also being partly funded by Bradford Council, who saw the development of rugby league as the means to another more important end. For them, encouraging participation in rugby league was a way of getting kids off the streets, turning them away from a life of crime, encouraging inter-racial social cohesion and all that sort of stuff.

Fortunately, at first, I was lucky enough to have Andy Harland to help guide me through this political minefield and show me the ropes. In fact I believe that it was because of my awareness of those issues - thanks to the working relationship I already had with Andy - that I was given the job in the first place. The other candidates all came to their interviews saying how they would hold training camps, take the game into local schools and build up a strong relationship with the Bulls. That was fair enough but they weren't answering the right questions for the council. In my interview, I must have shown a greater awareness of the bigger picture, over and above the promotion of the city's biggest professional rugby club.

Not that the Bulls themselves weren't well aware of the wider social benefits of rugby league, because they were. Back then, the club had a very strong reputation for getting involved in community development work and they did it very well. To Bradford, it was as much a part of their marketing philosophy as colourful pre-match entertainment, the sale of replica shirts and having a big cuddly mascot. Players like Robbie Paul - who was a fantastic role model - would travel out and about, spreading the word not only about the club but also discussing healthy lifestyles, the importance of education, the perils of bullying and positive ways to live your life and so on, usually in school assemblies. The bottom line, though, was that all those positive messages translated into huge crowds at Odsal on a weekend.

Now, on one level, there was nothing wrong with that. Bradford Bulls RLFC is a commercial organisation which needs to attract paying spectators through the turnstiles in order to survive and thrive. But that did make for a very complicated picture behind the scenes. The result was that I was constantly being pulled in separate directions, which is a very uncomfortable position to be in.

Even so, I gave the job everything I had. As well as working every hour under the sun, my wife and I moved from the house we were sharing with our Tony at Holt Park, in Leeds, to Clayton, in Bradford. And a lot of my problems weren't really to do with me at all, they were caused by a lack of understanding and compromise between the two groups of managers at Odsal and the council. Sure, they met and had dialogue from time to time, but nothing concrete was ever agreed. It all just kept falling back onto my shoulders.

For example, the Bulls might make a suggestion which was beyond my remit or, maybe, clashed with what I was already doing elsewhere. I would assure them that I would like to help out but that, first, they should speak to my council bosses. In short, both the Bulls and the council saw me as their own employee and that created difficulties, particularly as out-of-town areas like Keighley also came under my jurisdiction. Keighley didn't have a big say, because they didn't have the resources, but they did have a say because they were part of Bradford Metropolitan Council.

Inevitably, as a result of this confusion, we had a few verbals and disagreements and looking back, from my own perspective, there are ways in which I might have handled the situation better. I ended up falling out with the development guys at Odsal - Darrel Shelford and, later, Paul Medley - and it all got personal, which was ridiculous. We should have dealt with our problems as professionals.

Then there was the infamous - to me anyway - meeting with Gary Tasker, who is now the Rugby Football League's Director of Development. Back then, Gary fulfilled a similar role with the Bulls. If I remember rightly, Darrel was in on the meeting too and it was then that I was accused of what I considered to be some pretty petty stuff, such as not returning telephone calls. I asked them for dates and times but, not surprisingly, they either couldn't or weren't prepared to produce any. It was a nonsense allegation. As far as I am concerned, I return all my phone calls as soon as I get them.

I was also doing a Level 3 coaching course at the time, and Gary asked me why that was. 'What do you mean?' I said. 'It's part of my development.' 'Yes, but that's not what we want,' he replied. 'Yes, but I don't just work for you ... I work for the local authority too..'. I had been in the job for no more than eight months, but it was already clear that the situation in its present form was not going to work. They told me that what went on in that meeting didn't leave the room and that, if anything did come out, they would just deny it.

I remember another time too. We had a local authority community centre in which we organised a six-week coaching course. At the end of it, players from Bradford Bulls were scheduled to come and give the certificates out. When the time came, one of those players didn't turn up. When he was asked about it, Darrel Shelford just said: 'Speak to Ikram Butt, he's the development officer for Bradford.' In other words, blame me. But it wasn't up to me to provide players from Bradford Bulls - that was up to the club. This wasn't the only occasion that something like this happened either. I was once managing a camp at Ampleforth and the Bulls' minibus, which was booked to take the kids, didn't turn up. The parents, quite obviously, weren't best pleased and again I got the blame, even though it turned out that one of the club's employees was using it elsewhere. People began to side against me. Basically, the Bulls were setting me up for a fall and it all got a bit naughty.

Admittedly, my inexperience in the job meant that I found it difficult to deal with for a while, especially after Andy Harland had gone to the RFL. And that, of course, led to accusations that I didn't know what I was doing. Then I got to hear things like: 'What does an Asian lad know about rugby?'. That was the sort of nonsense that was coming out. I was also earning more money than the lot of them, which didn't help to ease the personality clashes.

Since then, whenever I have told the tale of those days, I have often been asked if I thought that racial prejudice was the underlying cause of my treatment. My answer is that while there must have been some of that - 'What does an Asian lad know about rugby?' - I am not so sure that it was such an important factor; after all I was once good friends with Darrel Shelford and Paul Medley. There may have been resentment that I was so heavily involved in developing links with Bradford's Asian community - as I said, Manningham and Girlington were areas that I was employed to deal with - rather than just concentrating on getting people through the gates at Odsal. And it's true that most of the schools that the Bulls went into were predominantly white and Church of England. But, at the end of the day, Bradford schools predominantly *are* white and Church of England, if we are talking about the whole district. No, I prefer to hope that the Bulls' unhappiness was more down to me not doing what they wanted me to do. Simple as that. The council were saying one thing; the Bulls another. I needed them both to sit down together and sort it out, but neither was strong enough to do that. I was pulling my hair out.

Anyway, after my meeting with Gary Tasker, I went away and thought long and hard about what course of action to take. I spoke to my brother, Tony, and also to various colleagues on Bradford Council, asking them what they would do in the same circumstances. In the end, I thought that if I told my bosses at the council about what had happened, things couldn't get any worse than the way they were now. So I told my boss and he told his. The upshot was that, after the two sides had another meeting, I was able to stick pretty much to the council's side of the fence and the Bulls stuck to theirs.

The stand-off didn't last forever. It was during this period that the former London and Bradford winger Abi Ekoku was in charge of the rugby league players' union, the RLPA, and so I asked for his advice too. Then, in January 2000, after a short spell in a similar role at Keighley Cougars, Abi replaced Gary Tasker as chief executive at Odsal which saw my relationship with the club improve dramatically. For one thing, Abi had himself become the first black CEO in the history of English rugby, so maybe that gave him a greater understanding of my predicament, I don't know. He was certainly up against it himself. There was a lot of arrogance in the attitudes of the people supposedly beneath him: who is Abi Ekoku to tell us what to do - that sort of thing. Abi tried to do things differently at Odsal and a lot of people didn't like that.

For me personally, though, things were very much better there for a while. If ever there was a conflict of interest I would go and see Abi and he would sort it out. He understood the political problems in the partnership and worked out a deal whereby it was the council who now employed me and not the club, although I would go on working in the interests of both. Eventually, though, he was forced out of the door and, although I didn't really need the Bulls' assistance by that stage and was confident enough to do the job on my own, that was very disappointing.

The thing is, away from Odsal, I was busier than ever. Along with the work I was doing in Manningham - you have to go where you are funded - there were similar schemes that I was involved with right across the district, including one in the mainly white area of Ravenscliffe, which I will come to in a moment. At one point I also helped to form an all-white youth team in the Wyke area of the city, which is still going strong today. In fact, that Wyke club is one of my proudest achievements in the sport, although it is hardly ever mentioned.

Another time, when Paul Medley took over from Darrel Shelford at the Bulls, I also co-ordinated the Bradford service area, which is the way that rugby league structures its youth development programme. On account of my recent history with the Bradford club and the fact that they obviously had a big say in the service area strategy, the situation was never less than difficult. After a while, Paul took over from me but he only lasted a few months in the role. Maybe he realised that it wasn't as easy as he thought. I may be biased, but during my time at least we had regular meetings. When the Bulls were in charge there never seemed to be any meetings at all - no one in the district had a clue what was going on.

However you dress it up, the fact is that in a city the size of Bradford, with such a large Asian population, neither of its professional sports clubs - Bradford Bulls or Bradford City - have historically done anything like enough to develop the Asian talent in their own backyard.

In the case of rugby league, for all that the Bulls were very keen to go into schools, that is the easy bit. Kids in schools are a captive audience, aren't they? It's what you do with them afterwards that is the important thing; how you move it all on to the next level, after-school clubs and so on. We were doing a lot of community stuff and, as time went on, the Bulls weren't. And you could level the same accusation at the wider game and British sport in general.

When it comes down to it, a vision for what might be achieved and a greater willingness to engage with the Asian community has to come from the top.

I honestly believe that if I hadn't been employed as the city's development officer, then Bradford Bulls would hardly have bothered with the Asian community at all. It was a constant battle to get them interested.

# 13

*

# Taking the Bulls by the Horns

To be fair, like many other sports' governing bodies, the Rugby Football League has - in more recent years anyway - at least paid lip service to the idea of attracting greater numbers of Asians to the game, whether that be as spectators or through wider participation. And sometimes they have even gone further than that.

In March 2000, for example, the RFL re-launched 'Tackle Racism in Rugby League', the continuation of its 'Tackle It!' campaign which first kicked off in 1996, in association with the Commission for Racial Equality. The original campaign had come about because a study compiled by Leeds Metropolitan University had found a 'small but significant problem' with racism in the game, and the RFL responded by coming up with a thirteen-point plan and, in 1998, becoming the first sports governing body to formally adopt an equal opportunities policy. Admirable stuff.

Over the years that followed the campaign was rolled out and rebranded, with differing amounts of success, on an almost annual basis. The launch in 2000, then, was just one more step along this particular road, although a very welcome one at that. In effect, though, it was little more than a pilot scheme and one that only featured amateur clubs in Bradford and Keighley at that.

Launched at the Manningham Sports Centre in Bradford, this latest campaign required clubs to undertake 'achieveable tasks', including the implementation of an internal club complaints procedure for racial incidents. Clubs were also asked to issue a statement against racism, make regular contact with local ethnic minority organisations and community groups, ensure the removal of graffiti from club premises and appoint a representative to oversee the implementation of the programme.

In a small way, the scheme worked very well. Keighley Albion, for example, were rightly praised for the way they had translated a team recruitment leaflet into Urdu, which was quite groundbreaking in its way. Every player at Victoria Rangers signed an anti-racism code of conduct, while Queensbury issued a ten-point action plan, geared to combat racism, to all club members. All in all, very encouraging, so much so that a national roll out of the programme was anticipated in 2001.

I remember going to the 2000 launch. Abi Ekoku was there and so was Dr. Mohammed Amran, who is a very good friend of mine, of the Commission for Racial Equality. Although I have always, by and large, had a good working relationship with rugby league's governing body, it was particularly good to have the CRE involved because, otherwise, every time the RFL were questioned about their track record in attracting Asians to the game, they could say: 'Oh, we have got Ikram Butt,' even though I actually worked for Bradford Council. Politically, the CRE could press for tangible action.

Having said that, I did get on very well with Neil

Tunnicliffe, who was the chief executive of the Rugby Football League at that time, and his other members of staff. I was handy for public relations purposes and I understand that. In the end, it is the same with the RFL as it is with their clubs. If they thought or were reminded about the issue of racism often enough, then they were up for fighting it. Ultimately, though, when push came to shove, they had 'greater' priorities. That's where we had our differences. Attracting more of the Asian community into rugby and sport generally should be a major priority too.

The most praise for rugby league's involvement in the Tackle Racism campaign should go to Ian Cooper, who was chief executive of the British Amateur Rugby League Association - otherwise known as BARLA - at the time. If anyone drove the project it was Ian. He was a super chap, although I have lost touch with him lately. I remember how before I even got the development job, his wife, who was a teacher in Batley, asked me to come down and do some rugby sessions with the kids, which I was more than happy to do. That was when I first got to meet Ian and we got on really well. I could see he was genuine and passionate about getting more Asian kids playing the game.

Ian realised that there was a big gap here that the game should be working to fill. With Ian and myself taking the message far and wide and later in conjunction with Sporting Equals, which was a partnership between the Commission for Racial Equality and Sport England, rugby league's anti-racism campaign soon began to earn a very good reputation with other sports, particularly football and cricket. Look around now and you will see loads of similar initiatives and I believe that we behind rugby league's Tackle it! campaign were pioneers in that. It was a really good scheme driven by BARLA, and involving the RFL, which showed other sports just what might be achieved.

Unfortunately, after that initial burst of activity, which also included putting out our own *Tackle It* magazine in association with the GMB Union, edited by no less a figure than that great rugby league writer Harry Edgar, the original 'Tackle Racism in Rugby League' campaign fizzled out instead of going national as planned (although the 'Tackle It' name limped along in one way or another for a little while yet). That was a real shame. In Bradford and Keighley, all the amateur clubs had signed up to it, in order to prove that they were a part of the process. If they hadn't done so, it would have affected their funding applications and future development plans. But when Ian Cooper left BARLA that was that and the idea was quietly shelved. There was the odd half-hearted attempt to get the concept back on track but the big problem then was that no club would be forced to take part. Unless a campaign is actual policy, clubs can do what they like.

I am sorry to say that in the decade since I first got the rugby league development job in Bradford, the situation in this area has not really got any better - in fact you might say it has grown worse. With the end of Tackle It! there seemed to be a long period when, instead of moving forward, rugby league was just standing still. It was a huge opportunity missed. However, we must always look to the future, and it does seem as if things might be again about to turn for the better, with one significant proviso. Personally, I would prefer a targetted approach to specific problems rather than the RFL's latest catch-all campaign, Respect, which is as much about encouraging people not to abuse referees as about promoting equity and diversity. To me, that's a sideways step, as big important issues get diluted. Still, I suppose we must play the cards we are dealt with and things could certainly be a lot worse.

All in all, under the chairmanship of Richard Lewis,

rugby league has moved forward. Before he left BARLA, Ian Cooper developed a really good relationship with Emma Rosewarne at the RFL, which Emma and myself have maintained since his departure. Emma's attitude is very warm and understanding with regards to this area and she is extremely supportive in all that I try to do. Emma has been fantastic. The Rugby Football League now also has its own equality and diversity manager, Sarah Williams, who also does a load of good stuff.

\* \* \* \* \*

Despite all the behind the scenes political fall-outs, I got lots of useful work done - often in tandem with Bradford Bulls - during what became a productive nine-year spell as a Bradford Council sports development officer - as the title later became broadened out to.

I was able to make an impact in a number of key social areas like deprivation, education, health, crime, racism and drugs, all through the medium of greater involvement in sport, and particularly rugby league. A number of those initiatives and projects gained local, regional and even national recognition, and are still being used as models of good example by sporting bodies and other organisations and agencies to this day.

One such idea that I became involved with was Connecting Communities, an initiative in partnership with the same Youth Charter for Sport, Culture and Arts that I later became an ambassador for. It was under the Connecting Communities banner that we were able to bring young people from Bradford together with kids from nine other communities throughout the country and attend the XVII Commonwealth Games in Manchester. Afterwards, the young people were invited into the VIP area to socialise with such illustrious individuals as Prince Edward and his wife, Sophie Rhys-Jones, the Countess of Wessex, which was fantastic.

The 2002 Commonwealth Games were also an exciting time for me, seeing as how the RFL put my name forward as a runner in The Queen's Jubilee Baton Relay. Jason Ramshaw was nominated for Keighley and I was nominated for Bradford. I was chuffed to bits with that, especially as there were some very famous people doing the same thing in other towns and cities, such as Linford Christie, Falklands War veteran Simon Weston and the 1966 football World Cup final hero, Sir Geoff Hurst. I only ran a short distance, but the fact that I was involved in such a high profile event gave me a memory to treasure and I will always be thankful to the Rugby Football League for giving me the opportunity.

At the Commonwealth Games itself, I was also able to watch Sri Lanka compete in the rugby sevens tournament and they did very well. They were playing union rules, of course, but it did leave me wondering why it is that rugby league doesn't try to become involved in global events like this. These are enormously popular international events and if rugby union is involved, then why not rugby league too? After all, the thirteen-a-side code is a commonwealth sport too. You wouldn't need to have thirteen players on each team. Maybe you could have union sevens and league nines, a number that suits the rugby league game better anyway. Or maybe why not just a combined event, so that league players are having a presence and making an impact.

Other initiatives I was either partly responsible for or co-ordinated during my tenure with Bradford Council included the Sportsweb Project, which was used by Leeds Met University and Sport England as an example of good practice working in the areas of Sports Development within the South Asian communities. We undertook loads of school coaching programmes, where it was great to see a host of well-known rugby stars and that grand old man of Great Britain and Bradford, the now sadly-departed Trevor Foster, keen to pass on their valuable experience and knowledge. And we staged kabaddi matches, special fun days during the half-term holidays and a school 'Bull Tag' project, held to coincide with rugby league's 2000 World Cup.

'Bull Tag' for those who don't know, involves grabbing a velcro tag from your opponent's waistband rather than actual tackling, so it is ideal for encouraging younger boys and girls. In our event, based on the World Cup itself, eight local primary schools took part and each one was allocated to a competing country. As well as playing in a tournament at Manningham Sports Centre, the youngsters learned about the history and culture of their nominated nation, and made posters and flags during schooltime. The only downside, I see now, was my quote to the *Asian Eye* newspaper. 'Many of the children are Asian,' I said, 'and by the time the next Rugby League World Cup comes around in 2004 [sic] I am hoping that Pakistan will be competing.' Ah, well. You can't win 'em all...

\* \* \* \* \*

Perhaps the most exciting project I was involved in while working as a development officer in Bradford, and certainly the one that got the most media attention, was when a group of us decided to form a kids team called the Manningham Bulls.

The idea had its roots in the coaching courses we had run from time to time at the Manningham Sports Centre. As I said, this was one of the first things I had been involved in back when Andy Harland was in charge and, when I took over from Andy, I was keen that the good work would continue.

The first time I organised it we had twenty five local schools taking part and Leon Pryce and Stuart Fielden from Bradford Bulls came along to present the prizes. There was also a Bull Tag course for girls, held by Great Britain women's rugby league international Chantel Patrick, that attracted more than eighty girls. But the activities in Manningham really began to grow into something more solid when I came out of retirement and began playing for the Bradford amateur side Victoria Rangers in October 2000.

Believe me, no one was more surprised than me that, somehow, I had suddenly found a reason to pull on my boots again. When I finished at Hunslet, I had breathed a huge sigh of relief. Now 31 years old, I didn't have to train anymore. And I didn't have that day-to-day pressure on my mind about having to play well. One or two clubs kept asking me to join them, but I was enjoying my retirement and didn't feel that I wanted to.

Gary Moorby - who is a super chap - asked me to go to Keighley Albion, for example, because he understood the implications of an Asian playing for a team in a town with such a large Asian population. Undercliffe were another club who were after my services.

But although I appreciated the interest, as far as I was concerned I had retired from rugby league forever. I hadn't played at all for three years and, physically, I was like a barrel. I had put a lot of weight on, didn't want the pressure and, anyway, couldn't devote the time because of my job.

It was during this time, though, that I was building a very close relationship with a chap called Nigel Goodings from Victoria Rangers. Mainly as a result of Nigel's influence, the Rangers club was very ambitious and played in division three of the Pennine League on the mainly white Ravenscliffe estate, Eccleshill, in the north of the city. Ravenscliffe estate was one of five in the area that, taken together, were known as Newlands, the beneficiaries of an urban regeneration project directed by Bradford City Council. Newlands was quite a rough and hostile environment, so rugby was a useful outlet for plenty of otherwise unchannelled aggression.

As chairman of the club, Nigel was also in charge of Rangers' junior set-up at the same time as I was heavily involved in co-ordinating the Bradford rugby league service area. We formed a close working relationship and long-lasting friendship. Nigel had played 'A' team rugby for Castleford, his home town, and had lots of knowledge to share, and not just about rugby league. He knows law and was once a professional golfer and weightlifter. He was warm, friendly and supportive of the objectives that I was trying to get across; i.e. making rugby league more inclusive and reaping the wider social benefits from doing that.

So when he asked me to turn out for Victoria Rangers on a Saturday afternoon, suddenly it made sense to do so. Not only would I be getting fit again, it all tied in with my day job with the council. One more good reason for joining Rangers was that my old mate and colleague Phil Hellewell was head coach there. And only being in division three, there was little or no stress. All in all, it was a tremendous opportunity.

Even so, my first game back, from the bench in a 38-4 home win over Queensbury's 'A' team, was horrendous. I couldn't last the full match and nearly had a heart attack I was blowing that hard. Boy, did I struggle. Even at that level, rugby league is the toughest team sport on the planet and you really do have to be on your toes. As the weeks went by, though, I began to enjoy myself and it was great to be back involved with the amateur game which, after all, was where I came from.

A bit older and wiser by now, I could also see the huge

amount of hard work and dedication that goes into running an amateur club. It's not just about turning up and playing. It left me with enormous respect for what they have to do just to survive. In amateur rugby league, money is almost always tough to come by unlike, say, in club rugby union, where you tend to get more middle class businessmen involved. And yet the work amateur rugby league clubs do in often under-resourced communities is fantastic and often goes unnoticed. The people who keep the amateur game going don't do it for the glory or local prestige, they do it out of the love of rugby league and know the benefits it can bring.

Anyway, at Victoria Rangers, we had a very successful year. For one thing, we finished top and won promotion and it's always nice to be winning at whatever level you play. Everyone gets on so much better. You make lots of new friends and the camaraderie was second to none. The relationships I was making there also continued to help me in my development work, although one or two people outside the club did accuse me of favouritism, which was nonsense. I did take a mate of mine along with me called Rashid, who had played for Queensbury and he slotted in very nicely. I was also able to use the club as a very effective development tool for lads such as Saqib Murtza, who went on to play for Dudley Hill and the Bradford Bulls academy. Later, he signed for Salford, Batley and Sheffield Eagles, where he still plays at the moment.

In fact, I enjoyed myself so much at Victoria Rangers that I ended up staying for another three seasons after that and, in 2002 and 2003, we were champions again. Then in 2004 I became assistant player-coach although, being a former professional, I had helped Phil with the coaching duties right from the start. Player-coach suited me as I couldn't really give the commitment that a full-on coach had to.

As a club, Victoria Rangers were very progressive and forward thinking, not just Nigel but also a chap called John Hodgson, who was the president and chief fund-raiser. His son played for the club. Together, Nigel and John had a combined vision of Rangers being one of the best clubs in Bradford; they were already one of the oldest, having been formed in 1891. Since then, they'd had a varied history, with their high point being two games against Widnes in the 1903 Challenge Cup. They drew at home but then went down narrowly in the replay at Widnes. And no, I wasn't on the wing, before you ask.

The club had been quite successful in the late 1950s and early 'sixties too, winning many an amateur league title or cup. But in more recent years they had fallen on hard times. Based at Peel Park, in the mid 1990s the club had almost had to fold after only being able to gather together nine players for their side. Thankfully, they hung around a while longer and when the struggling Bradford League cricket club, Eccleshill, was forced to quit its own home ground in 1996, Vic' Rangers moved in, rent free, with the help of the council.

With Nigel and John in charge, it wasn't long before things began to get better. By the time I arrived, Rangers were in the middle of a ten-year plan, running two teams with fifty open-age players, and no less than nine junior sides as part of a very impressive youth policy. In May, the under-12s won the club's first trophy in thirty-five years and we held a number of fun days in the school holidays, at which Leon's dad Dennis Pryce also coached, which attracted lots of publicity.

Along with the club's home ground on Harrogate Road, they were also able to use and improve a number of pitches at nearby Eccleshill Upper School, where they made many improvements in the way of training facilities, changing rooms and so on. In its first year, the Newlands regeneration fund put £80,000 into the club, by way of paying for security fencing and floodlights, while Rangers also won planning permission for a hundred-space car park, a thousand-seater stand and a new equipment store. Unfortunately, these last two never happened. Nigel and John had targeted an eventual place in the National Conference League too, the pinnacle of amateur competition in England, and were keen to utilise their links with Bradford council in order to make their club more welcoming to the broader community. The club also loaned more than £1,000 worth of equipment to the sports college at Tong School, which was used by pupils from Tong, the Yorkshire Martyrs catholic school and Bradford Cathedral College.

Best of all, from my point of view, was that Victoria Rangers considered themselves to be a multi-racial club in which Asian youngsters and girls were welcome to take up the game. In keeping with the 'Tackle Racism in Rugby League' campaign, every player, at whatever age, had to sign a contract which agreed that neither he, she or the club would not tolerate racial discrimination. In 2001, after a 49-16 victory over Blackpool Stanley in the National Cup (in which I scored a try!), Nigel was quoted as saying: 'Whether it's colour, religion, ethnic background or, in this area, poverty, we will welcome anyone.' The kids were charged a pound a week subscription, which gave them three training sessions and a game every Sunday morning. Leon Pryce was a club patron and Rangers could boast around twenty players in the Bradford Schools squads.

So, with the Newlands scheme, these were busy and exciting times. But along with my involvement there, I was also still busy in Manningham, which isn't all that far from Ravenscliffe, and Nigel and John were keen to link in with my work in that area as well.

# IKRAM IS KEEN TO HELP EVERYONE HE COMES INTO CONTACT WITH...
## Pav Singh

*Bradford City FC Academy coach,*
*West Riding County FA football development officer*
*and FA 'Football For All' Ambassador*

I first met Ikram when he came to run a rugby development course for the council at a leisure centre I worked at in 2000, shortly before I began to work at Bradford Council myself.

We clicked straight away and he helped me to apply for my first job in sports development, as a project co-ordinator for the Manningham area. Afterwards, I grew to become his line manager, but we started off as friends and that is exactly how it has stayed since. Ikram has always been there for me, and I for him. We are like brothers.

My own primary interest is in football rather than rugby, but everything that Ikram has achieved in the oval ball game, I have tried to replicate to some extent in soccer. Nowadays, I am the only Asian employed by a County FA in the whole of England and was one of the founders of the National Asian's Football Forum. I left Bradford Council recently to take up the role at the West Riding County FA, where I am now in charge of co-ordinating and managing coach education across the whole of Yorkshire.

Ikram and me spend hours and hours on the phone - my wife calls him 'my second wife'. We can talk forever about how we are going to change this policy or that policy ... we have always been passionate about the development of sport, particularly within the Asian communities. We share the same way of thinking about what needs to happen. When I was his line manager in Bradford, we used to have one-to-one meetings in the famous Mumtaz restaurant, with a chicken massala and a couple of naan breads.

I was born and raised in Bradford and my family moved to Leeds when I was about ten. For me, it was always about football. I represented Leeds City Boys, like Ikram, and we were the first team from that city to win the under-15s cup. After that, I had a few offers to sign schoolboy forms but ended up choosing Leeds United where I spent a year before leaving when I didn't get offered a scholarship. After that, I spent a few seasons in the Bradford City youth team as an extended schoolboy, because my dad was determined that I should concentrate on my education as well.

Around the same time, I had the opportunity to make the England under-18s side and reached the final thirty before, one Saturday morning in Scunthorpe, I broke my leg playing for the Bradford City youth team. It was quite a nasty break - both tibia and fibia - and it put me out of the game for quite a while and made me really focus on where I wanted to be. So I worked hard, did my degree and then, as a semi-professional, spent a lot of years with Harrogate Town, Farsley Celtic and Liversedge, where we nearly got to the first round proper of the FA Cup. I now play for Bradford Albion Sports, who have reached the FA National Carlsberg Cup on two occasions. I also wanted to coach, though, and took all my badges before getting a job on the development staff at Leeds United and now at Bradford City.

Like Ikram, I had my own experiences with the racial

aspects of British society and sport, especially when I was growing up. When we moved from Bradford to Leeds, for example, I went to a predominantly white school. There must have only been four or five Asian lads in the entire place, although nowadays it is full of Asian kids. Back then, there was very little understanding of our culture and, as a result, a lot of racism to contend with, so we all had to stand by each other. Fortunately for some of us, we could play a bit of football and so that helped to break down the barriers; sport has a way of doing that. Any potential bullies could see that we were tough and would just back off rather than start any trouble.

Some of the things we got up to would make you shake your head now. I remember we used to have a blacks versus whites game on the tennis courts: six of us against around twenty white kids. One of our mates, Daniel, a white kid, used to play for us instead, so they called him 'Daniel Singh'. And can you believe it, we were that good at football that we actually used to win! Mind you, it could get quite nasty towards the end. The teachers protected us as much as they could and my sister was in the year above. She was quite tough and would stick up for us too.

So that was school, but when I then got selected for the Leeds City Boys team things got even hotter, especially when we travelled away. I was often the only Asian around and people would look at me funny, as if to say: 'What's he doing here?'. Once, when I was in the under-14s, I can remember being stared at by all the parents and their kids as I got onto the coach for an away trip. For a young lad, that can be very intimidating.

All in all, if you are going to get on as an Asian sportsperson, character and mental toughness are really important - as well as the willingness to go out there and mix, and not be afraid. That's especially so in rugby, I am sure. Football is quite a flowing game so, usually, you come up against opponents one at a time. In rugby league, they are lined up against you right across the pitch! In all sports, though, you are going to hear comments from time to time. One classic, for me, came when I was playing semi-professional football up in Cumbria, at a place called Netherfield. I was just warming up and I heard a young boy across the way say to his mum: 'Look at that man over there, he's got a sun tan'. 'No,' says his mum. 'He's a Paki.'

So that was interesting. I went back into the dressing rooms and told the manager and my team-mates what I had just heard and they all started laughing. So I had no real choice but to make a joke of it myself, did I? In sport, that's often how it is. You can't show any sensitivity or weakness. To some people, I dare say that calling someone a 'Paki' might not seem all that big a deal, but if that's the way parents are teaching their children, well, it's pretty obvious that someone needs a proper education and it isn't necessarily the kid, is it?

I know from our long talks together (and the telephone bills!) that Ikram has been through plenty of experiences like the above and more besides. The thing about him, though, is that he has a big heart. I have grown so close to Ikram because I have always trusted him and been grateful for his support. He is the embodiment of everything that I have the most admiration for.

As I said at the start, Ikram and me have become like brothers over the past ten years or so. But it isn't just me. He always has time for anyone, whoever they are, and nothing is too much trouble. Ikram is as keen as mustard to help everyone he comes into contact with, whatever their culture, race or religion. It is fantastic to see that, in these troubled times, his hard work is finally getting the recognition it deserves. But, as Ikram himself would admit, his work has only just begun. And that goes for all of us.

# 14

*

# Rebuilding in Bradford

The real motivation behind the formation of the Manningham Bulls, though, was the Bradford Riots in July 2001, which kicked off just as things were going so well for us development-wise.

In essence, the riots were the result of tensions caused by a planned - and later banned - National Front march through Bradford city centre and a competing rally by the Anti-Nazi League. There are varying accounts as to how the actual trouble started but, however the spark was lit, there was no doubting the damage it caused, whether to property, people or the city's fragile sense of racial unity.

At the time of the confrontation, Bradford had the UK's second largest population of Asians, which meant that there were approximately 68,000 Pakistanis, 12,500 Indians, 5,000 Bangladeshis and 3,000 other Asians living in a city that otherwise had a white majority of 78.3 per cent (according to available statistics). By the end of it, the estimated damage ran to a cost of around £7 million - and just think of the good deeds that could have been done with money like that.

There were 297 arrests in all - with 200 jail sentences amounting to a total of 604 years between them - and around 300 police officers injured, not to mention who knows how many members of the public. Homes, cars and businesses were targetted by at least 1,000 rioters over three terrible nights including, most famously, the Manningham Labour Club, which was firebombed by a gang of youths while twenty-eight regulars were drinking inside. They were terrified and locked themselves in the cellar! My old Commission for Racial Equality mate Mohammed Amran was even quoted as saying: 'No one expected this sort of trouble on this scale. It has destroyed Bradford.'

That was probably putting it a bit strongly, but the impact of the rioting was severe, there's no doubt about that. For a while, Manningham was a no-go area for non-Asians. White taxi drivers would refuse to drive down certain roads and so on. Nor were Asian faces particularly welcome in mainly white areas, such as the Newlands estates. Fortunately, in my own case, I found that I was still able to move through all of those areas freely. Wherever I was, everybody knew me and I was well thought of. I was associated with rugby league and that was a real positive focal point, especially in Newlands.

All in all, though, the outbreak of the riots was a very worrying time, soul destroying even. Part of my role, after all, had been to develop confidence between communities and to promote joint aspirations. I had been keen to preach a bit of self-discipline and self-help, if you like. A lot of great work had already been done but, almost overnight, it was put back years and we knew that trust would take ages to rebuild. In Bradford, we had already come such a long way in healing the damage caused by the Salman Rushdie affair in the late 1980s and now, just as it looked as if that was all behind us, here we were again.

Until the riots, our programme in Manningham was going ever so well and part of the project was to identify and train local people as qualified coaches which, in turn, would help to give them a pathway into wider employment. After the riots, nobody in the white community wanted to work with them, because some of those lads had got themselves caught up in the situation and landed themselves in trouble. Basically, it felt as if were right back at square one.

If anything, though, rugby league is about taking big hits and then getting straight back on your feet. How does that song go: 'I get knocked down, but I get up again, you ain't never going to keep me down...'? That could be the rugby league national anthem. And although I don't remember seeing him on the touchline at Featherstone, Billy Ocean had it right when he sang: 'When the going gets tough, the tough get going...'. So, just one week after the violent disorder in Bradford, the Bulls and ourselves organised another multi-racial Bull Tag tournament at Odsal. Around forty schools took part and the local paper, the *Telegraph and Argus*, described it as: '...an impressive example of how youngsters from different racial and cultural backgrounds in the city can join together.'

While all that was great, we knew that we would need something a bit longer lasting if we were really going to help to heal the city and get back to the good work we had being doing before. The result was that after sitting down and talking about it, it was decided to form a youth team called Manningham Bulls, which was a joint initiative - I would be the last one to say it was all my own idea. We brought some of the coaches down from Victoria Rangers and suddenly they were coaching hundreds of kids, especially during the summer holidays, which was something that had never happened before. We also turned that around and took some budding Asian rugby league coaches up to Ravenscliffe, so they could gain experience. We took a few of the most interested kids to play up there too.

When the project began, there was a fair bit of suspicion and prejudice from both sides of the racial divide, as you might expect given the recent troubles. But we were determined to see it through. Mind you, things were a bit dodgy at first. It was all 'you white or black b*****d', or 'Paki this and that...'; there was lots of fighting and name-calling. All in all, though, we knew it was an educational process that needed to begin somewhere and so we stuck with it.

I remember one council initiative was that we should take them all up to a weekend rugby league training camp at Ampleforth, in the north Yorkshire countryside, which is what we did. Not surprisingly, as inner-city kids who had never experienced anything like this before, it wasn't long before they were all at each other's throats. By the end of the weekend, though, they had bonded absolutely and everyone was best mates.

After that, we took the team up to Glasgow to take part in the annual games there organised by the Scottish Ethnic Minority Sports Association (SEMSA). We had eleven lads from Manningham and eleven lads from Ravenscliffe in our squad and ended up winning the tournament. In fact, the two teams we entered were so successful that they ended up playing each other in the final, with five Asian lads and five white lads on each side. The boys' parents came too, which was also part of the educational process.

The thing is, whatever their racial make-up, the residents of both Newlands and Manningham lived in disadvantaged areas. And when the white kids and their parents came down to train or play in Manningham, or even attend a Christmas party as they were later invited to do, they were surprised and taken aback at the conditions they saw there.

Throughout history, everywhere in the world, a

country's economic and social problems have often been blamed on its ethnic minorities, hence the reason why right-wing extremists like the BNP have been able to win so many votes in deprived white working class areas recently. The kids and parents from Newlands could see that life in Manningham was every bit as grim as it was on their own patch; and vice versa. It took away their sense of resentment that: 'you Asians get all of the money'. They could see that any funding the area received was badly needed, as it was in their own area. It broke down barriers and did away with ignorance, which has to be a good thing, surely?

\* \* \* \* \*

However useful they were in the long run, Manningham Bulls - whose name shows how much I wanted a good relationship with Odsal - were always intended to be a development tool rather than a club.

As I tell people all the time, setting up an actual club in a development area can sometimes be the last thing you want to do. You have to be realistic. For a club to work, you need loads of volunteers who are all willing to give up their weekend every weekend. Otherwise, unless you have the time and resources to organise absolutely everything yourself, it will eventually die a death. It's far better, at first anyway, to just bring the players together when needed and try to encourage something to grow from that. Another thing we did with the Manningham Bulls, in 2005, was take them to Twickenham as part of the biggest charity rugby event ever staged.

Rugby Aid was organised by rugby union's International Rugby Board (IRB) in aid of that year's Indian Ocean tsunami relief effort. The match match saw a Northern Hemisphere team take on its Southern Hemisphere counterparts in a special one-off international featuring players like Lawrence Dallaglio, Brian O'Driscoll, George Gregan and Tana Umaga. The curtain-raiser, though, was a seven-a-side junior rugby tournament involving ten specially selected inner-city teams from across the country and the Manningham Bulls represented Bradford.

This time, our side featured twelve 10 and 11-year-olds from four local primary schools, Atlas, St. Barnabas', Miriam Lord and Spring Wood. And again the local paper reported on our participation. 'The thing I'm looking forward to most is winning hopefully,' said 10-year-old Shafaqat Ali, who also added that he wanted to be '...a professional rugby player for the Bradford Bulls and England' when he grew up. Meanwhile, his team-mate, Humayoun Shahid, said: 'I'm really excited. My favourite player is Jonny Wilkinson - I try to play like him.'

By now, it had become obvious to me that while most of the kids in Bradford thought of 'rugby' as league and would tell you that they supported the Bulls, or maybe Keighley, if they had to give an answer, what they really enjoyed doing was running about with a ball in their hands. It didn't really matter to them whether it was league or union. And why should it? Sport is supposed to be fun. Leave the politics to the adults.

So as my work with Bradford Council increasingly took me more down the route of being a sports development officer rather than just a rugby league development officer, it seemed a reasonable tactic to become more involved with the Rugby Football Union too. After all, what really mattered was getting the kids off the streets and giving them something positive to focus on, whether that be league, union, football, cricket or rounders. As a result, after a meeting with the RFU's ethics and equity manager Steve Farr in June 2004, I embarked upon a partnership with them that would seek to develop 'rugby' within the Asian community in inner-city Bradford. As the RFU already had similar programmes going in the North East and Leicester, our work in the city would fit in with their aims perfectly and nor, so far as I could tell, was their involvement solely motivated by a wish to tread on rugby league's toes. One of the potential partners identified by the RFU's development framework was Bradford Bulls RLFC.

The move to get involved with the RFU coincided with another long-cherished project of ours, the launch of the British Asian Rugby Association - aka BARA - which the RFU was also pleased to support and endorse. As the name suggests, BARA was neither a league or union organisation, it was committed to both codes and it came about as we tried to put some meat on the bones of another earlier idea; the world famous South Asia Bulls. Apart from myself, the directors who made it all happen were Nigel Goodings (chairman), Jug Johal (technical director), Jag Johal (rugby union director), Junaid Malik (rugby league director) and Shaid Rafiqe (commercial director), who designed a really great website. Without the energy of this group of lads, BARA could never have succeeded.

The idea behind the formation of the South Asia Bulls had been that it should - like the Manningham Bulls, but with adults - be an occasional team that got together from time to time for a clear purpose. And in bringing together players from differing South Asian backgrounds, we hoped both to build bridges with other communities and address long-standing issues within our own, whether it be Hindu, Sikh or Muslim, Indian or Pakistani. By doing that, we would also be providing positive role models for the aspiring Asian youth. It was pretty pioneering stuff.

Anyway, we launched the South Asia Bulls in Leeds on Monday 27 May 2002, backed by Sporting Equals, the BEM

Sports Forum, of which I was an executive member, Bradford Council, the City of York Council and the Rugby Football League. The reason York Council were involved is that our first outing as a team would be in York, at that city's Golden Jubilee Rugby League 9s Festival at Heworth, on Bank Holiday Monday, June 3. Along with ourselves, there were similar teams from the rest of the UK, plus Ireland and France too.

As with the Manningham Bulls, when we thought of the South Asia Bulls we also wanted to address wider social issues that were raging at the time. In this case, it was the troubles in India and Pakistan over Kashmir, which were of keen interest to a lot of people in Bradford. We bought ourselves some website space, had a logo knocked together, found ourselves a sponsor in Sporting Equals and got in touch with York 9s organiser Lionel Hurst, who made us one of only two teams to get an invitation to the event, the other fourteen clubs had to apply. Nigel Goodings of Victoria Rangers had a big part to play in the formation of the South Asia Bulls too. I have always had a close affinity with Nigel. There is very strong bond between us. We used to discuss a lot of things.

Basically, the people behind the South Asia Bulls were the same people who would go on to form BARA, and we dragged in friends and colleagues from all over the country like Amar Siddiq, Rashid Mahmood and our Tony to make up the side. And such a team was very much needed, believe me. In rugby league, there was only one player of Asian origin currently playing professionally - Saqib Murtza - out of some seven hundred and fifty who were registered, although black players did have a much stronger representation.

In the end, we did reasonably well at York. We were knocked out in the quarter-finals by the French semi-professional side Lézignan, who went on to win in the final.

We went back to Heworth in 2003 and 2004, too, and actually won the Plate on our last visit. That was a tough game. We played the York Ironsides in the final, the home team, so it was a great result. Harry Jepson presented us with our medals, which was nice. Since then, though, Lionel Hurst is no longer involved with the event and they have thrown it open to professional teams, too, which in my opinion defeats the object of what it was set up to do. They still invite us and maybe the South Asia Bulls will play there again, but I did prefer the York 9s when they were about helping international development.

There are other rugby events, though, and true to our philosophy of being open to both codes, in 2003 we took part in the Pocklington 7s, which is one of the biggest and oldest rugby union tournaments in Yorkshire. It was staged over the Easter bank holiday, so that really did help us to raise the profile. Back in rugby league, we also went south, to play in the Haringey Council Middlesex 9s at the New River Stadium. At that event, we got through to the semi-finals which earned us a nice useful cheque of £250. In fact, we enjoyed ourselves so much that we went back the following year, this time sponsored by the Asian Jewel Awards, and were beaten by South Africa in the quarter-finals. That was another tough game. We had gone there expecting to win, and put a very strong side out, but they were a very good team and battered us.

If there was a day when the South Asia Bulls really took off, though, it was in July 2003 when we played our first ever thirteen-a-side game, a 42-28 win over the Royal Air Force at Dewsbury's Ram Stadium.

Although we had already taken part in nines and sevens tournaments, this was our first proper game together. Beforehand, we tried to have a few training sessions but our boys, for one reason or another, could never all turn up at the same time, so we just had to arrive on the day and hope to turn it on. Amazingly, that is exactly what happened which was really pleasing against such a well-drilled and organised side like the RAF. Afterwards, we went upstairs into the Dewsbury clubhouse for a buffet but, revealingly I felt, there no halal food available. An apparently simple thing like that showed how, for all the good intentions, clubs like Dewsbury still weren't doing their homework when it came to making themselves more open to the wider local community.

Just for the record, the RAF tries came from Gary Banford (2), Paul Wood, Butch Hainsworth and Stu Knight, while Damian Clayton - just back from a tour of duty in Iraq - kicked four goals. Paul Akaidere (6) and Junaid Malik kicked our goals, while there was one try for Shane Hussain and a brace apiece for Akaidere, Amjad Hussain and (cough) Ikram Butt.

\* \* \* \* \*

Although the South Asia Bulls were doing very good work, it was obvious that if we really were going to see a change for the better, in the longer term, we would need a structured organisation of our own. Until we had that, the Bulls would be little more than a public relations exercise really.

The result was BARA - the British Asian Rugby Association - an organisation intended, as our publicity material put it at the time, to emphasise the 'clear synergy between sport and social cohesion'. It had to happen really. For all the effort we were putting in ourselves, and for all the fine words from the governing bodies and clubs, we were growing more and more frustrated with the lack of any meaningful change to policy or attitudes when it came to creating greater accessibility for the wider BEM communities.

Primarily, BARA was set up to oversee rugby development within the South Asian communities in Bradford and throughout the UK. But our wider aims included providing positive role models for the aspiring youth, utilising rugby as a vehicle to address key social issues, and supporting the development of rugby in South Asian countries. That meant we had to establish links with India and Pakistan, an important development, we thought, because the South Asian communities are a vital and significant part of the fabric of modern British cities. Through our overseas links, we would enhance the credibility of our operations at home and provide a useful platform for a mutual exchange of ideas.

In Bradford, for example, rugby is generally seen as a traditionally white game, working class in league, middle class in union. By bringing high-profile players over from Pakistan or India, we hoped to break down barriers between the white rugby playing community and the South Asian communities. One player who did come over on such a scheme was the Pakistan rugby union captain Kashif Khwaja, who swapped Lahore for Leeds and did a one-year business course at Leeds Metropolitan University. UK-based players would travel in the opposite direction too. And these exchange visits would send out a strong message to children and their parents about the unifying nature of rugby between different Asian communities, and between white, Asian and black communities too.

We realised that, for some people, the name British Asian Rugby Association might be a problem but, at the time, I believed it was important for us to call it that. For one thing, there were those in rugby league who had never understood why we weren't just a rugby league organisation; why bring rugby union into it, they asked. And it's important to remember that when we first launched South Asia Bulls, there were plenty in rugby league advising me against it. They didn't have a clue what we were trying to achieve. The most obvious reason for making it dual-code, though, was that a lot of my colleagues involved in the idea were rugby union lads. It wouldn't have been fair on them if I had just gone down the thirteen-a-side road.

Also, and pretty revealingly I thought, when we held the launch at the Mumtaz restaurant in Bradford, although the RFL were supposed to be supporting us, their original representative couldn't make it in the end, and his place was taken by Harry Jepson. The RFU sent a representative, a chap from Bradford & Bingley who was also the president of the Yorkshire Rugby Union, and BARLA's Maurice Oldroyd was there, along with representatives from Sport England, Bradford Council and the HSBC Bank.

Then there was the 'British Asian' bit. In an ideal world, of course, there would be no need for a British Asian Rugby Association, we would all be British rugby players and that would be that. But this isn't an ideal world, is it? And we were always open about how, somewhere down the line, we hoped to be able to integrate the aims of BARA into the mainstream. How long that took was up to the governing bodies themselves.

# IKRAM WOULD BE THE LAST TO SAY HE IS ACHIEVING ALL OF THIS BY HIMSELF ...
## Junaid Malik

*Former Amateur GB International and BARA co-founder*

I first met Ikram Butt in 2001, shortly before we set up the South Asia Bulls, although I had followed his career with interest since being a rugby league playing youngster.

Ikram, myself and a lad called Amar Siddiq, who plays for the Moldgreen amateur club, set up the Bulls at the Commission for Racial Equality building in Leeds. The South Asia Bulls' first game together was in the York Intermational Nines, although I didn't play because I was away in France with the Great Britain amateur team.

As I say, I had admired Ikram from afar as a kid, not only because, as a high-profile Muslim, he was a rugby playing role model, but also because he played alongside Terry Manning at Featherstone Rovers. Terry, Ikram's centre, came from Elland, which is where I was brought up. So whenever Featherstone came to play Halifax I would go along and watch them both play.

I began to play rugby league myself in Elland as a ten-year-old and I have been there ever since - I am now in my twentieth year with the club. Right from the start, I had an ambition to play rugby league to a high standard and so Ikram was a key figure for me. There just wasn't anyone else out there like him. I can remember watching him doing an interview with *Calendar* when he got picked for England, and that gave me great encouragement.

I was actually born in Pakistan but I took to rugby league like a duck to water. The reason I went down to Elland in the first place, though, was that the club was relaunching its junior section and my younger brother, Jerry, wanted to go, so I took him to training. It wasn't long before I caught the bug myself and I have never looked back. Playing rugby league just came naturally to me.

I would have no hesitation in describing Ikram as a role model although, when it came to making the decision to turn professional myself, I decided not to follow it through. There was a chance that I could have signed for Halifax, but I was studying at the time - I am a solicitor these days - and didn't want to give up my studies or amateur status for the sake of a possible few thousand quid. It was too much of a gamble, although if someone had come in with a serious financial offer then who knows what might have happened?

Instead, I threw all my efforts into amateur rugby league and, when the chance came along, the South Asia Bulls and, later, BARA. The motivation behind the Bulls was that the few Asians who were playing rugby across the country had no central organisation to gravitate towards. There was no information to tap into and it was easy to feel isolated.

And then when we launched BARA, the whole thing moved on to another level again. Ikram took up the post of general manager, while I became director of rugby league. Jag Johal was director of rugby union. The introduction of BARA has been a massive step forward and Ikram has played an crucial part in that. Through BARA's involvement with the All Party Parliamentary Groups - in both codes - the spotlight is now on British Asian rugby players like never before. There is still a lot of work to do, of course, but at least there is now a structured way forward and we are making progress, both here and in Pakistan and India.

BARA is now starting to get more backing from the governing bodies too, but the most pleasing thing is seeing more and more young players taking up rugby, although we could always do with attracting more. If those lads - and lasses - end up playing as internationals or in Super League then great, but the most important thing is that it has a snowball effect and they take the sport back into their communities, with more kids playing the game as a result. Rugby is a wonderful sport and it should be enjoyed by everyone.

Ikram would be the last person to say that he is achieving all of this by himself; it is the result of a lot of hard work by a growing number of very committed people. But you can't ignore the particular impact that he has had on the British Asian communities himself.

Ikram put down a marker, both in terms of playing for England - which is an amazing achievement for someone of his background - and in terms of what he has achieved since retiring from the professional game. As my own experience testifies, Ikram's influence has been phenomenal. And like the continued growth of BARA, it is only set to get bigger.

# 15

*

# Viva South Asia!

My own visit to South Asia - the very first of my life, I am embarrassed to say - had come the year before, in September 2003. The opportunity came out of the blue. This chap from Newcastle rang me up and said he was involved with the Indian rugby union. At the time, he sold it as wanting me to come out and help to coach the team at the 70th All India & South Asia Rugby Tournament. I thought - fantastic. That was exactly what I had wanted for ages.

My debut as an international coach had already taken place in September 2001, when I was player coach of England in the Student Rugby League European Cup. The tournament was held in Kazan, Tatarstan, and it was an experience to say the least.

I had always been keen to get into coaching rugby league, and helping out with the students fitted in well with my role as a development officer. Earlier in the year, I had also coached Great Britain and the Bradford District side at under-13s. I was a student myself at the time - doing a diploma at Leeds Met University. Apart from the studying at home, I only had to go in for one day a month but I did qualify in the end. I rang up Niel Wood, who works in Rugby League Services now but, back then, was in charge of the student game, and he said to get involved. So I took a couple of lads who were students down from Victoria Rangers. I didn't really want to play myself, that wasn't the idea. I just wanted to get involved in the background. But the coach, Simon Tuffs, who I knew because he had played in Australia at the same time as me, already had an assistant. It was Richard Agar, Allan's son and the current coach of Hull FC. He was a bit of a character, Simon; I remember them chasing him out of Australia in the finish because he almost wrecked the place!

Anyway, we carried on training and the lads got picked in the squad for the European Cup. I was a senior player at first and just helping out, but then Simon injured himself in an accident or something. As a result, Richard was promoted to head coach and I became his assistant. That was fine by me.

The trip out to Russia was very memorable. We flew to Moscow and had a day out there, visiting the Kremlin and so on. Then we had a long train journey east, which was like going back in time. As we travelled through the Russian countryside we would stop at all these little stations in the middle of nowhere and people would crowd around the train trying to sell us stuff. Scotland, Ireland and Wales were competing too and all of the British squads stuck together. I seemed to know someone from every country. It was a sleeper train, but you couldn't really get any kip. The bunks were too small and there was too much going on.

When we arrived in Kazan, the organisers put us in a sports complex, where massages were available and everything. The meals, though, weren't to our liking. It was their traditional food so we didn't want to disrespect it, but we ended up going to McDonalds or into town to buy our own pasta pots just to keep our energy levels up.

As for the tournament itself, the pitches were good, the stadium was good and we were well looked after. It seems strange to play in a ground surrounded by minarets and we went to visit a mosque in the village, but it was closed. For a Muslim, it was a strange situation. Although there were plenty of other Muslims around, it was obvious that for most of the locals religion was now some way down the line in importance behind communism. Knowledge of religion took second place to the daily realities of political life.

But back to the rugby league and the event was a roaring success from the start - especially for England. Over 16,000 people turned up to watch the opening ceremony which featured a game between hosts Tatarstan and Ireland. And as well as ourselves, Wales and Scotland, teams from Australia and Russia were also taking part. Eventually, though, we were the ones who came out on top. Although I didn't play - I had a pulled hamstring - England beat Tatarstan 34-16 in the final.

As things turned out, that was the one and only time I got involved with the England Students. I did have a great time, though, and we had a lot of good players in the team, many of whom went on to become professionals. There was Andy Raleigh, a big strong second rower, hard as nails, Paul Thorman, Jermaine Coleman, Robin Peers, Craig Firth and Andy Poynter, who went on to sign for Sheffield. Plenty of Geordies among them and a good set of lads.

So having had such a good experience in Kazan, when the chance came to coach in India a couple of years later, I didn't need to be asked twice. It was just the sort of open door that I needed and I jumped at the opportunity.

The chap from Newcastle told me that I would be coaching Bombay Gymkhana, who were the official base of the Indian Rugby Union in Mumbai. Yet when I got there, I discovered that I wasn't coaching at all, just playing. The mindset, it seemed, was that we'll get Ikram Butt in there and then we will win the final. Never mind, I told myself, it isn't really a problem. Finally, I had made my long-awaited first visit to South Asia and I was bound to make a lot of useful contacts, including a number of people who dealt with the Pakistani Rugby Union.

Nor had I travelled out there alone. Junaid Malik and Jag Johal went with me, although I am making that sound much simpler than it actually was. You need a visa to travel to India, and that is easier said than done, especially if you are Pakistani. And at this point, on my first visit, I was a bit naïve about the process. First I went to the consulate in Birmingham, without any success. They said they were being stringent for security reasons. I then carried on going backwards and forwards until, with my flight scheduled to leave on the Saturday, I was told to go up to Edinburgh. Apparently, there was a Sikh guy up there and he was known for being more liberal. He said where was your dad born? And I said Jalandhar, a place in the Punjab. He accepted it straight away. Until I got the visa in my hand I was sweating. I thought he was going to ask me to step into his office or something. Nowadays, if we are travelling on BARA business, it is a lot more straightforward. Since then, we have been able to sit down with the consulate, have a cup of tea, and explain what we were about.

Anyway, with my visa in my pocket, I drove all the way back to Bradford, got my stuff, and drove straight down to London. I left my car in a twenty-four-hour parking place and just ran for the plane because I was late. When we landed in India, I phoned my mate, Sadiq, and told him to go and pick up my car. He said: 'Sure, where are your keys?' I said: 'Here, with me'. I told him to just smash my side window but, fortunately, he had a bit more sense than that and just rang the guys who owned the car park to explain the situation. They said: 'Look, there's no point breaking into it, just leave it here and we'll only charge you half price.' The usual bill would have been £600 but they let me have it for £300.

Junaid's attempts to get a visa were even more desperate than mine, as he was actually born in Pakistan. But as I said, Gymkhana were intent on winning this competition - hence them bringing over three British players. Fortunately, the president of the IRFU, Pramod Khanna, had a brother called Vinod, who was a government minister and a Bollywood legend, so he was quite an influential person. In the end, Mr Khanna made a phone call and Junaid was allowed into the country.

To be honest, the tournament itself wasn't all that hot in terms of class and skill, but we did reach the final as expected and played a team from the Sri Lanka police. I scored a try, Jag scored a try and Junaid kicked all the goals. So the British lads got all the points but the Sri Lankans still beat us, 17-15. The referee was a guy called Salim Tyebjee, one of Bombay Gymkhana's own. The winning score came when the Sri Lankans pointed to the goals, indicating that they were going to kick a penalty. But then, as our backs were turned and we all walked back to the line, they tapped it, passed it wide and scored. We complained but it didn't do us any good. All the Gymkhana lads were in tears. They had won the event four years on the trot before then.

\* \* \* \* \*

The formation of BARA the following year coincided with the new organisation sending five players to Asia, as part of the 19th Asian Rugby Football Tournament in Hong Kong.

Two of us - Amraz Hamid and myself - would be playing

for Pakistan, while the other three - Newcastle's Simon Patel and Amarveer Ladhar, plus Ajay Subherwal - lined up for India. In keeping with BARA's aims, we were intended to be ambassadors as well as players and what with this being the first time that Pakistan had participated in an international rugby tournament, it felt like quite a historic occasion. Funded by the RFU, I also did a bit of coaching for local schoolteachers while we were there.

By now, I had already been out to Pakistan on the back of the contacts I made the year before in Mumbai. So, when I had heard the Hong Kong games were coming up, I put my CV together and said: 'Look, I would like to help you out.' After a while, the president of the Pakistan Rugby Union got back to me and asked how much I would like. I said: 'No, no, it's not about money. I am genuinely doing it because I want BARA to help to develop the game.' So we agreed some dates and I went to do some training with them in Islamabad and Lahore. After that, we discussed bringing some other lads over from the UK to represent Pakistan in the Hong Kong tournament.

As it was Pakistan's first tournament, nothing much was expected of us and that is exactly how things turned out. Because of its British colonial background, rugby union in India was much longer established and they were certainly at a higher level than Pakistan who, despite having seen its first game of rugby in Karachi in 1926, had only officially been part of the union since 2000. Unfortunately, we found ourselves having to play them and, to cut a long story short, they walloped us. Mind you, India at this time had around eighteen or nineteen teams going, while Pakistan had two, if that.

So that was BARA's first official experience of international rugby union. And it was already obvious that the fifteen-a-side code takes international competition very seriously. The ARFU - Asian Rugby Football Union - is a very well-funded organisation. All our flights to Hong Kong were paid for, we stayed in five star hotels ... it was all a very impressive and professional set-up. The actual games weren't a sell-out by any means and we played at Hong Kong football club, which had an artificial pitch. But the weather was great and we even had the Pakistani high commission come along to watch us. So the diplomatic wheels were well and truly oiled.

And a year later, in September 2005, things moved up a whole other gear when an entire BARA team went on a ten-day tour to play in the 72nd All India and South Asia Rugby Tournament in Mumbai, as a follow up to the earlier visit by Jag Johal, Junaid Malik and myself in 2003.

We prepared for the tour with another thirteen-a-side match against our old foes the RAF, this time held at Odsal as the curtain-raiser to a Bradford Bulls versus Salford City Reds Super League game, in front of hundreds of fans. In the end, we lost 25-24 thanks to a dramatic last-minute drop-goal, although it was a really entertaining game that could have gone either way. The most important thing was that it helped us to get some moves together and get to know each other's ability as players. As usual, group training sessions were very hard to come by so any chance to play together a month before the trip was always going to be worthwhile.

In the RAF match, our shirts were kindly sponsored by the Royal Air Force, but for the tour we developed a partnership with Leeds Carnegie Metropolitan University. In fact, that was what it said on our shirts: 'Leeds Met South Asia'. We were purposely taking a team made up of mixed backgrounds, cultures and religions and a number of them, like me, were either studying at Leeds Met or university alumni. Carnegie were increasingly keen to do a lot of work in India themselves and so the relationship made sense.

Right from the start it was a successful visit, not just on the rugby field, but out there in the schools that we visited too. My brother, Tony, also went on the tour and enjoyed himself as much as anyone. There was one school, though, that we arrived at late. And the headmistress was not happy at all. She wanted to cut our planned talk in the school assembly short, but we had one particular character in our team called Rashid Mahmood Khan.

Now, on tour, you always get the one person who is the self-appointed entertainments manager and Rashid was that man. We went to the school, where we were to get involved with the kids' activities, present rugby balls, that sort of thing. Anyway, Rashid got up on stage and took the microphone from the head teacher. He said he would like to thank her for letting us visit the school, thanked my colleagues for organising the tour and the kids for being there. And then, totally out of the blue, he turned to the headteacher and asked if she would mind if he sang everyone a song. Her and the other teachers looked at each other as if to say: 'What's going on here?' Anyway, a bit reluctantly, she said: 'Fine, go ahead.'

There was a film out at the time called *Sholay*, a Bollywood blockbuster. To this day, it has not been matched in termed of box office takings. No matter what age group you were, kids, old folk, everyone, you knew about *Sholay*. Anyway, Rashid suddenly burst into a song from that film, something about being friends forever. Soon, absolutely everyone, including the headmistress, was joining in. It was one of the funniest things I have ever seen. Everyone was in fits of laughter. And later, when we went to a special reception at the Embassy, he did exactly the same thing again in front of all the posh dignitaries.

On the playing front, unlike some teams, we didn't get any byes once the event got underway, we had to play our way through from the start. We eventually met Bangalore in the final. On the way, we had a 37-0 win over the Indian Army that would have been greater if we had managed to convert more than one of our eventual seven tries. We also played the Police, who no one in the ground seemed to like very much at all. In fact, our Tony overheard someone in the Police team complaining that everyone in the crowd was supporting us Brits rather than them. They were all chanting for BARA. Other teams in the tournament included Bombay Gymkhana, the favourites Chennai Cheetahs, Lahore RFC and two teams from Delhi, the Hurricanes and the Lions.

Our opponents in the final, Bangalore, were captained and coached by a chap called Phil Woodward who came from Leigh, and also played full-back. His wife was a teacher in Bangalore and Phil was helping to develop rugby there and had one or two overseas players in his side too. In fact, there were loads of South Sea Islanders and Maoris around and some of them played for the team we met in the semi-finals, Chennai. Even so, we had the measure of them although the thing I most remember the game for is that I was sent off! I had never been sent off before in my life, but the referee gave me my marching orders and that was that. All right, it was a late tackle, but it was in the last ten minutes of the game. Fortunately, the organisers agreed to let me play in the final.

We had seen Bangalore play in the earlier rounds and knew we had the beating of them, but a final is a final and there is such a thing as being over-confident. In the end, though, we did run out comfortable 27-3 winners. We had them on the back foot from the start and our full-back, Amraz Hamid, scored the first try in the 14th minute. On the half hour, Jug Johal, playing at hooker, got our second and Ben Kerr's conversion gave us a 12-0 half-time lead. In the second half, Ben, Paul Akaidere and Rehan Mansoor got three more five-pointers, while Bangalore could only manage a penalty goal in response.

It hadn't been a bad way for BARA to end their first overseas tour, had it? And when we got home, there was a nice reception waiting for us at Headingley, organised by Leeds Met Carnegie, which was fantastic. The boss of Leeds Rugby, Gary Hetherington, was there and so were Dave Jackson and Dave Braham of Leeds Met, who came with us to India and have since become very good friends of mine. Several of the players who play at Leeds in both codes were there as well. And a few months later, we showed off the championship trophy - an original replica of the Calcutta Cup now played for by England and Scotland - at the Pocklington Sevens. It was the beginning of a successful partnership between BARA and Leeds Carnegie that has continued ever since.

\* \* \* \* \*

Although we had very much enjoyed ourselves in Mumbai, now was the not the time for BARA to rest on its laurels.

In April 2006, my friend and fellow BARA director, Jug Johal, flew back out to India for another ten-day visit. While there, he met with Punjab sporting officials and visited still more schools. And then in June, one of our old boys, the London-based Glaswegian Shahid Rafiq, became the first Scottish rugby player to represent Pakistan when a total of thirteen British Asian rugby league and union players flew off to represent India and Pakistan in a series of rugby union Test matches.

Along with Shahid, the Pakistan side could also boast myself, Rashid Mahmood, Amraz Hamid, Junaid Malik and Rehan Mansoor, all based in West Yorkshire, in its line-up. And after an intensive week-long training camp with the rest of the squad in Pakistan, early in June we were scheduled to play in group five of the Asian Nations Series, sponsored by Malik Finance, with the Pacific islanders of Guam and our hosts, the Philippines.

Meanwhile, another seven players would represent India in their own two-game series against Malaysia in Kuala Lumpur on June 5 and Thailand in Bangkok, two days later. Those lads' names were: Amarveer Singh, Simon Patel Knowles (both Newcastle Falcons), Tim Wilkes (Darlington Mowden Park RU), Francis Brown (Harlow RFC), Manmandir Samra (Moseley RU), Ajay Subherwal (Dungannon) and the captain, Nasser Hussain, who played for Tynedale RU while he was studying in England.

As things turned out, India, who were in a division above us, didn't have a very good time of it at all. They lost 61-20 to Malaysia and then 50-28 to Thailand. Us Pakistan lads, though, had a much more positive experience and carved out a bit of history while we were at it. First, in a warm-up game during our week's training camp, we beat the Islamabad Rugby Club 25-5 and then, in the tournament proper in Manila, got past Guam 27-22 and the Philippines 24-3. Not surprisingly, the Pakistani Rugby Union was delighted - it was the country's first ever international trophy and BARA had more than played its part. And to top it off, the six of us were given a civic reception at Bradford Town Hall on our return, where the city's Lord Mayor, Choudhary Rangzeb, spoke very highly of BARA's work in the local community.

At first, our success in Manila enabled us to build a strong relationship with the Pakistani Rugby Union although, to be honest, it has struggled a little since. After the wins over Guam and the Philippines we had a bigger say on training schedules, forward planning and so on and identified more key players to bring out. Our victories also meant that we were promoted a division, which proved to be a mixed blessing because, later, we were hammered by India, Thailand and Malaysia in Bangkok, and the honeymoon was over. The PRU establishment didn't take too kindly to that, but I had grown a little bit disappointed with the organisation there. I couldn't see any positive, concrete developments. Then again, in a lot of ways, we had done what we wanted to do. Through BARA, we wanted to build a relationship with Pakistan and we did. The guys there know me now, and they know that I am a straight up and down chap.

In any case, for all our work overseas, BARA's direct involvement with the South Asian community in Britain continued to take up most of our time. Along with my own day-to-day development work, in July 2006 BARA played a one-off representative match against rugby league's amateur English national side, the England Lionhearts, intended to act as yet another relaunch for the RFL's 'Tackle It' campaign, among other initiatives. Played at the South Leeds Stadium, Hunslet, the thing I remember most about that day was the searing heat. Believe me, it was hotter in Hunslet than it was in the Philippines! Anyway, the Lionhearts won 24-14 although it took a couple of late tries and we pushed them all the way.

And then, in August, we played another of our matches with the Royal Air Force, which by now had become an annual fixture. This year's game was again played at Odsal where, this time, we went down 36-24 after a very disappointing display in front of around 1,000 fans. The reason for such a big turn-out came afterwards. Our game was played as a curtain-raiser to an international kabaddi match between India and Pakistan, in which players representing those countries from within the Bradford area put on a great evening's entertainment that Pakistan finally won 21-11. The money raised went towards the Kashmir Earthquake Trust and the Bradford Bulls Foundation.

It was also in the Autumn of 2006 that we launched our own newsletter - BARA Rugby News - and relaunched our website with a view to enhancing our exposure to the world. And in November of that year, a group of eight of us found ourselves playing for the Islamabad Jinns RFC, in the IRB's prestigious Dubai Sevens event. And not only that, after playing six games over three days, we eventually won in the Plate final, 34-0, against a team called the Wild Wadi. The star of the show was my mate, Junaid Malik, whose skill, vision and pace was outstanding throughout.

\* \* \* \* \*

Individual awards have never been the be-all and end-all for me. What matters most is that BARA itself gets recognition, enabling us to carry out the work that we feel it is so important to do. If myself or the organisation is nominated for big prizes, then that gains wider credibility which, in turn, means the governing bodies have to take us more seriously.

Another useful thing in this regard is the development of a healthy relationship with politicians and national Government, an area in which, I am pleased to say, we have come on in leaps and bounds since BARA was first formed in 2004. But more of that in a moment.

Having said all of the above, I wouldn't be entirely honest if I didn't admit to at least a little glow of personal satisfaction whenever my name gets put forward for an award. I have been nominated for the Sony Sports Awards - later renamed the British Asian Sports Awards - four times, but being on the shortlist has been as far as it has gone.

When I arrived at Café Royal in London on the first time

I was nominated in 2001, although I hadn't expected anything beforehand, when I looked at the seating plan I thought I must be in with a really good chance. The thing is I was on the same table as the vice-chairman of Sony TV, Rajan Singh, and Keith Vaz, the Labour MP for Leicester. I was also one of three people in the Outstanding Achievement category, the others being Harwarinder Singh Athwal, a competitor in the World Transplant Games since 1989, and Ajit Singh Kalirai, a 73-year-old who had competed at international level for the past twenty-five years in the Veteran Athletics Championships. So although I had nothing prepared, I did begin to wonder. And then, when they read out the nominations, all the television cameras came straight over to our table. Quickly, I began to rehearse a speech in my head but then, when they read the name out, it was the athletic Mr. Kalirai and not me. That taught me a lesson, I can tell you.

The thing is, as any Oscar nominee will tell you, even if you lose you have to keep smiling or else you look a right miserable sod. I'd be lying if I said that I wasn't disappointed not to have won, but I have got to the stage now where I realise that the important thing is raising that profile, not only of myself, but also the people who work so hard around me. In my time, I have also been shortlisted in the Muslim News Awards for Excellence in 2002, and the Lloyds TSB sponsored Asian Jewel Awards in 2005. My last British Asian Sports Award nomination came in February 2008. Looking back, however, I would have to agree that when you look at the quality of the people I was up against, no one could find any fault with the judges' decisions.

There have been a number of other notable awards nights along the way too. BARA were shortlisted in the prestigious Yorkshire Sports Awards, in which we won the category but came third overall. I myself won the Vision award for Bradford, which was nice because it is always good to be recognised in your own back yard. But my most recent personal achievement was to be included in the Asian Power 100 - a huge event held at the Hilton in London in December 2007, at which I won the 'Future Leaders - One to Watch' award. That was a huge evening. The cream of celebrities and business were there and I was the guest of Leeds Met, who sponsored a table. When my name was announced, there was a right racket of applause from the audience. Maybe that was because I had been on the circuit for a fair while by then, and a lot of those present were disappointed that I had never won anything, Also, the timing was right. A lot of people in sport are starting to push the BARA agenda now and that can only be a good thing. We had a wonderful time at the London Hilton

Out of all the award nights I have been to, the Asian Jewel Awards and Asian Power 100 were far above the rest. Khalid Darr, chairman of the event organisers Carter and Anderson, had belief in BARA and myself right from the start, when few other people shared our vision. At the Power 100 in particular, it was good to win in such good company. Simon Lee, who was then vice-chancellor of Leeds Met, was on our table. Although he has left the university since, I will never have anything other than huge admiration for the pioneering work that Simon put in during his tenure.

Meanwhile, in the wider political circles, we are also starting to make a very strong strong impact. Also in 2007, Prime Minister Gordon Brown praised BARA for our good work during the Prime Minister's Question Time just up the road in Westminster, and we were also officially endorsed by Sports Minister Gerry Sutcliffe MP.

BARA's involvement in the national political arena really got going when we were invited to a meeting with the All Party Rugby League Parliamentary Group in February 2007.

The All Party Group is an official gathering of like-minded parliamentarians who take a special interest in rugby league and the benefits of the sport to the well-being of the nation as a whole. In the past, for example, they played a very important role in campaigning for a free gangway between the two rugby codes, during the days when rugby union systematically banned anyone from taking part in the 15-a-side code who had ever had anything at all to do with rugby league - amateur or professional. In short, they are a body who can lobby on behalf of organisations like ourselves and they meet every month.

The meeting was organised by my old friend Spen Allison, who is the chairman of the British Amateur Rugby League Association (BARLA). It was Spen who made the first formal approach to Neil Turner MP, a Wiganer who is also secretary of the All Party Parliamentary Group. From that introduction, Neil invited us to one of the Parliamentary Group meetings and asked us to deliver a presentation about the British Asian Rugby Association. We told them about our development plans and stressed the need for governing bodies and Government itself to invest in encouraging participation amongst *all* ethnic communities. BARA is an inclusive organisation.

I must say that Spen has been wonderful on BARA issues from the off and he knew that we would benefit greatly from the MPs' involvement. And we were very pleased with the reception they gave us, particularly from people like Neil Turner and Greg Mulholland, a Leeds lad whose constituency is where I grew up in Headingley. Greg continues to be very supportive of our endeavours, as are all the other group members. Since then, our relationship and bond with the group has strengthened greatly.

After that initial meeting, I began to go down to London more often. I wanted to attend regular meetings and find out for myself what the body could actually do and what it is all about. What part could the All Party Parliamentary Group play within what BARA wanted to achieve? By doing that, I built close relationships with a number of very important people.

One of those is Gerry Sutcliffe, MP, the current Government Minister for Sport. Although Gerry is not actually a member of the group itself, he has attended meetings. I knew him before anyway via my role with Bradford Council. Gerry is also the Labour MP for Bradford South, which is the area that Odsal Stadium is in, and so he knows all about what we do and is very much behind what we are trying to achieve.

But being involved with the All Party Rugby League Group also helped us to get involved with rugby union's governing body, the RFU, and the All Party Parliamentary Rugby Union Group too. From our very the first meeting with the league MPs, we made it clear that we were about promoting rugby, full stop. League and union. The response was interesting because some of the league MPs couldn't understand why we would want to involve rugby union as well, given the historical background between the two codes and union's far from inclusive reputation in that regard. That first meeting only lasted ten minutes or so and it was difficult to get our whole message across. But over time, with more dialogue and conversation, they started to see where we were coming from and then they were all on board.

After all, as politicians, it didn't take them long to realise that there enormous social benefits to be gained from getting more Asian kids involved in sport, as we in BARA have been saying all along. To give just one example, currently in the UK we are struggling with high levels of childhood obesity - and that applies to every community. Then there is the issue of social cohesion. At the moment, certain parts of Britain have a big problem with communities living in isolation. The power of sport - and it doesn't matter which sport - can break down those barriers and build bridges. Sport can also help to fight political extremism, which is a major cause of the troubles we see in the world today. It can channel negative energies in a more positive direction and encourage teamwork, stressing our similarities rather than our differences all the time.

If we look at the Asian situation, for example, and then break that down into Asians who happen to be Muslims, sport can help to dispel the myth that all Asians are terrorists. On the contrary, Asians are individual people like you and me. If we can incorporate that into the political system, the British public as a whole, Muslims, Christians or otherwise, will all have a greater understanding of one and other and get along so much better. Sport is a form of dialogue and when dialogue stalls, well, that's when you begin to have problems.

Whatever your political agenda, people always claim that the Government could do more to help and we at BARA are no different in that regard. Having said that, though, I don't underestimate the difficulty of the situation that this present Government finds itself in. On the one hand they have to be seen to be acting tough on the issue of terrorism, but on the other they need to champion sensible social attitudes, and pursue an inclusive policy that allows every member of the public to feel themselves a valued part of this country, whatever their religion, lifestyle or colour of skin.

And you can't get much closer to the heart of the UK than being invited to the Houses of Parliament, can you? As a group, it was a huge honour for BARA to be asked to speak there but for me, individually, Ikram Butt, a normal kid from a terraced house in Leeds, it was quite a moment too. The place is awesome and absolutely dripping with history, and you can't escape the symbolism of it. You are directly at the centre of the British establishment, aren't you? We BARA reps were given a tour of the building and it was fascinating to see all the architecture. Like most places, it looks much smaller than it does on the telly, but it is still pretty impressive.

Beyond all that, though, that meeting really laid a platform for us as an organisation. And having the ear of friends in high places is always helpful, especially when you are dealing with governing bodies that, until then, may not been quite as wholehearted in promoting BARA's aims as we might have liked. In rugby league's case, it wasn't so much the man at the top - RFL chairman and new Sport England chief Richard Lewis - who was the problem. Richard has never been anything other than receptive to our cause and continues to be so. The problem, if ever there is one, tends to be with lower-level management, who sometimes struggle to see the value in BARA and what it can offer, or so it seems to me.

Still, with the All Party Group on our side, we have a lot more influence. And, as it happens, the All Party Parliamentary Rugby Union Group has a longer history than its rugby league counterpart and is equally supportive. A certain number of individuals in both groups are on other sports bodies too, so that can only be a good thing in terms of expanding the reach of what we are trying to do.

# IKRAM IS A FORMIDABLE OPERATOR WHO IS ABLE TO GET PEOPLE ENTHUSED...
## Neil Turner MP

*All Party Parliamentary Rugby League Group Secretary and Government Ambassador to Rugby League*

I never had the chance to watch Ikram play professional rugby league, but I am told by people whose judgement I trust on these matters that he was the finest Asian player in the game.

I had no difficulty believing this, despite the fact that it was Ikram himself who told me, because at that time he was the *only* player from an Asian background who had broken into the highest echelons of professional rugby league.

Rugby league has a long and proud history of being colour-blind. Black players who were being kept out of other professional and amateur codes because of covert or too often overt racism or prejudice were eagerly snapped up by rugby league clubs and provided tremendous entertainment for fans as they paraded their admirable skills at Wembley and in British Lions shirts. But the Asian community was blissfully unaware of the joys of playing and watching the game, and, unlike in cricket, had no player the young could identify with and want to emulate.

## Tries and Prejudice

Ikram loved playing rugby league, and knew that the game provided opportunities for the individual to develop their physical prowess, their temperament, and their self - discipline, as well as working in a team which recognised only the skill you had and effort that you were prepared to put in to see your team win. He wanted the Asian community to be made aware of these and take part in playing and watching rugby league at all levels. But getting them to take notice was going to be no easy task.

But being a professional rugby league player makes you see problems like that as mere obstacles to be overcome. And so he formed the British Asian Rugby Association - BARA. Working mainly in the Leeds/Bradford conurbation, and initially using a non-contact version of the game, he was able to introduce young children to the joy of handling a rugby ball at speed, and the thrill of scoring a try after a well-worked move.

The All Party Parliamentary Rugby League Group exists to promote the game in Parliament and help its development in any way we can. It was suggested we invite Ikram and his colleagues to speak to the group and tell us of the progress that had been made, but also the challenges still to be faced. To say we had our eyes opened would be the classic understatement. No-one in the APPG had any inkling that such good work was going on, and so successfully in areas of our country with severe deprivation and where there was the potential for racial conflict.

Our group was anxious to help BARA in any way we could, and when Ikram promoted the idea of a match between Parliamentarians and Rugby League All Stars at The Stoop, home of Harlequins RFU and RFL Clubs, we jumped at the chance. Events like that don't just happen, they take a lot of organising which someone has to do. Ikram threw himself into this with what I now know is his customary zeal and persuasiveness, and I was able to marvel as a galaxy of heroes paraded their not very rusty sublime skills before my dewy eyes as memories of eight winning Wembleys in a row for Wigan came flooding back.

But most importantly, we raised the profile of BARA and the work it was doing to a level it would have otherwise taken many more years to reach, with radio and TV coverage, as well as many newspapers carrying the story.

That was when I realised that Ikram was a formidable operator, able to get people enthused and involved, and want to be part of making BARA and the work they are doing a success.

His driving ambition for the game and his vision in seeing that it can be a vital element in promoting community cohesion and understanding, while breaking down the barriers of suspicion and prejudice, is exemplary. Through Ikram Butt's work, children of all religions and both sexes are learning that rugby, as a team sport, is a microcosm of life, where who you are and how you use and develop the talents you have are the essentials, not the colour of your skin.

# IKRAM SMASHED ANY RACIAL STEREOTYPES MY PLAYERS EVER HAD...
## Andy Reed MP

*All Party Parliamentary Rugby Union Group*

After twenty-five years playing rugby union I finally made my league debut at Leeds Carnegie in the summer of 2008, aged 44. Our coach that day was Ikram Butt, a 'legend' I had met the previous year. We didn't manage to beat the press in our game that day, but I did manage to score two points at the end by converting our try.

Since then I have recruited Ikram to play a full role in our Commons & Lords rugby union team, where he has paired up with former England star Rob Andrew in a formidable midfield partnership at Twickenham. Ikram has not lost the skills and strength that made him such a great player.

But this is only part of the Ikram I have grown to know and it is for his other work with BARA that I most admire his skills. His passion for it is infectious.

I chair my local County Sports Partnership in Leicestershire and have seen many people driven by their enthusiasm for sport. But Ikram takes this to another level. And of course his mission with BARA is entirely right.

I know that the rugby governing bodies are keen to do more to encourage wider participation in the game. But I am particularly supportive of BARA and Ikram because they are determined to provide greater opportunities at every level for people from the South Asian communities, both in the UK and abroad. For too much of the rugby world this is still a largely untapped group of people, particularly in Leicestershire and Loughborough, my own constituency, where more work needs to be done.

BARA's principle aims are to provide positive role models, break down cultural and religious barriers, promote community integration, personal development, healthy living and encouraging participation in sport and physical activity, especially in rugby. All of this can help in a place like Leicestershire and, whilst Ikram cannot take all of this work on himself, I do see him as the sort of person who will be able to drive forward a longer lasting legacy for BARA around the country because of the vision and passion he puts into his work. I didn't take much persuading to give him a hand, but he has certainly nudged me further out of my comfort zone. Too often we talk a good game in sport about equity issues, but there is still so much more we need to do to break out of our racial stereotypes for instance.

An example of Ikram's commitment came in May 2009, when he travelled from Bradford to Leicestershire to play in my local President's XV at Birstall RFC. This is grass roots rugby, certainly not the glamour fixture of Twickenham, but Ikram gave his time generously and with great humility. By bringing along Hrishi Pendese, the captain of India's rugby team, who is currently based at Loughborough University, he certainly made the case for Asian rugby in our country by their sheer presence on the pitch.

As a result, I now have a club interested in what more it can do to hear and listen to the BARA message. Living his own message, Ikram and now Hrishi certainly smashed any racial stereotypes my club players ever had about the quality and strength of Asian players. Let us hope that Ikram and BARA have broken the log jam and can continue to overcome such barriers, so that South Asian communities get a thirst and hunger for rugby of both codes and that clubs up and down the country open up their doors to this untapped resource of players. Rugby, in particular, will be the winner. Ikram and BARA can take the credit for moving this agenda on.

From our working relationship to genuine friendship in such a short space of time. It is testimony to Ikram that the greatness he showed (and still shows) on the pitch, not to mention the drive and enthusiasm that enabled him to thrive in a tough professional sport, now makes BARA and his own work with it so pivotal to the future health of sport in this country.

# 16

\*

# Playing for Keeps

It was a little daunting at first dealing with all these political men in suits who, if you believe the newspapers, have a bit of a reputation for wheeling and dealing and saying only what they think you want to hear. I soon came to realise, though, that everyone is a politician really. We all have some agenda or other and we all want to influence people and get them on our side. But what I am finding is that, increasingly, BARA's concerns are shared by the politicians themselves. That is why we are being given so much valuable support.

Not that it is all about talk, we have started to play quite a bit of actual rugby too. That began when the Parliamentary Groups asked us exactly what it was that we wanted them to do. Did we want them to write on our behalf to local authorities or governing bodies? So I said, let's build a healthy relationship before we go into all that and one of the things we could do is play a game. Initially we talked about the rugby league MPs identifying one Super League player each who could play on their behalf. But the MPs were keen to have a go themselves, which was great.

So the BARA celebrity team was born. The idea was that high-profile individuals in the worlds of media, business or sport would come together and form a team in order to raise awareness and keep BARA in the public eye. So, for example, in the first game we played at the Twickenham Stoop in June 2007, Martin Offiah was amongst those taking part, along with the Welsh rugby union international Colin Stephens, former Great Britain rugby league star and Sky Sports pundit Phil Clarke, Abi Ekoku and Saima Hussain, Great Britain's first female Asian rugby league international. Our opponents were a side made up of MPs and politicians and the game we played was christened BARA Tag Time, a version of Bull Tag, which we had already used effectively across thirty five schools in West Yorkshire. Before we went on, there was also a kids game between Oriel School of London and Springwood School of Bradford. As it happens, the BARA team won by a single try but that wasn't the point of the exercise.

That game at the Stoop was something of a watershed for our organisation and BARA Tag Time proved so popular that we have been playing it ever since. The following year we took the idea up north to Headingley and, in June 2009, went back to the capital. BARA Tag Time is an exciting idea that we hope to develop even more in the years to come.

When it comes to rugby union, their All Party Group has had its own Parliamentary team for a number of years. And they don't play BARA Tag Time, they play proper 'rugger', with the bumps and bruises to show for it. In April 2009, I was a guest player for them myself, at Twickenham, after having already played once before in 2008. The side is known as Commons and Lords RFC and we played against a team representing the Cystic Fibrosis Trust, with all the proceeds going to that charity. The Commons and Lords side plays regularly, throughout the Six Nations and so on, and I was invited to go with them on tour to South Africa but my work commitments made it impossible.

This year, my own biggest contribution to the Commons and Lords RFC cause was to be given a dead-leg taking an inside ball from Rob Andrew - yes, that Rob Andrew. He shouted: 'Ikram, cut in off my shoulder,' so I did and missed the ball completely before colliding with a lad on the other team. I was limping for days. Gerry Sutcliffe was my inside centre, and his winger was Jim Fitzpatrick, a 57-year-old MP. In the forwards, we had Lord Addington, a super chap, who really loves his rugby. Later on, Rob got drawn into an on-field scuffle. The other side were taking it all a bit too seriously and I was forced to come to his rescue. Good job I don't hold grudges, eh? The MPs love the physicality of it all and it is great to be involved.

* * * * *

And so, as we come to the last few pages of my autobiography with plenty of work behind us and - God willing - lots more still to do, what does the future hold for BARA and the development of rugby within the South Asian community?

Well, overseas, I am convinced that things are about to get very exciting. As I write, we are working on our relationship with the Pakistan Rugby Union and have never stopped providing players for the country's national team. BARA are the representatives of the Pakistani Rugby Union in the UK - not the sole representatives - but they ask us to suggest players in the positions they need and we are happy to recommend them. With India, we still send players out to their training camps and, if those players are selected, the IRU reimburses their travel expenses. Pakistan are still a little way down the IRB pecking order behind India, but since they were fully endorsed by the Asian Rugby Football Union (ARFU), the Pakistani Sports Board and the Pakistani Olympic Board, they can pay air fares too now which makes the funding of such enterprises easier.

At the beginning of our relationships with the Pakistani and Indian Rugby Unions, I made a verbal promise that I wouldn't come in and try to introduce rugby league right at the start. I'm sure they knew, though, that my background was in rugby league and that, eventually, I would be bound to want to give it a go. And now, some eight or nine years down the line, that time is at hand. India, in particular, are happy for me to begin coaching rugby league once the 2010 Commonwealth Games are out of the way, which is extremely understandable because India is hosting them and taking part in the rugby sevens. The Indian IRU and I have, though, already held talks in which I suggested that, rather than having two separate governing bodies which may conflict, India should pioneer the concept of having one governing body for both codes. They seemed to like that idea, so we will see what develops.

With Pakistan, it is not as smooth as that. Pakistan has a different way of looking at things to India - not better or worse, just different. Sometimes, I am not so sure that they have entirely embraced the full vision of what we are trying to do.

As a result, I have felt that there is little point discussing rugby league with the PRU because they would not take the benefits on board as well as the Indians have. So, instead, I have begun to introduce rugby league into the country from a different angle. In trying to develop the 13-a-side code, we have built a very strong relationship with the Islamabad Rugby Club, who I get on extremely well with. We decided that if we were going to launch rugby league anywhere then the best place was Islamabad since they have been using rugby league as part of their training regimes right from the start.

At the end of 2008, Kevin Rudd, who is the Rugby League European Federation's development executive, and myself flew out to Pakistan on the back of reports I had compiled from previous visits, including one occasion when I travelled there with Spen Allison. Having someone as well respected as Spen with me helped to gain access to schools and won us meetings with head teachers, local politicians and so on. The message was very clear: schools in Pakistan are eager to get involved in the game of rugby league, so the timing of Kevin's visit couldn't have been better.

On the whole, Kevin's trip to Pakistan was mainly about him coming out and seeing for himself what was going on at first hand. I know he was pleasantly surprised at the activities taking place but, more importantly, Kevin was able to have discussions with potentially important individuals and see how passionate people were about the game of rugby league.

We visited Islamabad, the Pakistani capital, which has the only purpose-built rugby pitch in the country; another reason why it is the perfect place to begin. And we also visited schools, and in particular Beacon House School, which has a number of parish schools up and down the country and also around Europe and America. So by aligning ourselves with this school we are tying rugby league into an important network, not only across Pakistan but in other parts of the world too.

Kevin met the head teacher of all the Pakistani schools in Beacon House, and it was a very positive meeting indeed, to the extent that they were telling us that they had the perfect green area on which to build a pitch just for rugby league. So it was all very encouraging and that was very satisfying from my point of view, because I had been going to Pakistan for a number of years, trying to get people interested and involved. The visits of Spen and Kevin endorsed what I had been saying all along.

Long term, of course, the success of the venture will depend on the people actually out there on the ground. But in the short term we have established a committee composed of parties who are interested in establishing rugby league in Pakistan. It is a constitutional group and the next step will be for Pakistan to become part of the International Federation, which will allow them to meet and play other countries who are at a similar stage of development. Again, that will be useful dialogue where one country's experience can help another. It's always good to talk and learn about other people's experiences.

Over the past decade or so, there have been quite a number of nations who have started with nothing - rugby league-wise - and then through dedication, hard work and passion, quickly developed to a very good standard. Look at a place like Lebanon, for example, whose progress in recent years has been nothing short of outstanding, despite being ridiculed in the 2000 World Cup. Finance always plays a large part and can help things run a lot smoother, but the Lebanese proved that money isn't everything. Just as important are genuine people who are keen to be involved for the long haul. If the going gets tough, they still hang in there because they are determined to see rugby league flourish.

I have no doubt that will be the case with rugby league in Pakistan and India, too, and that we will soon see the 13-a-side code played regularly right across South Asia. As is the case here in the UK, people say that South Asians are not interested in sports like rugby, but rugby union is quite widespread there and there's no reason why rugby league can't be too. I am very optimistic that, with BARA's support, rugby league will soon be on the map. In fact, on one small level, it already is. We have done a couple of tournaments there and, during Kevin Rudd's visit, staged the first two full games between two teams of adults and two teams of children, along with a number of workshops in schools.

\* \* \* \* \*

And what about here in the UK? What does the future for BARA hold here?

Well, obviously, my ultimate dream would be that both codes of rugby will become truly inclusive on every level, amateur or professional, attracting children and adults whatever their background. Individuals would not be judged on their colour of skin or religion, but on character and ability alone. And as I have said all along, if that fine day ever did occur, there might no longer be any need for BARA at all. In fact, when it comes to greater engagement with the South Asian community, it is time for the whole of British sport to move on, not just rugby.

For me, personally, it is time to move on too. I will still be as heavily involved with BARA as ever but, from May 2009, I left my job as a development officer with Bradford Council for a new role at the Leeds Rugby Foundation, in partnership with Leeds Carnegie. The job's official title is 'Connecting Communities' manager and I will be working within the wider community - primarily through rugby - in the areas of education and health. It is a very exciting challenge and I feel that the timing of the move is perfect.

For all that we have managed to achieve in a short period of time and despite our growing political connections, BARA has, relatively speaking, never quite had the sort of weight behind it that it needs if it is to really get things done. In this new job I will have one of the biggest - if not the biggest - rugby clubs in the world and a huge sporting and educational institution like Carnegie behind me. So, although initially it is only a three-year project, I feel that we will have a much better chance of getting sport's governing bodies to understand how sport should be used as a vehicle for positive change.

Yes, I will be sad to leave Bradford, especially after having worked there for over nine years. However, my relationship with the city is not quite over yet. I shall carry on living there and my new role takes in Leeds and the whole of Yorkshire anyway, so I have no doubt that we will continue to build on the good work already done there. I may be off to new pastures, but Bradford will still play an important role in all that we do.

One of the most important tasks, for me, is to try and persuade the governing bodies that although they at times do launch some very useful initiatives, lasting change won't come until the suggestions made by BARA are actually written into constitutional policy, otherwise clubs are going to feel free to do whatever they like. One club may see the development of relationships with the black and ethnic minorities as a good thing, another may see it as a waste of valuable resources. Until clubs are forced to take action in this area, we will only be scratching the surface of what might be achieved, both in terms of sport and the needs of wider British society.

Speaking of wider British society, two organisations that are very close to my heart and who I hope to work with even more closely in future, are football's Kick It Out campaign and an organisation called Mosaic, founded in November 2007 by HRH Prince Charles. Each combats racism in a slightly different way and I am proud to be an ambassador for both. Much like myself, the Kick It Out campaign uses sport as a means of getting its incredibly valuable message across, while Mosaic uses volunteering initiatives to highlight and champion the enormously positive contribution that the Muslim communities make to the well-being of the United Kingdom.

When it comes to Mosaic, though, one aspect of their work which particularly appeals to me is their set of mentoring and volunteering programmes, which link successful Muslims to schools and community groups across a five to twenty-five year age range. Such activity is now going on in Lancashire, Yorkshire, Leicester, the West Midlands and London.

Perhaps the most interesting aspect of that to me, though, is the prison mentoring service that Mosaic also provides, in which Muslim young offenders who may be ostracised by society in general and even their own communities, are given new opportunities and positive role models, in order to raise aspirations and support the achievement of individual goals. I think that is absolutely wonderful work. But given my own experiences, why wouldn't I? Did you know that Muslims currently constitute nearly ten per cent of the entire male and female prison population? That is more than three times their representation in the total population, with some 10,000 Muslims in custody on remand or serving custodial sentences (statistics www.mosaicnetwork.co.uk).

Whichever way you look at it, those figures are just terrible, aren't they? And for me, personally, it's certainly food for thought when you consider how, in a number of high-profile cases lately, certain non-Muslim sports personalities have escaped prison sentences despite having committed far more serious crimes than the one I was put away for. In the years to come, I intend to help Mosaic all I can.

\* \* \* \* \*

Anyway, back to rugby league - the sport that first launched me onto this incredible and enlightening journey as a hormonally challenged youth all those years ago? How do I see the future panning out there?

Well, the first thing to say is that rugby league, at the top level anyway, seems healthier than ever, and each of my former five clubs have made great strides since I left them - some quite a bit further than others.

As I said earlier in this book, I was always in favour of the launch of summer Super League. I am just a born optimist, I suppose, and it seemed like the dawn of a bright new era. Nor did I mind the new nicknames that came in - Rhinos, Bulls, Warriors and so on. In fact, I quite liked them. It showed that the clubs had finally realised that they were a part of the entertainment business and would have to work a bit harder to get people through the gates from now on, especially the younger generation. For those clubs with the imagination to make the most of it - such as Bradford - it also opened up all sorts of revenue streams and, as we know, financial income has been a problem for league clubs since the break from rugby union in 1895. Even so, rugby league has stood the test of time and it is a sport for the whole family.

Having said all that, there are still one or two things I am not too happy with. The scrummaging is just silly these days and I am disappointed that we still haven't got a strong Super League club up in Cumbria, a real rugby league stronghold if ever there was one. Maybe someone up there could form a regional Super League side, with Barrow, Whitehaven and Workington continuing under their old names as feeder clubs in the lower divisions. Maybe that could work, although my own experience at Featherstone tells me that the fans there wanted to see their own team - Featherstone Rovers - playing at the top table, so then again maybe not. Either way, something needs to be done.

Fortunately, when it comes to my former clubs themselves, with the possible exception of Hunslet, who continue to struggle to get by in Championship One, it has been pretty much good news all the way. As I write, Huddersfield are perhaps the biggest improvers of the lot, getting some great crowds into the Galpharm Stadium these days and now very much at home towards the top of the Super League table rather than wallowing about in their traditional position at the bottom. London Broncos have ditched most of their Australians, begun to develop some exciting local talent of their own, moved back to the Twickenham Stoop and been renamed as Harlequins RL. Although big crowds are still tough to come by, under Brian McDermott, the Quins play an exciting brand of rugby and the development of amateur rugby in the capital over this past ten years has been phenomenal. And my childhood favourites Leeds, well, what can you say about current champions Leeds? After a slow start to the Super League era the Rhinos are now one of the true rugby powers of the land. Their team is packed with genuine world class superstars and, best of all, nowadays they actually win the odd trophy! Long may that continue.

Perhaps the biggest improvement, though, can be found at the club that will always be closest to my heart, Featherstone Rovers. They may still be outside Super League but, on the quiet, 'Fev' have always been quite a forward thinking club. Even at the height of the merger row, you got the feeling that while the supporters might have been up in arms from the start, the club itself was at least prepared to think the idea through. The committee at Post Office Road was always aware of the need to attract not just today's fans, but also the fans of the future.

I am very pleased to see that, although things have been difficult at times for my old club, Featherstone have never given up hope of getting back to rugby league's top tier. And as far as I am concerned that just demonstrates the truth of their argument from the start - that they could hold their own if given the chance. They have even started going to Spain for pre-season training - they never did that when we were there, more's the pity! I am excited for the future of

Featherstone Rovers. They are a club that is moving forward.

Eventually, of course, it will all come down to having a suitably modern stadium. And like many traditional clubs currently outside of the top flight - I'm thinking Widnes, Leigh and Halifax - Rovers are sharpening their off-field act. That means there will come a time when the Super League structure itself will need to be looked at if everyone is going to be accommodated and reasonable ambition is not to be ignored. Otherwise, it is going to be hard to fit everyone in. We are already complaining about players having to play too many games in a season, and the impact that has on our national team. So you can't simply keep adding teams willy-nilly. Personally, I think twelve clubs is the ideal number, playing each other once, home and away, although since the arrival of Salford and Celtic Crusaders in 2009, we have now gone back to fourteen.

One idea that I do like is to aim, eventually, for two conferences with twelve teams in each - either split by geography to keep the big local derbies intact, or by a random pre-season draw - a bit like American Football. The teams in each conference could play each once, home and away, and you could have a handful of cross-conference games to make up the numbers. Then you would get the play-offs, as usual, and aim towards a Grand Final, where the champions of each Conference would play off to be Super League Champions. It could be rugby league's very own Super Bowl. With the more powerful clubs - i.e. Leeds and St. Helens - in separate conferences, so-called lesser clubs would also have a better chance of making a final. And can you imagine what a game the Grand Final would be if it was the first time that, say, Wigan had played Bradford all season? Obviously, we are not yet at the stage where that is a realistic prospect, but it is definitely worth working towards.

Finally, and given the dual-code philosophy of BARA, I am

often asked whether I ever see the day when there will only be one code of rugby - a combination of both league or union. My answer to that is simple. No. As things stand now, after almost one hundred and fifteen years of separate development, there is no reason why both codes cannot work together in harmony, but continue to do very well on their own individual paths. These days, I very much enjoy watching rugby union - particularly on an international level - and playing it too. But, apart from the shape of the ball, it is a different game all together to the thirteen-a-side code. As a league man through and through, I consider rugby league to be the greatest game in the world, bar none, but there is plenty of room for all. In both codes, attendances are rising, clubs are investing in infrastructure and the future looks bright.

For me, though, there remains one obvious caveat and it applies just as much to one code as the other. It is that long-standing personal disappointment of mine about the lack of home-grown Asian players operating at the highest echelons of the engage Super League or Guinness Premiership.

Where is England's next Ikram Butt?

One thing I do know is that with the ongoing challenges and political uncertainties facing all our communities, there has never been a more important time to use the unifying power of rugby as a way of bringing people together in an environment of mutual understanding and respect.

Now, more than ever, we need to inspire in our young people the shared values of wisdom, moderation and inclusivity. Real change often takes generations; it probably will in rugby too. But if *we* don't start to break down the walls standing between us, then who will?

# MY ALL-TIME FAVOURITE XIIIs
## (All teams to be coached by Peter Fox)

### Featherstone
1. Chris Bibb
2. Ikram Butt
3. Terry Manning
4. Paul Newlove
5. Owen Simpson
6. Ian Smales
7. Deryck Fox
8. Leo Casey
9. Trevor Clarke
10. Steve Molloy
11. Gary Rose
12. Chris Burton
13. Brendon Tuuta
*Subs:*
14. Martin Pearson
15. Richard Gunn
16. Gary Price
17. Andy Fisher

### Great Britain
1. Joe Lydon
2. Jason Robinson
3. Paul Newlove
4. Jonathan Davies
5. Martin Offiah
6. Garry Schofield
7. Andy Gregory
8. Lee Crooks
9. Keiron Cunningham
10. Kevin Ward
11. Denis Betts
12. Andy Farrell
13. Ellery Hanley
*Subs:*
14. Shaun Edwards
15. Jamie Peacock
16. Paul Sculthorpe
17. Adrian Morley

### BARA Team
1. Amraiz Hamed
2. Phil Khan
3. Ikram Butt
4. Tajiv Masson
5. Shearer Singh
6. Junaid Malik
7. Omar Mehdi
8. Jag Johal
9. Andy Ali
10. Tony Butt
11. Usman Malik
12. Rehan Mansoor
13. Rashid Mahmood
*Subs:*
14. Aman Boughan
15. Jug Johal
16. Amjad Hussain
17. Amit Mistry

# IKRAM FILLS THE ROLE OF SPOKESPERSON SO WELL - HE'S BEEN THERE, DONE THAT...
## Zeshan 'Zesh' Rehman

*Zesh Rehman (born 14 October 1983) is an English footballer of
Pakistani heritage who finished the 2009 season playing for
Bradford City, while on loan from Queens Park Rangers.*
*'Zesh' was the first British Asian to play in the English Premiership
and is the first to have played in all four divisions of professional
football in England. He also captains the Pakistan national team -
the first Pakistani international to play professionally in England*

I grew up in the Aston area of Birmingham, close to Villa
Park, where whites, blacks, Asians and everyone else all
played football in the street. Football was the one way of
bringing all those communities together.

In my youth, I used to encounter the odd bit of racism
here and there, but if you want to be a professional
sportsman then you soon learn to deal with that. We played
in mixed teams, so everyone was integrated.

I was quite lucky because my dad, Khalid, loved football.
Right throughout the 1970s and '80s he would go to games,
even at the height of hooliganism. He loved the game and
that love just filtered through to me.

I left the Midlands when I was 12-years-old, when my
dad took me to London so that I could pursue my
footballing dreams. Eventually, through hard work and
determination, I made my way through Fulham's junior,
youth and reserve sides before making my full debut against
Liverpool, at Anfield, in 2004. In doing that, I became the

first British player of South Asian origin to start a Premiership match. You can imagine what a thrill it was for me to play and hold my own against such stars as Alan Shearer, Wayne Rooney, Thierry Henry and Jermain Defoe.

Over the next couple of years, I made 30 appearances for Fulham before leaving in 2006. During that time, I also spent time on loan at Norwich and Brighton. The month after I left, I signed a three-year contract with my current club, Queens Park Rangers and have since been back to Brighton - and Blackpool - on loan again.

At the back end of the 2009 season, I spent three months with Bradford City. That not only allowed me to add to my list of 'firsts' by becoming the first British Asian to play in all four professional divisions, it also introduced me to Ikram Butt. I first bumped into Ikram while he was sitting in the Cedar Court Hotel, writing this very book, just down the road from Odsal Stadium.

Hopefully, we will now speak more often. I enjoyed hearing Ikram's thoughts on his ways to attract more Asian children into sport in this country, the importance of providing a positive role model and so on. More often than not, he and I have similar opinions.

Like Ikram, I too am actively involved in sport's international dimension. As captain of the Pakistan national football team, I am very proud to help to promote the round ball game in South Asia, although it was a tough choice to make between playing for Pakistan and waiting for my chance with England, who I represented from the under-17s to under-20s. Eventually, I decided that a full England cap was unrealistic and chose Pakistan instead - one of the hardest decisions of my life.

It was a decision that didn't go down well with everyone, but that's another story which you can read when my own autobiography comes out!

Personally, I think it's vital that Asian kids in this country should be encouraged to embrace the British culture while, at the same time, not forgetting their roots. No matter what your background, you must always remember who you are and where you have come from.

Sport in general - whether it be rugby, football, cricket or whatever - is the perfect vehicle to educate. As Ikram says, we should all of us try to understand one another's cultures and not just stereotype people based on race, religion or anything else.

Having said that, as a professional sportsperson there is often a fine balance to be struck between voicing opinions and concentrating all your energies on the thing which gave you that voice in the first place: sport. If you are not careful, you can be accused of taking your eye off the ball. So, in that regard, it helps most if you do your 'talking' on the pitch, by being the right sort of influence.

Once the playing is over and done with, then the next stage can come into play - as Ikram has shown. He is not just outspoken for the sake of it. He fills the role of spokesperson so well because he has been there and done it.

Me, I have always been 'football first'. But as you get older, you do become more aware. I set my own website up and get letters and so on, which makes you realise there are issues bigger than football, but which football can help to address.

I don't see my position as a burden. I am in a responsible position and if I can offer advice then I should.

More people should be engaged in the sort of work that Ikram is doing. He is offering a hand and trying to make a difference for the next generation.

I am glad that I met him. It really is great to see that there are people like Ikram Butt in British sport who are trying to do something positive, over and above what's in it for themselves.

# IKRAM CONTINUES TO PUT ALL THAT PLAYING EXPERIENCE TO GOOD USE...
## Hasan Pooya

*Chairman of Islamabad Rugby Club*

'Ikram Butt....great guy, you really must meet him.' That was what the boys of Islamabad Rugby Club told me after Ikram's first visit to Pakistan. I didn't pay much heed at the time and, by virtue of circumstance, almost a year went by before our paths did finally cross.

I must admit that I was a little wary of Ikram at first, half expecting a conceited rugby player from England who had come in to teach the 'locals' a thing or two. Instead one had the pleasure of meeting a softly-spoken, straightforward and humble individual blessed with the ability to communicate to the extent that one finds it difficult to get angry or upset with him over anything; including the time he made me fly to Manchester from Karachi on forty-eight hours' notice only to disappear upon my arrival and resurface fourteen hours later. (Haven't forgotten that one bro'!)

Rugby is one of the toughest team sports in the world and one finds its players in general to have a very humble and positive outlook (barring the inevitable few moppets).

Maybe that's because of the exhausting nature of the game, which requires a combination of courage, fitness, skill and teamwork. Or perhaps it is the camaraderie and routine of continuously taking hard knocks, shrugging them off and carrying back on with the game.

Ikram continues to put all that playing experience to good use and works earnestly to reach out and bridge communal barriers. Be it arranging tag rugby for Bradford schoolkids, training sessions for the youth of Islamabad, organising matches for a local UAE team, creating events for Members of Parliament, supporting the efforts of the Pakistan national team or simply playing a few games in Mumbai; he succeeds not only for himself but those of us who have collectively grown richer in our relationships due to his patient efforts and selfless attitude.

I am happy that Ikram Butt has written his autobiography. Surely this will be a source of great encouragement to many of our Asian friends, residing in the UK, to take up rugby.

Here at the Indian Rugby Football Union, we appreciate Ikram's contribution to rugby among the Asian community, as well as for having built a strong bond between BARA and the IRFU. We look forward to a continued pleasant relationship as we both seek to develop, promote and take rugby to higher levels in the Asian region.

**Pramod Khanna, President - Indian RFU**

As the first Asian-origin rugby league player to represent England, Ikram Butt has left footprints and created a strong support system for others to follow. Ikram has dedicated his life to promoting and fostering goodwill and understanding across communities. He has seamlessly transcended all obstacles with dedication, sincerity and incredible humility.

Ikram will undoubtedly scale greater heights and continue to inspire people to believe in themselves and their talent. His story is truly unique and fascinating and it will touch and enlighten everyone who reads it.

**Chaitanya Sinh, former India Captain
and Managing Director A La Concierge Services Pvt. Ltd**

Ikram Butt is a positive role model all young people. Not only because he made the most of his considerable talent; not just because he had to overcome more barriers than most of his peers in order to succeed; but because of how he lives his own life and his timeless efforts to improve the lives of the people in the communities in which he lives and works.

Ikram inspires everyone. He is a fantastic ambassador for Bradford and I am proud to know him.

**Tony Reeves, Chief Executive,
City of Bradford Metropolitan District Council**

Ikram and myself represented the City of Leeds under-11s schoolboy team against the St.. Helens schoolboys team in a curtain raiser to a senior Saints versus Leeds match. I was at full-back and Ikram played at hooker. It was a cracking game which we eventually won.

I knew then that Ikram had the potential to go all the way. He was very pacey, had a good step off either foot and very strong. We continued to play our amateur rugby league together for many years until I broke my leg in a game. This was a major setback as, up until then, like Ikram, I had a number of scouts watching me and making offers. Ikram and I are like brothers and almost did everything together when we were young. There is a special bond between us which has lasted since we were young kids. I am very proud to call Ikram my brother.

**Matloob Khan, former team-mate**

As BARLA chairman I am keen to provide opportunities for everyone in rugby league, regardless of their background.

BARLA has an excellent reputation for welcoming and encouraging participation in all our diverse communities in the UK. And, personally, I had the pleasure of being invited by Ikram and the Islamabad Rugby Club to see first hand how rugby is developing out in Pakistan.

It was an eye opener. I was able to see for myself how passionately enthusiastic the Pakistanis are about rugby. In addition, I was able to experience the warmth of the people, who made me feel very welcome. The experience also gave me an understanding of culture and religion in Pakistan.

Ikram & BARA continue to do excellent development work here in the UK and abroad. We are delighted that BARA are associate members of BARLA.

**Spen Allison,**
**Chairman of British Amateur Rugby League Association**

# Acknowledgements

My grateful thanks go to a number of people, most of whom either contributed to this book or are mentioned in its pages. Most obviously, I offer deep love and gratitude to all my family, especially Bushra, Aamina, Ruqayya and Hayan, and my mother and late father, brothers, sisters, nephews and nieces.

Others who have provided tremendous inspiration include Khalid and Arif Darr at Carter Anderson; Hanif Malik, Starr Zaman and everyone at HAMARA; and Junaid, Usman and Jerry Malik of the Malik Group. I would also like to thank Billoo Malik, Mohammed Sadiq, Rashid Mahmood, Huggy Osman, Dr. Mohammad Amran, Chaudhrey Khalid Bhalot, Chaudhrey Aurangzeb, Paula Hellewell, Saima Hussain, Harish Tekchandani, Imran Farooq, John Hodgson, Phil Hellewell, Basil Richards, Talish Butt and Jerry Hussain, who have always been there for me.

All the BARA committee deserve the highest praise, especially Jug, Jag & Shahid, as well as all the players, including Paul Akadaire, Rehan Mansoor, Amraiz Hamid, Amar Saddique, Phil Khan, Parminder Singh, Zahoor Ahmed and Andy Ali. I recently ended nine wonderful years working with Bradford Council, for which I would especially like to thank Tony Reeves, Pav Singh, Jane Glaister, Phil Barker, Cllr. David Ward & Amjad Hussain.

I am currently greatly enjoying working with the All Party Parliamentary Rugby League and Union Groups, in particular Neil Turner MP, Greg Mulholland MP, Andy Reed MP and Gerry Sutcliffe MP.

Emma Rosewarne, Richard Lewis, Kevin Rudd and their colleagues at the RFL continue to be a source of great support, as are Spen Allison and the team at BARLA. Equally helpful to the BARA cause are Martyn Thomas, Nick Bunting and

Hamish Pratt at the RFU. Simon Lee, Peter Rodgers, David Jackson, David Braham, Joy Kumar and Ismail Dawood at Leeds Carnegie have supported me through good times and bad.

In India and Pakistan, the assistance and friendship of everyone at the PRFU and IRFU is much valued. And I would also like to thank all the guys at Bombay Gymkhana, especially Rahul, Chait, Faisal, Mukka, Muffi, Nasser, Maneck, Hrishi, Pramod and Agha; everyone at the Lahore and Islamabad Rugby Club, especially Zubair, Pasha, Hajji, Hasan, Khashif and Farid. Back in the UK, I am also hugely grateful to Sir Herman Ouseley, Danny Lynch and the rest of the 'Kick It Out' team for their ongoing support.

Organisations who have financially backed BARA include the Asian Jewel Awards; RFL; RFU; Leeds Rugby; Bradford Bulls RLFC; Mumtaz Restaurant; Lucky's Takeaway and Fortune Cookie; Jaz Chatta and Mick Turner of Ravensport; Sporting Equals; B.E.M. Sports; the RAF; Sekon and Firth Solicitors, Bradford.

A big thank you, too, to each of my previous rugby clubs, especially the fans, staff and players of Featherstone Rovers RLFC, and also to Rob Wilkinson of PR Promotions. Finally, I am grateful to my friend Tony Hannan and all at Scratching Shed Publishing Ltd for their invaluable expertise in turning this book idea of mine into reality.

# Available now or coming soon from Scratching Shed Publishing Ltd...

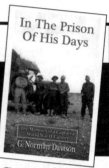